Post-War British Fiction

Realism and After

Andrzej Gąsiorek

Lecturer in English Literature
University of Birmingham

Edward Arnold
A member of the Hodder Headline Group
LONDON   NEW YORK   SYDNEY   AUCKLAND

First published in Great Britain 1995 by
Edward Arnold, a division of Hodder Headline PLC,
338 Euston Road, London NW1 3BH

Distributed exclusively in the USA by
St. Martin's Press, Inc.
175 Fifth Avenue, New York, NY 10010

British Library Cataloguing in Publication Data
A catalogue record for this book is available from the British Library

ISBN 0 340 57215 9

5 4 3 2 1 99 98 97 96 95 95

Typeset in 10/11 Palatino by
Textype Typesetters, Cambridge
Printed and bound in Great Britain by
J W Arrowsmith Ltd, Bristol

Contents

Moim rodzicom, Basi,
i małej Lidce

Preface

This book is not a survey of post-war British fiction; I had better admit that at once. I omit several novelists whose work I should have liked to discuss, space permitting. Names such as Samuel Beckett, Anthony Burgess, William Golding, Iris Murdoch and Muriel Spark spring to mind. But I do not attempt to provide a comprehensive overview of developments in the novel since 1945; I examine, rather, the conflict between realism and experimentalism as it manifests itself in the work of a wide range of writers. The book's title is not meant to suggest that realism is a spent force, which has been superseded by various postmodernisms. On the contrary, I argue that whereas 'traditional realism' has been challenged in numerous contexts the impulse to represent a changing social world with the greatest possible fidelity remains central to much post-war writing. This book, then, is concerned neither with those novelists who revert to nineteenth-century realism nor with those who favour extreme linguistic experimentation. It focuses instead on writers whose works deliberately fall somewhere between what Barthes calls the *scriptible* and the *lisible*, and which tend to try to reconceptualize realism rather than to reject it outright in the wake of modernist and postmodernist critique. The novels of these writers suggest that distinctions between 'realist' and 'experimental' or between 'traditional' and 'innovative', which were of such significance to the modernists and the avant-garde in the earlier part of the century, are so irrelevant to the post-war period that they should be dropped altogether.

The realism/experimentalism dichotomy is formalist. It construes realism as a set of narrative techniques, and experimentalism as their subversion. This is inadequate. Realism, I argue, needs to be seen as a heterogeneous phenomenon. Only then can the post-war writing practices that engage with it be seen in their full diversity and complexity. To take but four examples, the reasons for which a socialist such as John Berger, an anti-colonialist such as George Lamming, a feminist such as Angela Carter, or a liberal humanist such as Angus Wilson depart from earlier realist modes are quite different. Their multifarious reworkings of these modes can be understood only if they are analysed within the specific contexts in which they are produced. How the novelists who are dealt with in this book react against, reject, or extend realism depends on their prior account of it, on whether for them it is aligned with, say, liberalism, socialism, colonialism, or patriarchy, or perhaps simply seen as an outmoded concept whose association with nineteenth-century narrative modes thoroughly discredits it. Following Brecht, I view realism not in terms of more or less fixed formal techniques but as a family of writings that share a certain cognitive attitude to the world, which manifests itself in a variety of forms in different historical periods. On this view, there is no necessary link either between particular narrative strategies and the goal of accurate representation or between realism, however it is conceived, and any given political position. My examination of novels by Ivy Compton-Burnett, Henry Green, V. S. Naipaul, George Lamming, John Berger, Doris Lessing, Angus Wilson, John Fowles, Angela Carter, Sara Maitland, Graham Swift, Julian Barnes and Salman Rushdie seeks to bear out these claims.

One other observation. This book is in certain respects a modest exercise in retrieval. Postmodernism is so often invoked as a cultural dominant that a diverse range of literary forms come to be seen in a homogeneous fashion as part of a general 'crisis of representation'. This is in my view deeply misleading. To read authors who engage in quite different ways with the epistemological and aesthetic difficulties entailed by representation as though they are all participating in the same pursuit is to 'flatten out' the post-war period in a way that can only contribute to the very dehistoriciz-ation that critics of postmodernism lament. One of my most basic assumptions in the writing of this book has been that careful attention to the specific political and aesthetic contexts in which writers work militates against the subsumption of their quite diverse novels to the current preoccupation with postmodernism.

Various colleagues, friends, and family members have contributed to the writing of this book. I owe an enormous debt to them for helping to make it happen. I would like to thank my editor, Christopher Wheeler, for being so patient and helpful while I was writing it; he has been everything I could have wished for in an editor. Special thanks go to Teresa Shergold, Danusia, Janusz, Krzyś, Leszek and Michał Gąsiorek for their generous support, their frequent advice, and their unfailing good humour; in addition, the computer expertise of my three brothers has proved a gold-mine. Several friends and former teachers in Canada read earlier versions of some of the work that has found its way into this book. My thanks to Paul Coates, Stewart Cooke, Maged El-Komos, Tim Gauthier, Kerry McSweeney, Brian Trehearne and Gary Wihl. I would also like to mention those former colleagues at the University of East Anglia who read parts of this book and helped me to clarify my thinking. My thanks go to Andrew Higson, Vic Sage, and Roger Sales. I owe my greatest scholarly debt to David Aers; his encouragement, criticisms, intellectual example, and friendship have made this book infinitely better than it would otherwise have been. Above all, I would like to express my deep gratitude to Basia Gąsiorek, who has helped me in more ways than I can here acknowledge. Without her this book would never have been written.

Andrzej Gąsiorek
April 1994

Acknowledgement

An earlier version of my work on Angus Wilson appeared as 'Resisting Postmodernism: The Parodic Mode of Angus Wilson's, *No Laughing Matter*', in English Studies in Canada, 19, 1 (March 1993). I am grateful to the editors for permission to reprint a revised version of this article.

1

Realism in the Post-War Period

After Modernism

Even a cursory glance at the numerous discussions of the novel's future in the aftermath of the Second World War reveals that many writers shared certain concerns. They thought the novel was under pressure from the events of recent history, which seemed not only to be unrepresentable but also to have shattered pre-war illusions; from mass culture in the form of radio, cinema, and later television; and from the after-shocks of modernism. These concerns fall into two categories: the first concentrates on external events (war, social change, cultural transformation); the second focuses on developments internal to the novel (style, technique, form). Between them, they were used to explain a perceived crisis of fiction. Modernism had produced often dazzling works of art but had driven fiction so deeply into subjectivism that it had been left with few resources for dealing with social issues. The war, in turn, had had a devastating impact on the imagination, stifling writers' creativity and destroying their confidence in the form. Fiction was becoming journalistic, and its story-telling function was being taken over by cinema. The novel, exhausted as a form, unable to meet the demands placed on it by a changing world, and challenged by the mass media, was thus thought to be in terminal decline.

Debates about the state of the novel and its precarious future are not new. They have been going on ever since the form's earliest days. The first half of the twentieth century was no exception, as the famous disputes between James and Wells, Woolf and Bennett, and Lawrence and Galsworthy attest. In each case, competing theories of fiction clashed, while their respective proponents declared that the novel was unlikely to survive if their opponents' views prevailed. In each case, moreover, the innovators were convinced that their new techniques were better equipped to evoke changing perceptions of reality. The rallying cry was not to 'make it new' but to make it real – to break free from established conventions in order to portray reality with greater fidelity and artistic vision.[1] The early post-war period, in contrast, was marked by a gamut of emotions ranging from uncertainty to despair. Whereas the modernists perceived themselves as an avant-garde, and frequently made a good deal of literary capital out of such self-promotion, post-war writers saw themselves as fighting a rearguard action to preserve a form threatened with extinction. The modernists cast giant shadows over their successors' work, since they seemed to have taken the novel as far as it could go, leaving the latter to scrabble about among the leftovers. Post-war writers lacked zest and a sense of excitement. On the one hand, the horrors of the war seemed to outstrip the literary imagination, and, on the other hand, the move towards a democratization of society brought about by Education Acts, public building programmes, nationalization of key industries, and the introduction of a national health service provoked fears of massification among what was a predominantly conservative literary intelligentsia. Evelyn Waugh compared the period of the first Labour government to enemy occupation.[2] And Elizabeth Bowen articulated many widely shared anxieties when she declared that the imagination was being undermined by 'the aching, bald uniformity of our urban surroundings', which provided nowhere for 'fancy to dwell' since it was everywhere confronted by 'new soaring blocks of flats' and 'mushroom housing-estates'.[3]

Alex Comfort's *The Novel and Our Time* (1948) provides a good example of the persistent concern in the 1940s with the difficulty of confronting the changed landscape of post-war social life. To understand the malaise of the contemporary novel, he wrote, people should look not to literature for an explanation but to society. The latter had become 'totally fragmented'; it was a 'non-civilization' that was at an 'end-point'. Comfort required novelists to display 'a coherent attitude to history and events' and to resist escape into pure form or pacts with barbarism, but he acknowledged that most were failing in both respects. The novel was 'patently not succeeding in coping with the material . . . being presented to it'.[4] The argument was commonplace. V. S. Pritchett had 2 years earlier suggested that contemporary literature had been 'overshadowed by the events of the last ten years' and that the confused novelist had unwittingly 'become the historian of the crisis in civilization'.[5] For Rose Macaulay 'life has during the past years been disintegrated, broken into odd, unshapely bits, one not fitting into another', with the result that 'fragments, impressions, brief glimpses' had become the prevailing mode.[6]

The old critical view which saw the 1940s as a moribund period exploded by the eruption onto the scene of the so-called Angry Young Men, who subsequently presided over a period of neo-realist dominance, is misleading. The 1940s not only witnessed fierce debates about the present and future direction of the novel but also produced novels by writers as diverse as Nigel Balchin, Elizabeth Bowen, Ivy Compton-Burnett, Lawrence Durrell, Henry Green, Graham Greene, Rosamond Lehmann, Wyndham Lewis, Malcolm Lowry, Nancy Mitford, William Sansom, Angela Thirkell, Philip Toynbee and Evelyn Waugh. Despite this, it was for some time widely held that the period from the 1940s to the 1960s could be characterized in terms of a straight conflict between experimental writers and realists. The present book is primarily concerned with novelists who sought a *rapprochement* between experimentalism and realism; but it is important to consider the opposition between them posited by writers like Kingsley Amis, William Cooper, and C. P. Snow on one side and writers like Christine Brooke-Rose, Eva Figes, and

B. S. Johnson on the other, since this opposition clarifies the nature of two dominant directions in post-war fiction and goes some way towards explaining why other novelists felt it to be unsatisfactory.

Both groups saw themselves as battling for the future of the novel. Whereas one saw innovation as indispensable to the form's health, the other considered it to be the cause of its malaise. Kingsley Amis declared that 'the idea about experiment being the life-blood of the English novel is one that dies hard'.[7] His own avowed goal was to counteract this notion. He described his novels as 'believable stories about understandable characters in a reasonably straightforward style: no tricks, no experimental foolery'.[8] This is the language of empiricism and Anglo-Saxon common sense. Experimentation is aligned with 'tricks' (deceitfulness) and 'foolery' (triviality). Cooper was more acerbic. The experimental novel represented an attack on 'intellect in general, made by intellectuals so decadent that they no longer mind if intellect persists'. Cooper's words, like Amis's, reveal how powerful a hold modernism had taken on the minds of post-war novelists. It was against modernism that realism needed to be defined: 'we saw that . . . the Experimental Novel had got to be brushed out of the way before we could get a proper hearing'.[9] Snow was in the vanguard of the attack on experimental writing. His two main charges were that modernism was inward-looking, obsessed with subjectivity and the personal vision, and that its attention to form and style reduced the novel to a linguistic construct that made little or no reference to an external world. Modernism was thus incapable of dealing with social questions.[10] For Snow, influential writers such as Hulme, Joyce and Pound had bought into the Romantic conception of the artist as an outsider, a *poète maudit*, whose main desire is 'to contract out of society'.[11] His own concern with writing novels that explored social experience, the workings of power, and the impact of science on twentieth-century life led him to favour realism.

The realist defence was contested by novelists such as Brooke-Rose, Figes, and Johnson. They argued that modernism was necessarily the point of departure for post-war fiction. The contemporary novel should investigate language, reveal its own provisional and fictional status, and refuse what they perceived as realism's univocal perspective. They thus rejected the return to conventional forms exemplified by 1950s realists and deplored their treatment of modernism as an aberrant interlude in the history of the novel. Figes claimed that 'the novels of the past were portraying a false reality' and that 'new models' were required; writers like herself, Brooke-Rose, and Johnson were 'concerned with language, with breaking up conventional narrative, with "making it new" in our different ways'.[12] Brooke-Rose, influenced primarily by Pound and Beckett, spoke of drawing attention to 'the fictionality of fiction' and described herself as an 'auto-destruct artist' who wrote in order 'to solve specific problems' and to play with language and narrative.[13] Although she repudiated a progressivist conception of literature, such a view frequently underpinned the work of the post-war avant-garde. For Johnson, the novel was 'an evolving form' and this meant that 'where Joyce left off should ever since have been regarded as the starting point'. According to Johnson, the writer should search for new forms not only because Joyce and Beckett had between them exhausted the old modes but also because reality is mutable and new representations of it are required. The novelist, like a Lévi-Straussian *bricoleur*, 'must evolve (by inventing, borrowing, stealing or cobbling from other media) forms which will more or less contain an ever-changing reality'.[14]

The intensity of feeling in both camps meant that opponents' views were often caricatured. John Wain's parody of Joyce's *Finnegans Wake* in *Hurry On Down* was crude, to say the least: 'Clout bell, shout well, pell-mell about a tout, get the hell out. About nowt'.[15] But Johnson's claim that the writing of nineteenth-century fiction is 'anachronistic, invalid, irrelevant, and perverse' was hardly more subtle.[16] A variety of writers rejected these extreme positions in favour of a more catholic conception of fiction. Angus Wilson, who had early been associated with the return to realism, was one of the first to display his impatience with the narrowness of vision promoted by both perspectives, writing that 'we may make use of all that experiment has taught us, may indeed experiment ourselves, without losing contact with our good old English tradition, the true husbandry needs old and new alike'.[17] Wilson was aware that the dichotomy bedevilling British fiction relied as much on political as on aesthetic grounds. Indeed, what passed for purely aesthetic judgement was frequently underpinned by covert political assumptions. To defend realism in the 1950s was to be aligned not only with 'good old English tradition' (empiricism, common sense, social comedy along the lines of Fielding and Dickens) but also with a broad commitment to liberal humanism. Experimentalism was thus attacked on putatively artistic grounds, but because political criteria were slipped in it could at the same time be dismissed as decadent (Cooper), politically reactionary (Snow), and elitist (Amis). Wilson singled out Snow's reviews as good instances of this strategy, regretting the latter's tendency 'to confuse aestheticism and concern with formal experiment with a political regressivism, to associate the traditional novel form he likes with sound, progressive social principles'.[18]

This is an important point, since it indicates that although certain realists sought to gain credibility for their chosen mode by linking it to a general political orientation, such linkage is contingent and arbitrary. As Stuart Laing has argued, there are no 'fixed relations between literary forms and political/ philosophical positions'.[19] Wilson was quick to grasp this point and to distance himself from the realism he had initially championed when he saw that its apologists were using it to imply that experimental writing was *ipso facto* politically reactionary. Such a view was as misleading as the alternative claim that experimental writing was inherently progressive because its challenge to conventional narrative forms was homologous with a challenge to the social order.

A number of post-war writers have rejected the realism/experimentalism dichotomy. This book explores the work of some of them. But realism and experiment mean different things to different novelists. An account of the reasons for which writers either depart from or extend realist narrative modes must therefore begin with an understanding that there is no single crisis of realism as a form. Many Anglo-American critics of the novel have associated realism with liberalism and have thus sought to explain the former's difficulties as an epiphenomenon of the latter's crisis. I shall later challenge this view in detail but for now let it be said that I consider realisms to be multiple and believe that they can no more be equated with a particular political stance than with a given set of narrative strategies.[20] The work of the novelists I discuss in this book bears out this view, suggesting that realism is conceived in markedly different ways. It may be associated with an out-moded aesthetic that is incompatible with a certain form of social satire (Ivy Compton-Burnett, Henry Green); with a European tradition of writing that is inseparable from colonialism and imperialism (Wilson Harris, George Lamming, V.S. Naipaul); with a liberal humanism that is increasingly uneasy about its political impotence (John Fowles, Angus Wilson); with a socialism that is under pressure from the events of recent history (John Berger, Doris Lessing); with a corpus of works that frequently offers regressive representations of gender relations (Angela Carter, Sarah Maitland); or with conceptions of history and politics that can no longer encapsulate what is seen as postmodern reality (Julian Barnes, Salman Rushdie, Graham Swift). Some of these writers reject realism outright; others go beyond nineteenth-century forms and techniques in an attempt to break free from an ahistorical conception of realism. But how these novelists respond to realism depends on their prior conception of it, their politics, and their literary aims.

It is striking how persistently commentators linked the crisis of the novel with a crisis of society. The sense of fragmentation produced by the Second World War is understandable, but the 1950s and 1960s reveal an ongoing preoccupation with Britain's decline. John Holloway argued that 'a long partial holiday period is coming to an end for us as a nation, and that because of this we must be ready to re-think our position in fundamental terms, and perhaps transform our life in fundamental ways'. The problems Holloway identified were cultural rather than social, political, or economic. And despite the inclusive language of *English* nationhood, he was primarily preoccupied with the dilemmas confronting the intelligentsia and not the nation as a whole; the empiricist temper which he identified as typically English, and which he thought was unable to confront the present crisis, was 'distinctive of our intellectual life'.[21] But fear of decline was not restricted to liberals. E.P. Thompson argued that welfare-capitalism was not to be confused with socialism, and declared that the country was decaying because it was over-ripe for socialism. Eight years later, Perry Anderson offered a quite different Marxist analysis. Anderson attributed Britain's malaise to the failure of the English Revolution to transform the social structure and the failure of the Industrial Revolution to provide the working classes with an ideological legacy that would enable them to combat the ruling class. The Second World War, in turn, had left the country's infrastructure relatively undamaged, with the result that no major socio-economic reorganization had taken place. Anderson identified a widespread lassitude, a torpid economy, a backward education system, and a prevalent cultural philistinism as key aspects of the present crisis, which was 'a general malady of the whole society, infrastructure and superstructure – not a sudden breakdown, but a slow, sickening entropy'.[22] Arthur Marwick points out that although explanations of Britain's decline differed, since they depended on prior political convictions, the belief that the country was in crisis was shared right across the political spectrum.[23]

Writers and critics sought to explain the post-war novel's limitations with reference to this sense of national crisis, although it is important to see that commentators in fact perceived several crises (i.e. of socialism, welfare-capitalism, 'high' culture), each of which interpreted the country's demise in different ways. But the period's numerous debates about the state of the novel suggest that many observers believed that novelistic experimentation was required for social reality to be represented adequately. In 1956 John Lehmann published *The Craft of Letters in England*. Most contributions were sombre in tone, lukewarm in praise of current writing, and critical when comparing it with modernism. Lehmann focused on a general loss of faith in Marxism and Christianity, arguing that 'the problem of belief' had become central. Philip Toynbee – himself an experimental writer – echoed Lehmann's sentiments. The old forms were exhausted, and the contemporary novelist was 'on his own, struggling in a collapsed tradition, uncertain of his intractable medium and uncertain of his constantly changing material'.[24] In 1958, the *London Magazine* held a similar symposium. Contributors were equally cautious. They agreed on three general points in respect of contemporary British novelists: none was of major international stature; none had adequately responded to post-war social change; none was especially innovative. Most symposiasts saw some form of experimentation as necessary to revivify the form. Novelists revealed similar concerns. Iris Murdoch, for example, identified two dominant strands of writing, the 'crystalline' (symbolist) and the 'journalistic' (realist); she argued that neither mode could offer a complex account of human personality, of moral dilemmas, or of a social reality that both grounds and transcends the individual.[25] For many writers, realism was proving inadequate to the task of confronting the post-war world; crises in the social domain were held responsible for realism's – and thus the novel's – apparent decline. To understand the reasoning behind such claims we need to look at the powerful link between liberalism and realism in Anglo-American theories of the novel.

Realism, Liberalism and the Death of the Novel

The 'death of the novel' thesis was frequently put forward in the first two to three decades of the post-war period. The debate over the death of the novel is instructive because it reveals how closely intertwined the novel and realism are in Anglo-American criticism. Because the novel is, in this tradition, implicitly equated with realism, any undermining of the latter's pre-eminence is taken as a challenge to the genre as a whole. Post-war critics who saw realism as integral to the novel argued that a crisis of the realist novel betokened a crisis of the novel as a form. Because they further claimed that liberal ideology underpins realism, they suggested that this crisis reflected a concomitant one of liberalism, which had been undermined by recent history. The novel, equated first with realism and then with liberalism, was fracturing under aesthetic and social pressures into disparate narrative modes.

According to a dominant Anglo-American theory of the novel's origins, its genesis and subsequent development is inseparable from the establishment of capitalism and a liberal bourgeois ideology. The *locus classicus* of this view is Ian Watt's *The Rise of the Novel*. Watt accounts for the novel's 'rise' by seeing it as the representative form of an emergent mercantile class that developed concurrently with the social and economic changes instigated by capitalism. According to Watt, the 'formal realism' that emerged during this period represents the new form's 'defining characteristic' and is 'typical of the novel genre as a whole'.[26] His thesis has been widely endorsed.[27] An important critical tradition conceives the novel as inseparable from capitalism, an emergent bourgeois class, and liberal ideology. But the frequent invocation of liberalism poses a problem, for it is not always clear in what sense the word is to be taken. Does it refer to the values and ideology of laissez-faire politics, with the emphasis on Macphersonian possessive individualism? Or does it refer to a general humanist sensibility, which is characterized by open-mindedness, tolerance, and breadth of vision? Both senses of liberalism could plausibly be associated with the novel, but they are distinct. It is one thing to relate the eighteenth-century novel to the rise of a middle class partly produced by economic liberalism, and quite another to suggest that there is subsequently a necessary relation between liberalism and the novel form. W. J. Harvey, for instance, connects the novel's development with 'the growth of the bourgeoisie in a modern capitalist system' and describes it as 'the distinct art form of liberalism'. This is consistent with Watt. But when Harvey goes on to claim that liberalism 'is a state of mind' and that 'the novel cannot be written out of a monolithic or illiberal mind' he has slipped into another discourse. Liberalism is now a literary sensibility rather than an economic or political creed; it suggests pluralism, respect for diversity, tolerance. This second version of liberalism becomes the prerequisite of the form itself. The writer who does not share Harvey's assumptions is said to write 'a *kind* of fiction' but not a 'realistic novel', which is 'the central, classic tradition of modern fiction'.[28] Writers such as George Orwell, George Steiner and Lionel Trilling put forward similar views. For them, the novel has its origin in, and relevance to, a particular historical epoch; when that epoch faces disintegration, so does its pre-eminent literary form.

The powerful hold this view had on post-war critics can be seen by looking at Bernard Bergonzi's *The Situation of the Novel* and David Lodge's *The Novelist at the Crossroads*. Both writers rejected the 'death of the novel' thesis. Nevertheless, they were disturbed by the direction the novel was taking, fearing that experimentation was hostile to liberal culture and humanist values. Bergonzi worried that the novel was no longer 'novel' and had turned to the easy pickings of sub-genres and pastiche, which were incompatible with 'the ideology that sustained the novel for the first 2 centuries of existence, its belief in unpremeditated experience, in originality and individuality and progress'.[29] Lodge, in turn, revealed his doubts about experimental writing in the very terms he used to discuss it. He viewed 'with something less than enthusiasm the disappearance of *the novel* and its replacement by the non-fiction novel or fabulation'. The realist novel was seen as the novel's exemplar; other narrative modes were related, but somehow less significant, fictional forms. Because realism constituted the novel's central highway, 'these side roads will seem to lead all too easily into desert or bog – self-defeating banality or self-indulgent excess'.[30]

These assumptions are questionable. It is arguable both that realism represents fiction's acme and that the novel depends on it. A different line of argument suggests that the novel has been multifarious from the outset and that parody, pastiche, playfulness and fantasy have been as central to it as any mimetic impulse.[31] On a Bakhtinian interpretation, for example, the novel is not a modern literary form because it developed realistic techniques but because it discloses the heteroglossic complexity of early modern societies. For Bakhtin, the novel is neither associated with any particular social group nor defined by any given form. It is characterized by its fluidity, for its features belong to no 'system of fixed generic characteristics'. Moreover, because it is associated with 'low' parodic-travestying literatures that ridicule 'high' culture and undermine the language of hegemonic groups, it becomes a transgressive, anti-canonic form that discloses society's stratified and conflictual nature. The novel, Bakhtin argues, 'has no canon of its own. It is, by its very nature, not canonic'.[32] Following Bakhtin, one can elaborate an alternative genealogy of the novel, focusing on the early conflict between realism and romance, the comic–parodic strain running through Cervantes, Fielding and Sterne to the present day, and traditions such as gothic, fantasy and science fiction.[33] A detailed analysis of the nineteenth century alone, supposedly the period of realist dominance, reveals just how many different theories of fiction were competing for a hearing and suggests that supporters of realism were engaged in an intense debate over the direction the novel should take.[34] Realism is but one element in the novel's chequered history.

The view that the relation between realism and the novel is almost a necessary one is connected to the claim that realism is underpinned by liberalism. Orwell declares that the writer *'as a writer . . . is a liberal'*; Steiner claims that the novel 'is inseparable from the bias of a middle-class, humanistic culture'; and Lodge contends that if 'the case for realism has any ideological content it is that of liberalism'.[35] The novel is initially associated with (if not defined by) realism and then the latter is equated with liberalism, which is employed in at least two senses. This line of argument interprets the post-war challenge to realist fiction as a crisis not only of the novel but also of liberal culture. Such a view is for several reasons untenable: firstly, because the so-called crisis of realism in post-war writing is part of a wider rethinking of the problem of representation, the constituent features of which are diverse and cannot be reduced to the issue of liberal doubt alone; secondly, because realism has been differently conceived in different periods and continues to be interpreted and utilized in a variety of ways; thirdly, a corollary of this point, because there is no necessary relation between aesthetic forms (i.e. realism) and ideological positions (i.e. liberalism);[36] and, fourthly, because the link between the novel and realism is historically contingent. I am urging the view that the novel is a heterogeneous and mutable genre, which undermines its earlier forms in an ongoing search for new ways of engaging with a historically changing social reality. On this view it is misleading to speak of a general crisis of the genre when one of its key forms is challenged or superseded.

Rethinking 'Classic Realism'

The liberal account of realism has proved to be tenacious, as can be seen by looking at the post-structuralist critiques of it offered in the 1970s and early 1980s. The analysis of what was called the 'classic realist text' discloses that at a deep level there was a continuity between post-structuralist and liberal readings of realism; the positive valuation of realism within liberal accounts was inverted so that realism could be criticized, but it was still associated with bourgeois liberal humanism. For critics such as Stephen Heath in *The Nouveau Roman*, Colin MacCabe in *James Joyce and the Revolution of the Word*, and Catherine Belsey in *Critical Practice*, realism displays certain key features: a view of language as a transparent tool through which to view an external world; reliance on a reflectionist aesthetic; a concept of (relatively) stable character; reliance on a universalizing metalanguage that establishes a 'hierarchy of discourses' and produces the 'social' as the 'natural'; closure. Their conventionalist analysis of realism, which draws a good deal on Barthes, argues that realism is not a transparent way of describing the world but is a rule-governed signifying system that determines how perceptions of the world are structured.[37] Realism relies on an untenable theory of language, which casts its representations as reflections that 'mirror' the world, passing off its accounts as self-evidently veracious (natural) when they are in fact contingent (historical).

Realism's apparent naivety with regard to its own use of language and narrative stands at the heart of the post-structuralist critique. The function of realism, Heath argued in 1972, is 'the naturalization of that reality articulated by a society as the "Reality" and its success is the degree to which it remains unknown as a form'.[38] MacCabe notes the presence of a controlling metalanguage in realist writing and argues that it has a twofold role: firstly, to present itself as 'a window on reality' and by so doing to control the poly-vocity released by its object-languages; secondly, to establish its superiority (as auto-interpretation) over these object-languages by organizing them into 'a specific hierarchy of discourses'. The presence of a metalanguage that denies its own provenance, orders a text's discourses into a hierarchy, and creates a reading position by 'interpellating' the reader produces the 'classic realist text'.[39] Belsey's reading is similar. She begins by rejecting what she calls 'empiricist–idealist' assumptions about the relationship between world and language in favour of a post-Saussurean view in which 'language precedes the existence of independent entities, making the world intelligible by differentiating between concepts'. From this perspective realism cannot 'reflect' the world, but only 'the order inscribed in particular discourses'. In fact, because realism is forced to create 'juxtapositions and complexities out of what we already know . . . it is a predominantly conservative form'.[40]

This critique of realism rests on thoroughly conventionalist assumptions. The correspondence theory of truth is jettisoned; reality cannot be 'mirrored' in language but is produced in, by, and through it. Different discourses cannot therefore be measured against a 'reality' that could adjudicate among them, since there is no unmediated access to the world. Language signifies not because it makes reference to a mind-independent reality that pre-exists and constrains discursive structuration of it but because it is a system of differences that produces the world. This account of realism is valuable in as much as it draws attention to the dimension of language, which is on the whole downplayed in nineteenth-century realist writing, but it is problematic in other respects. It attributes a simple-mindedness to realist novelists that is impossible to justify; it operates with a crude conception of correspondence theory, which is already inapplicable to much nineteenth-century writing and still more so to the contemporary period; its account of metalanguage is monolithic, failing to distinguish between its uses in different texts or even within a single work; finally, it lacks historical specificity and thus offers a generalizing account of realism that portrays it in a misleadingly homogeneous fashion. At the heart of the conventionalist case against realism is an essentialism of the kind elsewhere deplored by post-structuralist critics.

The concept of the 'classic realist text' depends on analysis of nineteenth-century realism. MacCabe and Belsey buttress their arguments with reference to George Eliot's work. Indeed, Eliot seems to be every conventionalist's favourite classic realist writer; her novels are duly trotted out when realism's fixed form and inherent conservatism are to be exposed. Penny Boumelha has recently shown how this version of Eliot's novels presents at best a partial truth, since they are far more questioning and self-aware than it allows.[41] I shall not rehearse Boumelha's persuasive arguments here, but I want briefly to extend them with reference to Eliot's critical writings and to *Adam Bede* in order to challenge the notion that Eliot's work can be aligned with classic realism.

George Eliot's concept of realism is certainly inseparable from empiricism and from a correspondence theory. She says of Ruskin: 'The truth of infinite value that he teaches is *realism* – the doctrine that all truth and beauty are to be attained by a humble and faithful study of nature, and not by substituting vague forms, bred by imagination on the mists of feeling, in place of definite, substantial reality'. Realism directs attention to a mind-independent world; its task is to produce knowledge of that world through empirical observation, and thus to guard against the subjectivism that breeds solipsism. This doctrine is central to Eliot's work. But does it commit her to the naive representationalism associated with classic realism? The answer must be no. In the same review of Ruskin, Eliot acknowledges that art depends on selection and thus cannot reproduce reality entire: '*All* the truths of nature cannot be given; hence a choice must be made of some facts which can be represented from amongst others which must be passed by in silence'.[42] This emphasis on the artist's interpretative and synthesizing function goes hand in hand with a complex view of language, which is far from a 'mirror' theory:

> [O]ne word stands for many things, and many words for one thing; the subtle shades of meaning, and still subtler echoes of association, make language an instrument which scarcely anything short of genius can wield with definiteness and certainty. Suppose, then, that the effort which has been again and again made to construct a universal language on a rational basis has at length succeeded, and that you have a language which has no uncertainty, no whims of idiom, no cumbrous forms, no fitful shimmer of many-hued significance, no hoary archaisms 'familiar with forgotten years,' a patent deodorized and nonresonant language, which effects the purpose of communication as perfectly and rapidly as

algebraic signs. Your language may be a perfect medium of expression to science, but will never express *life*, which is a great deal more than science.[43]

It is hard to know in what sense this account can be taken to offer a view of language as a 'transparent window' onto the world, or, concomitantly, of realism as a 'reflection' of the world. This takes us straight to *Adam Bede* and to the famous excursus in Chapter Seventeen where the metaphor of the mirror is indeed invoked. I want to suggest that the excursus not only supports the complex view of language and realism already outlined but also undermines the metalanguage Eliot herself employs. The opening of the chapter disrupts the realist illusion. It alerts the reader to the novel's textuality and signals Eliot's awareness of the nuances entailed in the novel/reader contract; hence her attempt to anticipate criticisms that she expects her female readers to make of her refusal to idealize her clergyman. Whereas contemporary critics of realism portray it as inherently monologic, Eliot acknowledges the dialogic nature of writing and reading, and incorporates this dialogism into her text. The oft-quoted passage about the author's desire to reproduce events 'as they have mirrored themselves in [her] mind' proceeds immediately to announce the epistemological difficulties thereby entailed: 'The mirror is doubtless defective; the outlines will sometimes be disturbed; the reflection faint or confused'. An elaborate defence of Eliot's aesthetic follows. That Eliot feels such a defence is necessary suggests she is aware that there is no unanimous conception either of 'reality' or of the 'novel' but that she is involved in an ongoing debate over rival accounts of both. A concern with epistemology pervades the chapter, but Eliot's subsequent emphasis on the opposition between social life and abstract thought is of particular interest. She persistently attacks those 'select natures who pant after the ideal', arguing that such people are so enamoured of abstract thought that they fail to attend to the daily realities of other people's lives.[44] Although Eliot herself generalizes from the particular to the universal, she reveals her awareness of the dangers inherent in such 'lofty' speculation. There is an ongoing tension, foregrounded by the novel itself, between Eliot's commitment to a concrete, context-dependent mimesis and her penchant for generalizing from the particular. Her text thus employs a metalanguage but at the same time calls its own use of it into question.

Conventionalist critics work with an abstract notion of realism, paying scant regard to the historical period in which a novelist such as Eliot was writing and to the illocutionary force of her texts. Against whom was she writing? To what end was she defending realism? Such questions do not seem to trouble them. Yet the briefest of glances at essays such as 'The Natural History of German Life' and 'Silly Novels by Lady Novelists' reveals that Eliot's espousal of realism belongs to a concrete context – it is part of a broad challenge (Ruskin, the Pre-Raphaelites, Browning, the Higher Criticism) to academicist art, idealist fiction, sentimental novels of the 'mind-and-millinery species', prejudice against women's education, and myth-laden, unhistorical readings of scripture.

The conventionalist position also offers a misleading account of realism's epistemology. It is not just Eliot who eschews the naive reflectionism attributed to classic realism; her emphasis on the synthetic role of the imagination in processing experience is shared by Balzac, de Maupassant and James. Balzac famously describes himself as secretary to his society in the preface to *La Comédie Humaine*, which might suggest that he sees himself as a passive recorder of events, but the way he subsequently describes his role emphasizes just how active he is in organizing, selecting, and interpreting his material: 'En dressant l'inventaire des vices et des vertus, en rassemblant les principaux faits des passions, en peignant les caractères, en choisissant les évènements principaux de la Société, en composant des types par la réunion des traits de plusieurs caractères homogènes, peut-être pouvais-je arriver à écrire l'histoire oubliée par tant d'historiens, celle des mœurs'[45]. Maupassant, in turn, rejects any notion of a photographic realism in his preface to *Pierre et Jean*, arguing that realism does not reflect reality but analyses it through the creation of aesthetically ordered visions: 'Le réaliste, s'il est un artiste, cherchera, non pas à nous montrer la photographie banale de la vie, mais à nous en donner la vision plus complète, plus saisissante, plus probante que la réalité même'.[46] Henry James, that most subtle of realists, contends in 'Alphonse Daudet' that 'the main object of the novel is to represent life' in such a way as to bring about 'a miraculous enlargement of experience', but he immediately acknowledges the multiplicity of perspectives available to the writer, for 'may not people differ infinitely as to what constitutes life – what constitutes representation?'.[47] His own preference is clear. In the preface to *The Spoils of Poynton*, he contrasts art's 'discrimination and selection' with life's 'inclusion and confusion' and dismisses 'the fatal futility of fact'.[48] It may be that some nineteenth-century writers thought that realism 'mirrors' reality, but this can hardly be claimed of realists *tout court*.

Eliot is in many respects a conservative novelist. So much can be shown without difficulty. It is something else, however, to infer from this that realism is an inherently conservative form *qua* form. Such a claim ignores both the specific content of literary works and the determinate contexts in which they are produced and received. Raymond Williams, for example, argues that 'the diagnosis of "realism" as a bourgeois form is cant' and shows how realism has been used to further working-class politics.[49] But conventionalist critics make exactly this kind of formalist claim. They thereby reproduce the very transition from the particular to the universal that they deplore in realist fiction. 'Classic realism' is a case in point. To arrive at such a concept one must consider a variety of recurring textual features outside of the novelistic and historical contexts in which they find their meaning. One can then incorporate these features into a structural typology but only by severing them from the cultural practices that give them their point. The 'classic realist text' is a hypostatization that makes a generic 'type' out of what is in fact an irreducibly heterogeneous corpus of texts. It *produces* realism as a homogeneous form by taking it out of the contexts of production and reception through which it acquires its meanings. It occludes both literary specificity and the social nature of reading.

Four conclusions and one observation. Conclusions: firstly, many realist novelists have been aware of the epistemological and aesthetic difficulties involved in literary representation; secondly, if one wants to understand particular realist works in their historical contexts, they should be seen in relation to the socio-cultural 'forms of life' in which they participate; thirdly, realism cannot *a priori* be equated with any given ideological position or political stance;[50] fourthly, realism is internally fissured, frequently conscious of its own contradictions, and constantly mutating into new forms. An observation: the conventionalist account of realism sees it as conservative and bourgeois; nineteenth-century realist writers lack the epistemological sophistication of contemporary critics and cannot foreground social contradictions. This view rests on a theory of belatedness symptomatic of much postmodernist thought; it is 'we' who are doubting, ironic, self-reflexive and detached, whereas 'they' are innocent, gullible, benighted, and unable to stand back from the beliefs of the day. We pit 'our' self-reflexive scepticism against 'their' naive realism in an act of gross historical condescension.[51] If the preceding arguments carry any force, then this kind of historical dualism ceases to be sustainable. Equally, however, the current concern with reflexivity may result in realism being valued because it too can be shown to be theoretically up-to-date, rather than because of its cognitive power and its ability to challenge various contemporary assumptions about the nature of reality.

From Realism to Realisms

John Fowles concludes the twelfth chapter of *The French Lieutenant's Woman* with a question: 'Who is Sarah? Out of what shadows does she come?' Chapter Thirteen notoriously fails to provide an answer, sliding off into a metafictional disquisition on the problems of writing novels 'in the age of Alain Robbe-Grillet and Roland Barthes'.[52] Fowles's breaking of the fictional frame announces that his mock-Victorian novel is something of a pastiche. He thus suggests that it portrays nineteenth-century life in order to examine not only Victorian society as mediated by its literature but also the nature of fictional representation as it appears from a post-war perspective. Like all metafictional texts, *The French Lieutenant's Woman* offers a double-focus: it refers both to a reality outside the text and to the process by which that reality is fictionally constructed. This double-focus is common to many of the novels discussed in this book. Whatever the differences among them, they include the problem of representation as part of their subject matter. They thus enact a shift from the typical strategies of nineteenth-century realists, who, for all their awareness of the epistemological difficulties that represent-ation entails, tended to concentrate on the social domain being depicted rather than on the process of depiction.

The self-reflexivity introduced by this shift in emphasis, which is taken to be one of postmodernism's key characteristics, can be discerned in a wide range of otherwise different works. Any talk of realism in the post-war context must acknowledge that a return to the techniques of the nineteenth-century novelists is unlikely to be of much help. This book explores the work of novelists who, on the whole, remain committed to what I shall for now term referentiality but who are profoundly aware of the various ways in which the latter has been called into question by modernism, the avant-garde, and postmodernism. Realism continues to be a presence in the post-war period but not as a set of formal techniques. It functions, rather, as a constellation of discursive practices, making it more pertinent to talk of an impulse to represent the social world than of a particular narrative mode. This impulse is by no means shared by all writers; nothing could be more misleading than to suggest that this is the case. Many novelists have no interest at all in continuing to explore realism, and some of the writers dealt with in this book (Barnes, Carter, Compton-Burnett, Green, Rushdie, Swift) depart from it in important ways.

Realism is in any case a notoriously slippery concept that eludes easy definition. It can broadly be conceived in three ways: as a general mimetic orientation that can be traced back at least as far as Aristotle's *Poetics*; as a specific literary movement opposed to neo-classical ideals that began in France in the 1830s and spread across Europe; as a non-conventional approach to the representation of reality, associated with various avant-garde writers, which seeks to render a historically mutable reality by breaking with established criteria and canons. Realism, I suggest, is flexible, wide-ranging, unstable, historically variable, and radically open-ended. Wittgenstein puts it as follows: 'We are inclined to think that there must be something common to all examples of realism, and that this common property is the justification for applying the general term "realism" to the various writings; whereas "realistic writings" form a *family* the members of which have family likenesses'.[53] These likenesses enable us to identify different members of the realist family as, say, comic, ironic, liberal, magic, naturalist, socialist, and so on. But the existence of this multiplicity of siblings, some more closely related than others, suggests that realism, beyond certain general attributes such as a mimetic impulse and a commitment to some form of referentiality, is heterogeneous.

If realism comprises a multi-faceted family of writings that alter from period to period, then its various products need to be seen in a historical rather than a formalist manner. Realism discloses not so much a set of textual characteristics as a general cognitive stance *vis-à-vis* the world, which finds different expression at different historical moments, manifesting itself in a wide range of fictional forms. The formalist conception of realism, so passionately attacked by Brecht in his debate with Lukács, rests on an unchanging conception of literary form that in turn presupposes historical stasis. It 'fixes' both social reality and the literary work. At the same time it displaces attention away from the synthetic role played by the author, since it implies that realist representation is an epistemologically and aesthetically simple affair. The theory of realism, René Wellek writes, 'is ultimately bad aesthetics because all art is "making" and is a world in itself of illusion and symbolic forms'.[54]

The Aristotelian emphasis on 'making' is central to my argument in this section. Drawing on Aristotle's enormously rich account of mimesis and on Paul Ricoeur's hermeneutic reading of it, I want to suggest that many post-war novelists build a self-reflexive dimension into their works in order to disclose the constitutive function of language in human beings' articulations of reality. The double-focus discernible in so many of the novels examined in this book exploits the very doubleness that Aristotle considers to be at the heart of literary representation. Janus-faced, these texts look both outward to an external world that they attempt to depict in all its complexity and inward to the very processes by which such depiction is brought into being. We can thus see why the kind of writing favoured by someone like Eliot has been superseded and why the post-structuralist account of realism, despite its weaknesses, has highlighted the reasons behind the decisive break with nineteenth-century narrative modes ushered in by modernism and post-modernism. Eliot remains caught in a subject-object dualism that, however subtle her conception of language, conceives it as designative rather than constitutive. Post-structuralism's break with this conception draws attention to the way that language shapes, constrains, and to some extent determines, the terms in which reference can be thought of at all. It is on these simult-aneously creative and confining aspects of language that so many contemporary writers dwell.

Post-war novelists who do not reject realism outright but who write with the legacy of modernism at their backs are in a sense forced to bring the issue of representation to the fore. The issue of language thus becomes central, as Heath argues. A *Festschrift* for J.P. Stern provides Heath with the opportunity to offer a generously critical reappraisal of his earlier semiotic critique of realism, which was 'always open to formalist reductions'. He quite properly insists that the modernist emphasis on language (later developed in a variety of directions by post-structuralism) decisively alters how realism is conceived because it refuses to flinch from the realization that cognition, and any literary artefact that is its product, is linguistically mediated. This realization does not shatter the intimate connection between text and world but forces the link between them to be reconceptualized. The result 'is not a collapse of realism (into "self", into "language"), but a transformation of our grasp of their conjunction – that transformation affecting the given opposition of "subjective" and "objective" itself'. At issue here 'is not a loss of realism but a contemporary redefinition of it to include the awareness – the "language-consciousness" – of the terms of its production'.[55]

How can Ricoeur's hermeneutic reading of Aristotle contribute to this awareness of the complex interaction between language and world? As is well known, Aristotle's use of the word mimesis is usually mistranslated as 'imitation'. This is a mistranslation because imitation is only one of mimesis's many meanings; others are impersonation, mimicry, performance, enactment, copying, indication, suggestion, expression.[56] Stephen Halliwell favours 'portrayal' or 'representation', contending that 'imitation' is 'the least adequate' translation. Mimesis denotes a complex concept that supports a variety of related meanings, but for Aristotle its representations crucially depend on the writer's constructive activity. At its simplest, Aristotle's account describes the poet as a maker of plots, but the picture is a good deal more complicated than this suggests. Halliwell argues that Aristotle's view of mimesis entails a distinction between (non-mimetic) propositions, that may be true or false, and (mimetic) literary productions, that plausibly represent human actions. The distinction turns on the fictional status of literary works, on 'their concern with images, representations, simulations or enactments of human life, rather than with direct claims or arguments about reality'.[57] Gerald Else echoes this view, suggesting that in Aristotle's usage mimesis 'cannot mean simply "copying"'; rather, it refers to 'an act of construction' that is implicitly fictional.[58]

There is a doubleness in mimesis. It does not stand to reality in a relation of one-to-one correspondence, whereby the fiction depicts a pre-existent set of events, but is distanced from reality by virtue of the fact that it is a *fictional* representation. The criterion by which it is measured is that of plausibility, not truth, as the famous distinction between history and poetry confirms; whereas history describes what actually occurred, poetry deals with what could plausibly have happened but did not. It explores the possible and the probable rather than the real; it is invented, thought up, made. The demand that poetry be plausible means that it points back at the reality in which it is rooted, but its constructed nature ensures that it is simultaneously seen as something feigned. Mimesis is at some distance from any account of representation as simple correspondence or copying, and a good deal closer to Aristotle's later account of metaphor as the seeing of similarities between things.[59]

If mimetic works do not imitate actual events but construct invented actions, and if their success depends on their evocation of fictional worlds that are plausible rather than true, then to talk of referentiality, as I did earlier, is potentially misleading.[60] Such works, if one excludes various forms of 'faction', do not refer to what 'really' happened in the world but invent stories that provide accounts of what it is like to live in the world. They are analogues, evocations of social life that do not depict it as it is but enable human beings to see more deeply into it by portraying it *as* a fiction.[61] They are not isomorphic with reality, nor do they purport to be.[62] In as much as they are referential, their referentiality is irreducibly metaphoric; at the very moment that they announce their power to evoke reality they admit that they can only do so indirectly, since they must describe it as something other than itself. For Michael Davis, the *Poetics* is therefore 'about human action as constituted by the irresistible impulse of reason to *sullogizesthai* – to see this as that'.[63]

The analogical conception of mimesis proves enormously productive when it is extended to a discussion of contemporary realisms. It enables us to get away from a debilitating reliance on correspondence theories that all too often neglect language's constitutive and transformative role in the creation of meaning. Ricoeur returns to the *Poetics* precisely in order to connect the semiotician's emphasis on this aspect of language with Aristotle's account of mimesis, in the hope that he will thereby be able 'to extricate representation from the impasse to which it has been relegated' without ignoring the post-structuralist critique of it.[64] For Ricoeur, Aristotle departs from Plato in two important respects: he combines mimesis with poiesis, thereby emphasizing that the former is active and productive; he suggests that mimesis does not offer weakened copies of the world (which for Plato means that literature is twice removed from the true Forms) but evokes it so as to 'bring about an augmentation of meaning'. The key point, Ricoeur argues, is that mimesis 'does not equate itself with something already given' but 'produces what it imitates'.[65] Even when mimesis is considered as a form of imitation – which it is, though it is also more – it is *indirect* imitation in the sense that, although reality grounds its products, these are created analogues to it. Mimetic works must be plausible to be coherent, hence Aristotle's emphasis on the importance of the probable to plotting. It is the intelligibility of the plot, which allows a quasi-real fictional world to come into being, that allows readers to make sense of it by seeing how it connects with the reality they inhabit. The plot is not 'an effigy or a replica of action'; it 'imitates in that it is intelligible'.[66]

We are a long way from correspondence theories that rely on the metaphor of the mirror and on what James dismissed as 'the fatal futility of fact'.[67] The 'language-consciousness' identified by Heath informs every step that Ricoeur takes, leading him to stress over and over again that mimetic literature does not copy a pre-existent world but configures it in order to transfigure our understanding of it. What are the consequences of this view for the referential problem? Ricoeur suggests that the classical designative account of language is unsustainable. He argues that his account of mimesis 'splits open descriptive reference' and allows us to 'forge the notion of a non-descriptive referential dimension'. Reference in fiction is retained, but it is conceived as 'a productive form of reference' and not in terms of mirroring. In Charles Taylor's words, the designative model that underpins truth-conditional theories of meaning 'is not viable, not because it might be seen as too ambitious, but because it manifestly is not ambitious enough'.[68] Mimesis, then, 'imitates real action' not because 'real means already there and available' but because 'real means that human action is "effectively" refigured through the fact of being configured'.[69] Thus Ricoeur alerts us to the analogical doubleness inherent in mimesis; its works are not only about the world that they produce in fictional form but also about their own mediation of it. In the nineteenth century, emphasis tended to fall on the former; now, after the impact of modernism and postmodernism, it falls increasingly on the latter. Fowles's metafictional interventions in *The French Lieutenant's Woman* are typical features of post-war fiction, as is his avowed desire *'to create worlds as real as, but other than the world that is'*.[70]

Realism and Mimesis

Realism, I have argued, is best seen as an open-ended concept; it gives rise to different narrative modes, which derive from authors' particular projects, aesthetic and political convictions, and changing socio-historical contexts. As Brecht remarks, realism is 'much used by many people and for many ends' and 'bears the stamp of the way it was employed, when and by which class, down to its smallest details'.[71] I have suggested that it can be equated neither with the novel *per se*, since the relation between them is contingent, nor with liberalism, since the latter constitutes only one of its sustaining ideologies. But the humanist reading of the novel as primarily realist and essentially liberal has been influential. It has tended to pit realism against experimentalism, conceiving them as opposites rather than as writing practices that stand in a complex, mutually interanimating relation to one another. This book argues that the dichotomy between realism and experimentalism is misleading in the post-war context because numerous novelists have sought to transcend it in their writing. Their work is marked by the tension between a wish to represent various aspects of post-war reality and a recognition of the artistic difficulties thereby entailed. Some remain more or less within the orbit of a fairly traditional realism (Fowles, Lamming, Lessing, Maitland, Naipaul, Wilson); others depart from it in different ways (Barnes, Berger, Carter, Compton-Burnett, Green, Rushdie, Swift). The post-war novel is multifarious and heterogeneous, the product of an ongoing contest over the forms it can and should take. Realism, in turn, should in my view be seen as a capacious form whose general commitment to the representation of reality sanctions a diversity of narrative modes. It is not a monolithic entity; indeed, as Lilian Furst points out, we would do well to 'pay less attention to realism than to realisms'.[72]

If it is the case that post-war writers respond to realism in a variety of ways, thereby revealing that a multiplicity of traditions is at work, then it is misleading to speak of a general 'crisis of representation'.[73] Talk of such a crisis is usually taken to be one of postmodernism's key signatures, and Jean-François Lyotard's pithy description of the postmodern as 'incredulity toward metanarratives' remains a good basic definition.[74] This incredulity does not, however, hinder postmodernists from invoking a few metanarratives of their own, such as the reported deaths of the subject, history, epistemology and metaphysics.[75] Postmodernists are quick to point out that the phenomenon under discussion is heterogeneous and internally contradictory, but these metanarratives of dissolution reappear often enough to make them fairly constitutive of it.[76] Prevalent among such new metanarratives is the preoccupation with the waning of historicity and the aesthetic 'depthlessness' that is its corollary. The result, it is claimed, is a loss of temporality and a dehistoricized sense of the present, which flattens out the past. Jameson suggests that postmodernism has become the 'cultural dominant' in relation to which contemporary cultural practices must define themselves.[77] If this is so, then it is important to have some idea of when postmodernism started to be a force-field of such power; otherwise the entire post-war period itself becomes historically flattened out, since all the texts that engage with the problems of realism and representation will be seen to be doing so under the sign of the postmodern. Postmodernism then becomes a virtually useless catch-all, for, if the entire period is seen in terms of a general crisis of representation and historicity, we lose sight of the enormously differentiated responses to realism and modernism, to politics and history, evidenced by post-war British fiction. The all-important differences between and among post-colonialists such as Naipaul and Lamming, socialists such as Berger and Lessing, liberal humanists such as Wilson and Fowles, feminists such as Carter and Maitland (I could go on) disappear from view when postmodernism is too quickly identified with the contemporary. Part of this book's purpose is to resist the dehistoricization of the recent literary past by emphasizing the irreducibility of the texts under discussion to the currently influential metanarrative of postmodernism.

I shall also suggest that the old division between experimental and realist writing is untenable if that distinction is taken to support avant-garde claims that experimental writing is inherently radical (aesthetically and politically), whereas realist writing is essentially conservative. The link between artistic experimentation and progressive politics is at best a tenuous one, and Peter Bürger's *Theory of the Avant-Garde*, which shows how and why the various avant-gardes were incapable of fulfilling their political aims, has surely shown how questionable this connection is.[78] Post-war avant-garde writing in Britain has been no more successful in linking art with politics; the *nouveaux romans* of Christine Brooke-Rose, the Dada-inspired collages of Alan Burns, and the metafictions of B.S. Johnson offer increasingly rarefied versions of the earlier shock tactics, thereby revealing that they are the fag-end of a decaying tradition. Although overtly avant-garde writers would deny this, the work of the novelists treated in this book suggests that any simple distinction between experimental and traditional writing has long ceased to be pertinent. What marks the fiction assessed here is precisely the interanimation of forms, styles and techniques. Attention to language's constitutive role, the doubleness inherent in fictional representation, and the impossibility of unmediated access to the real, are everywhere apparent. Most of the writers whose work I examine break free from the stultifying opposition between a realism committed to narrowly conceived correspondence theories and an avant-gardism committed to non-mimetic linguistic polysemy. They cross-breed narrative modes, taking what suits them from a variety of genres, and creating new forms that cannot easily be classified. Whether or not their novels should be labelled realist is perhaps a moot point. But their persistent focus on the difficulties of mimesis bears out Heath's claim that 'exploration, demonstration, criticism of the terms of representation are now fundamental to any consequential realism'.

Notes

1. See Leon Edel and Gordon N. Ray (eds), *Henry James and H. G. Wells, A Record of their Friendship, their Debate on the Art of Fiction, and their Quarrel* (Westport, Conn.: Greenwood, 1979); Virginia Woolf, 'Modern Fiction', *The Common Reader* (New York: Harcourt, Brace and World, 1953), pp. 150–9, and 'Mr. Bennett and Mrs. Brown', *The Captain's Death Bed and Other Essays* (New York: Harcourt Brace Jovanovich, 1950), pp. 94–120; D. H. Lawrence, 'Morality and the Novel' and 'Surgery for the Novel – or a Bomb?' *Selected Literary Criticism of D. H. Lawrence*, ed. Anthony Beal (New York: Viking, 1956), pp. 108–13 and pp. 114–18.
2. Evelyn Waugh, 'Aspirations of a Mugwump', *Spectator* (2 October 1959), p. 435.
3. Elizabeth Bowen, *The Mulberry Tree: Writings of Elizabeth Bowen*, ed. Hermione Lee (London: Virago, 1986), pp. 58, 59.
4. Alex Comfort, *The Novel and Our Time* (London: Phoenix House, 1948), pp. 11, 13, 18, 21, 75.
5. V. S. Pritchett, 'The Future of Fiction', *New Writing and Daylight*, 7 (1946), pp. 75–81, at pp. 76, 77.
6. Rose Macaulay, 'The Future of Fiction', *New Writing and Daylight*, 7 (1946), pp. 71–5, at pp. 72, 73.
7. Quoted in Ruben Rabinovitz, *The Reaction Against Experiment in the English Novel, 1950–1960* (New York: Columbia University Press, 1967), p. 40.
8. Quoted in Blake Morrison, *The Movement: English Poetry and Fiction of the 1950s* (Oxford: Oxford University Press, 1980), p. 299.
9. Quoted in Rabinovitz, *Reaction*, pp. 6–7.
10. C. P. Snow, *Sunday Times* (27 December 1953), p. 3.
11. C. P. Snow, 'Challenge to the Intellect', *Times Literary Supplement* (15 August 1958), p. vi.

12. Eva Figes, *The Imagination on Trial: British and American Writers Discuss their Working Methods*, eds Alan Burns and Charles Sugnet (London: Allison and Busby, 1981), p. 33; Eva Figes, *Beyond the Words: Eleven Writers in Search of a New Fiction*, ed. Giles Gordon (London: Hutchinson, 1975), p. 114.
13. Christine Brooke-Rose, 'Interview', *Contemporary Literature*, 17. 1 (Winter 1976), pp. 1–24, at p. 4; Christine Brooke-Rose, 'Self-Confrontation and the Writer', *New Literary History*, 9. 1 (Autumn 1977), pp. 129–36, at p. 136.
14. B. S. Johnson, 'Introduction', *Aren't You Rather Young to be Writing Your Memoirs* (London: Collins, 1974), pp. 12–13, 16–17.
15. John Wain, *Hurry On Down* (London: Secker and Warburg, 1953), p. 57.
16. Johnson, *Aren't You Rather Young*, pp. 13–14.
17. Angus Wilson, *Diversity and Depth in Fiction: Selected Critical Writings of Angus Wilson*, ed. Kerry McSweeney (London: Secker and Warburg, 1983), p. 196.
18. Angus Wilson, *New York Times Book Review* (2 July 1961), p. 12.
19. Stuart Laing, 'Novels and the Novel', *Society and Literature, 1945–70*, ed. Alan Sinfield (London: Methuen, 1983), p. 256.
20. See Raymond Tallis, *In Defence of Realism* (London: Edward Arnold, 1988), p. 190.
21. John Holloway, 'English Culture and the Feat of Transformation', *The Listener* 77 (12, 19, and 26 January 1967), pp. 47–9, 85–9, and 126–32, at p. 89.
22. Perry Anderson, 'Origins of the Present Crisis', *Towards Socialism*, ed. Perry Anderson and Robin Blackburn (Ithaca: Cornell University Press, 1966), p. 47.
23. Arthur Marwick, *British Society since 1945* (Harmondsworth: Penguin, 1986), p. 274. For other accounts of Britain's post-war problems, see Anthony Arblaster, *The Rise and Decline of Western Liberalism* (Oxford: Basil Blackwell, 1984), particularly chapters 17, 18 and 19; Tom Nairn, *The Break-Up of Britain* (London: New Left Books, 1981); Martin Wiener, *English Culture and the Decline of the Industrial Spirit, 1850–1980* (Cambridge, Cambridge University Press, 1982).
24. Philip Toynbee, 'Experiment and the Future of the Novel', *The Craft of Letters*, ed. John Lehmann (London: Cresset, 1956), pp. 60–74, at p. 72.
25. Iris Murdoch, 'Against Dryness: A Polemical Sketch', *Encounter*, 16. 1 (January 1961), pp. 16–20.
26. Ian Watt, *The Rise of the Novel: Studies in Defoe, Richardson and Fielding* (Harmondsworth: Penguin, 1957), pp. 10, 294.
27. See Bernard Bergonzi, *The Situation of the Novel* (London: Macmillan, 1970), pp. 13, 34; W. J. Harvey, *Character and the Novel* (London: Chatto and Windus, 1965), p. 24; George Orwell, 'The Prevention of Literature', *Collected Essays* (London: Secker and Warburg, 1961), pp. 328–41, at p. 337; George Steiner, *Language and Silence: Essays on Language, Literature and the Inhuman* (New York: Atheneum, 1967), p. 82.
28. Harvey, *Character*, pp. 24, 25, 28.
29. Bergonzi, *Situation*, pp. 23, 34.
30. David Lodge, *The Novelist at the Crossroads and Other Essays on Fiction and Criticism* (London: Routledge and Kegan Paul, 1984), p. 22, emphasis added.
31. See Robert Alter, *Partial Magic: The Novel as a Self-Conscious Genre* (Berkeley: California University Press, 1975).
32. Mikhail Bakhtin, *The Dialogic Imagination: Four Essays*, ed. Michael Holquist, trans. Caryl Emerson and Michael Holquist (Austin: Texas University Press, 1981), pp. 11, 39.
33. See, for example, Ros Ballaster, *Seductive Forms: Women's Amatory Fiction from 1684 to 1740* (Oxford: Oxford University Press, 1992); Michael McKeon, *The Origins of the English Novel, 1600–1740* (Baltimore: Johns Hopkins University Press, 1987); Jane Spencer, *The Rise of the Woman Novelist: From Aphra Behn to Jane Austen* (Oxford: Blackwell, 1986); Janet Todd, *The Sign of Angellica: Women, Writing, and Fiction, 1660–1800* (London: Virago, 1989).

34. See, for example, Edwin M. Eigner and George G. Worth (eds), *Victorian Criticism of the Novel* (Cambridge: Cambridge University Press, 1985); Kenneth Graham, *English Criticism of the Novel, 1865–1900* (Oxford: Clarendon, 1965); Richard Stang, *The Theory of the Novel in England, 1850–1870* (London: Routledge and Kegan Paul, 1959).

35. George Orwell, 'Inside the Whale', *Inside the Whale and Other Essays* (Harmondsworth: Penguin, 1979), p. 48; Steiner, *Language*, p. 80; Lodge, *Novelist*, p. 33.

36. I am indebted here to Laing, 'Novels', pp. 257–8.

37. I borrow the characterization of these critics' account of realism as conventionalist from Terry Lovell's invaluable *Pictures of Reality: Aesthetics, Politics and Pleasure* (London: British Film Institute, 1983). Other influences on their work are Althusser, Lacan, Foucault and Derrida.

38. Stephen Heath, *The Nouveau Roman: A Study in the Practice of Writing* (London: Elek, 1972), p. 20.

39. Colin MacCabe, *James Joyce and the Revolution of the Word* (London: Macmillan, 1979), pp. 15, 16.

40. Catherine Belsey, *Critical Practice* (London: Methuen, 1980), pp. 38, 46, 51.

41. Penny Boumelha, 'Realism and the Ends of Feminism', *Grafts: Feminist Cultural Criticism*, ed. Susan Sheridan (London: Verso, 1988). Two important essays that approach the problem of realism in different ways from mine are David Lodge, '*Middlemarch* and the Idea of the Classic Realist Text', and J. Hillis Miller, 'Optic and Semiotic in *Middlemarch*', both in John Peck (ed.), *Middlemarch* (London: Macmillan, 1992), pp.45–65 and 65–84.

42. George Eliot, 'John Ruskin's *Modern Painters*, Vol. lll', *Selected Critical Writings*, ed. Rosemary Ashton (Oxford: Oxford University Press, 1992), pp. 247–60, at p. 251.

43. George Eliot, 'The Natural History of German Life', *Selected Critical Writings*, pp. 260–96, at pp. 260, 282.

44. George Eliot, *Adam Bede* (London: Penguin, 1985), pp. 221, 229.

45. Honoré de Balzac, *La Comédie Humaine: Études de Mœurs: Scènes de la Vie Privée*, Vol. 1 (Gallimard, 1976), p. 11.

46. Guy de Maupassant, *Pierre et Jean* (Paris: Louis Conard, 1929), pp. xiv, xi.

47. Henry James, 'Alphonse Daudet', *Partial Portraits* (Ann Arbor: University of Michigan Press, 1970), pp. 195–242, at pp. 227, 228.

48. Henry James, *The Spoils of Poynton* (London: Penguin, 1987), pp. 23, 25.

49. Raymond Williams, 'A Lecture on Realism', *Screen*, 18. 1 (1977), p. 30.

50. For similar claims, see Laing, 'Novels'; Laura Marcus, 'Feminist Aesthetics and the New Realism', *New Feminist Discourses: Critical Essays on Theories and Texts*, ed. Isobel Armstrong (London: Routledge, 1992), pp. 11–26, at p. 23; Rita Felski, *Beyond Feminist Aesthetics: Feminist Literature and Social Change* (London: Hutchinson, 1989).

51. I am alluding to E. P. Thompson's remarks at the beginning of *The Making of the English Working Class* (Harmondsworth: Penguin, 1980).

52. John Fowles, *The French Lieutenant's Woman* (Boston: Little, Brown, 1969), pp. 103, 104.

53. Ludwig Wittgenstein, *The Blue and Brown Books* (Oxford: Oxford University Press, 1964), p. 17.

54. René Wellek, 'The Concept of Realism in Literary Scholarship', *Concepts of Criticism*, ed. Stephen G. Nichols, Jr (New Haven: Yale University Press, 1963), pp. 222–55, at p. 255.

55. Stephen Heath, 'Realism, Modernism, and "Language-Consciousness"', *Realism in European Literature: Essays in Honour of J. P. Stern*, eds Nicholas Boyle and Martin Swales (Cambridge: Cambridge University Press, 1986), pp. 103–23, at

pp. 106, 108, 118, 120.

56. See Michael Davis, *Aristotle's Poetics: The Poetry of Philosophy* (Lanham, Maryland: Rowman and Littlefield, 1992), pp. 25–9; Gerald F. Else, *Plato and Aristotle on Poetry*, ed. Peter Burian (Chapel Hill: North Carolina University Press, 1986), pp. 74–89; Stephen Halliwell, *The Poetics of Aristotle: Translation and Commentary* (Chapel Hill: North Carolina University Press, 1987), p. 71.

57. Halliwell, *Poetics*, pp. 71, 72.

58. Else, *Plato*, pp. 74, 83.

59. Aristotle, *Poetics*, trans. Gerald F. Else (Ann Arbor: Michigan University Press, 1970), 59a4. In this connection, see Kendall L. Walton, *Mimesis as Make-Believe: On the Foundations of the Representational Arts* (Cambridge, Mass.: Harvard University Press, 1990), pp. 41, 102, 124–7, 300.

60. See Norman Gulley, 'Aristotle on the Purposes of Literature', *Articles on Aristotle*, Vol. 4, *Psychology and Aesthetics*, eds Jonathan Barnes, Malcolm Schofield and Richard Sorabji (London: Duckworth, 1979), pp. 166–76, at p. 174.

61. See Walton, *Mimesis*, p. 300.

62. See Tallis, *Defence*, p. 28.

63. Davis, *Aristotle's Poetics*, p. 4.

64. Paul Ricoeur, 'Mimesis and Representation', *A Ricoeur Reader: Reflection and Imagination*, ed. Mario J. Valdes (Hemel Hempstead: Harvester Wheatsheaf, 1991), pp. 137–55, at p. 137.

65. Ibid., pp. 137, 138.

66. Ibid., p. 143.

67. James, *Spoils*, p. 25.

68. Charles Taylor, 'Theories of Meaning', *Human Agency and Language: Philosophical Papers*, Vol. 1 (Cambridge: Cambridge University Press, 1990), pp. 248–92, at p. 279.

69. Ricoeur, 'Mimesis', p. 152.

70. Fowles, *French Lieutenant's*, p. 105.

71. Bertolt Brecht, 'Against Georg Lukács', *Aesthetics and Politics: Debates between Bloch, Lukács, Brecht, Benjamin, Adorno*, trans. ed. Ronald Taylor (London: Verso, 1982), pp. 68–85, at p. 81.

72. Lilian Furst (ed.), *Realism* (London: Longman, 1992), p. 22.

73. See Fredric Jameson, 'Foreword', Jean-François Lyotard, *The Postmodern Condition: A Report on Knowledge*, trans. Geoff Bennington and Brian Massumi (Manchester: Manchester University Press, 1984), pp. viii–ix.

74. Ibid., p. xxiv.

75. See Jane Flax, *Thinking Fragments: Psychoanalysis, Feminism, and Postmodernism in the Contemporary West* (Berkeley, University of California Press, 1991), Ch. 2.

76. See Linda Hutcheon, *A Poetics of Postmodernism: History, Theory, Fiction* (London: Routledge, 1988).

77. Fredric Jameson, *Postmodernism, or The Cultural Logic of Late Capitalism* (London, Verso, 1991), pp. 18, 6.

78. Peter Bürger, *Theory of the Avant-Garde*, trans. Michael Shaw (Minneapolis: Minnesota University Press, 1984). See also Felski, *Beyond*.

2

Late Modernism as Social Critique

C.P. Snow and his *confrères* saw realism and experiment as implacably opposed to one another, as we have seen. For Snow, modernism had led the writer 'to contract out of society' and thereby to create inward-looking and socially irresponsible works.[1] The realists' account of modernism was certainly simplistic; apart from anything else, they tended to equate it with subjectivism, ignoring the post-Flaubertian emphasis on impersonality, which was so influential for writers such as Ford Madox Ford, T.E. Hulme, Wyndham Lewis, Ezra Pound and T.S. Eliot. The work of Ivy Compton-Burnett and Henry Green belongs to this tradition. Both started writing well before the Second World War; after a false start with *Dolores* (1911), Compton-Burnett published her first significant novel, *Pastors and Masters*, in 1925, while Green began with *Blindness* in 1926. Although both writers established quite distinct styles of their own, their sensibilities were to a great extent moulded by the innovations associated with an impersonal modernist strain. Both exploited the possibilities of dialogue, developing externalist narrative modes that enabled them to offer biting social satire. But Compton-Burnett and Green are usually read in an ahistorical manner that trivializes their work. I shall argue that their scrupulous attention to style and technique informs their social critique, which suggests, in turn, that the view of modernism taken by realists in the 1950s was somewhat myopic.

Compton-Burnett's novels, which (with one exception) are set in the late Victorian and early Edwardian period, are inseparable from the historical context in which they are rooted. Her novels were all written between 1911 and 1969, but she dealt only with the *fin-de-siècle*, averring that she did not 'have any real or organic knowledge of life later than about 1910'.[2] Critics tend to celebrate her work either for its pioneering use of dialogue or for its exploration of power, construing the former formalistically and treating the latter abstractly. But Compton-Burnett does much more, for she focuses relentlessly on the economic and institutional bases of social power. Maurice Cranston's description of her oeuvre could hardly be bettered: 'She depicts a world where power counts above all things, a time when the bourgeoisie is at its moment of ripeness, with the rot already there but the disintegration yet to come; she sees all relations in terms of the family, and the family as an institution based on property; the class war is endemic in her novels, and history unfolds itself at once dialectically and inevitably'.[3]

The significance of Compton-Burnett's much-discussed style lies here. The artificiality and brittleness of the dialogue reflect the shaky foundations on which late Victorian society is built and the duplicitous façade behind which its structural weaknesses lie concealed. The non-realist mode and the crystalline language that is this dialogue's corollary make no attempt to reproduce the density of 'the real' but rather try to pierce that very density, as though with a lancet, in order to expose the horrors it covers up. Protagonists' pretensions and hypocrisies are punctured with deadly precision, but this is usually done by other characters and not by way of a controlling metalanguage (of the post-war novels, *Manservant and Maidservant* is something of an exception). Compton-Burnett's work aggressively parodies the universalizing tendencies inherent in common-sense truisms and proverbs, so it is not surprising that she tends to eschew metalanguages. Her novels persistently defamiliarize what appears to be natural; they not only display their own artificiality as texts but also dismantle the social world they depict, disclosing both its constructed nature and the insidious networks of power that sustain it.

Green, like Compton-Burnett, is difficult to place. Because his work is experimental yet hard to contextualize, he gets read either as a stylist or as an allegorist of the human condition; whereas one set of critics concentrates on his technical innovations, describing him as a pure artist, the other group interprets him in an emblematic way, disclosing the hidden meanings they perceive beneath the symbolist surface of his prose.[4] Both approaches ignore the broader social significance of his writing. How then are we to read Green? What are we to make of a writer who discounted direct literary influences on his work, remarking that 'Joyce and Kafka have said the last word on each of the forms they developed' and claiming that '[y]ou've got to dream up another dish if you're to be a writer'?[5] In my view, Green's solution to this dilemma was to develop narrative forms that could provide a *via media* between realism and modernism. He thereby challenged the reductive critical dichotomy between realist (read: social, public) and modernist (read: individual, subjective) practices. As Michael North usefully points out, 'the old opposition between Woolf's sensibility and Bennett's Five Towns' destroys 'the world in between where Green's fiction finds its existence'.[6]

Part of my purpose in this chapter is to show that it is precisely that 'world in between' an aestheticist modernism and a gritty realism that novelists such as Compton-Burnett and Green explored to great effect in the 1940s and 1950s. Both writers experimented with technique and form but resisted the subjectivism to which much modernist literature was prey. Green, in particular, adopted a detached standpoint that drew on an objectivist modernism whose roots lay in Hulme's and Pound's Imagism, and Lewis's Vorticism. His late theory of fiction led him to curtail the Symbolist tendency in his earlier work in favour of a spare prose style in which the authorial presence is resolutely suppressed. This style is inseparable from the subjects with which the novels deal; it reveals Green to be a social satirist who dissects the conflicts of everyday life as they manifest themselves through class tensions and sexual–domestic power struggles. Furthermore, the detached perspective and characteristic obliquity of novels such as *Nothing* (1950) and *Doting* (1952) are, I suggest, closely linked to the culture of 1940s Britain. Their hostility to the post-war settlement is signalled thematically, through their negative depictions of austerity and social reconstruction, and stylistically, through the minimalism of their narrative modes.

Ivy Compton-Burnett

Virginia Woolf's oft-quoted statement that human character changed around 1910 reveals a desire, shared by other writers in the first part of this century, to identify a clean break with the Victorian period.[7] Although there was no unanimity as to the rupture identified by Woolf, many writers agreed that the war begun in 1914 marked the end of an era. For Henry James, the 'plunge of civilization into this abyss of blood and darkness' exposed 'the whole long age during which we have supposed the world to be . . . gradually bettering'.[8] Ford Madox Ford's Christopher Tietjens perceived it as the final defeat of chivalry and honour: 'No more Hope, no more Glory, no more parades for you and me any more. Nor for the country . . . nor for the world, I dare say'.[9]

The language of rupture employed by such writers left a picture of the pre-war years as an untroubled idyll shattered by the depredations of twentieth-century history. It was a picture apt to encourage nostalgia. Writing in the aftermath of another war, Elizabeth Bowen was to describe nostalgia as 'a prevailing mood', arguing that the desire to escape to the safe haven of a mythological past betokened a 'loss of faith in [the present]' whose origins derived from 1914. Bowen had no time for the invention of a national heritage located in the Victorian era: 'England dwells on a picture of exuberance in a settled scene – unspoiled countrysides, tribes of ruddy-faced children raised in manors, parsonages, farmhouses, cottages with roses over the porch'. History, she pointed out, provides a more disturbing account of the past; nostalgia ignores not only the 'millions [who] went under leaving behind no trace' but also 'the dismay, the apathy, the brutalising humiliations of people for whom there was no break'.[10]

Bowen's comments return literary representations of the late nineteenth and early twentieth centuries to a proper historical context. This context, though lightly etched in, is central to any understanding of Compton-Burnett's work. Compton-Burnett once remarked that 'economic forces influence people a great deal, that many things in their lives are bound up with them. Their scale of values, their ambitions and ideas for the future, their attitude to other people and themselves'.[11] The material reality of her characters' lives and the forms of social organization based upon it – country house estates, primogeniture, strict laws of entail – shape their modes of behaviour. But Compton-Burnett is a complex writer and although she explores the effects of a particular socio-economic system on her characters she does not conclude that this system is the origin of the behaviour she describes.[12] For Compton-Burnett, it is not the autocratic, patriarchal nature of upper-class Victorian family life that produces abuse of power; rather, its circumscribed space provides the hothouse atmosphere in which egotism can produce its flowers of evil.

Compton-Burnett's novels are set in large manors – often country house estates – and they examine the workings of extended family life in the upper and upper-middle classes, focusing on the authority of a ruling figure and the effect his or her use and abuse of power has on various dependants. Because the novels primarily consist of dialogue and offer little extra-diegetic information, the structure of family life and the historical period to which it belongs must be inferred from the text. It quickly becomes obvious, however, that the action takes place roughly between 1875 and 1910, and that many of the novels represent oblique reworkings of the 'Condition of England' question that exercised writers such as C.F.G. Masterman, H.G. Wells, E.M. Forster and John Galsworthy in the early years of the twentieth century.

Post-war novels such as *Manservant and Maidservant* (1947), *The Mighty and their Fall* (1955), *A Father and his Fate* (1957), *A Heritage and Its History* (1959), and *The Last and the First* (1971) explore the gradual decay of the Victorian ruling class. They depict the same socio-economic world as that pilloried by Wells's George Ponderevo in *Tono-Bungay* (1909). George describes the semi-feudal Bladesover estate as 'a closed and complete social system' that so dominated social life that it 'seemed to be in the divine order'. But by 1909 Bladesover, and the class hierarchy it represents, exist only in appearance; the grand house offers a public façade that conceals 'how extensively this ostensible order has even now passed away'.[13] Bladesover is presided over by the decrepit matriarch Lady Drew, a figure who would be perfectly in place in Compton-Burnett's world. Here the rulers are either middle-aged or very old figures (reminiscent of Queen Victoria) who tenaciously hold on to power, continuing in the established way and refusing to pass authority on to their eager progeny. Would-be inheritors such as Simon Challoner in *A Heritage* have had to queue for so long that they feel their birthright has been denied them and that they have wasted their most productive years catering to the whims of seemingly immortal father figures. Strict accordance to the rule of primogeniture and the law of entail is thus responsible for the atrophying of these families, for those with vitality are forced to dissipate their energies. Furthermore, the closed quasi-feudal system is almost impossible to break through. In *The Mighty and their Fall* Lavinia is eventually assimilated; in *A Father and his Fate*, Verena is defeated; in *A Heritage*, Hamish lacks the strength of character to usurp Simon, but the latter, after waiting for years to rule, leaves everything as it was; and in *The Last and the First*, Hermia defeats Eliza in their battle for control of the family but looks to be merely a leaner, meaner version of her stepmother.

The issue of inheritance is of prime importance in Compton-Burnett's work. It raises the question of who will inherit England as much as that of who will rule the family, for, as Compton-Burnett once noted, her 'novels are in a way a microcosm of a larger society'.[14] Indeed, anyone who wants to read Compton-Burnett in an ahistorical manner, seeing her as dealing with a generalized human condition alone, must work quite hard to ignore the plethora of references she makes to specific financial and economic pressures, all of which point to the agricultural depression of 1875–1905. This depression hit country house estates particularly hard. Migration from the country to the city, a shift from agriculture to manufacturing, and cheap imports from abroad, which led to falling grain prices, led to massive financial problems.[15] Many of the great estates rapidly declined; faced with unpaid rents, high costs of maintenance, and unprofitable crops, landowners were forced to retrench in various ways: selling land, remortgaging it, renting their houses and moving elsewhere, granting substantial rebates to their tenants. Several estates were effectively broken up during these years, and references to wholescale economies are prevalent in the writing of the period.[16] Wilde's Lady Bracknell was to offer the wittiest description of the problem: 'What between the duties expected of one during one's lifetime, and the duties exacted from one after one's death, land has ceased to be either a profit or a pleasure. It gives one position, and prevents one from keeping it up. That's all that can be said about land'.[17]

Compton-Burnett does not belabour these issues but inscribes them into the weft of her works. Her novels are obsessed with financial issues, and various economies – such as giving up servants and governesses, moving house, renting, and selling land – are frequent topics of conversation. In *The Mighty and their Fall*, Ninian Middleton's estate-derived income has 'lessened in the manner of its kind' and 'seem[s] to return to its source, taking his energy with it'; he is forced to remind his family of their straitened circumstances, explaining that 'the land does poorly, and giving it my life does not better it'. In *A Father and his Fate*, the Lear-like Miles Mowbray tests his daughters' love by plausibly informing them that '[g]reat retrenchment must be made' and asking what sacrifices they are prepared to make for him. The Heriots, in *The Last and the First*, are almost forced to move out before an unexpected bequest saves them: 'Tithes and rents have fallen; farmers have failed; mortgages have been called in; general costs have risen. . . . We have never done more than strike a balance, and now the climax has come'. Like the owners of Bladesover, the ruling elite in Compton-Burnett's social world are in retreat, desperately hanging on to a life of economic privilege and moral authority they cannot sustain.[18]

Most of the estates depicted in Compton-Burnett's novels are run on despotic lines. As studies of the patrilineal families that comprise the governing class, the novels explore the institutional frameworks through which authority is conferred and power wielded. As I have already noted, Compton-Burnett is too subtle a writer to assume that the proclivity for power can be gendered in a facile way; her male monsters are more ubiquitous than her female tyrants, but then the social system – via primogeniture – gives them family headship far more frequently. The women who do gain access to power, because their husbands either have conveniently died or have no stomach for authority, are equally overbearing and egotistical. Compton-Burnett's texts emphasize that neither gender has an especial predilection for oppression. In her pessimistic worldview social structures encourage tyrannical behaviour but do not create it; rather they allow egotism to flourish because they grant certain individuals outrageous latitude in their exercise of power.

The Mighty and their Fall offers a typical example of socially sanctioned abuses of power. Ninian Middleton is a patriarch whose family belongs to him in much the same way as do his property and land. After his wife's early death he has treated his eldest daughter, Lavinia, as a surrogate partner, and there are hints that incest has taken place.[19] When he decides to remarry he attempts to blot out his past relations with Lavinia, imagining that they can easily be sloughed off. Hengist protests that as a result of all that has happened Lavinia can never be a child again, but Ninian dismisses him. His desire to deny recent family history is challenged by his future wife, who declares that '[y]ou can't undo what is past'. The novel subsequently bears her out. As with most of Compton-Burnett's tyrants, Ninian's besetting sin is that he treats his family in a purely instrumental fashion – they are the means to his ends. Ninian's stress on his right to happiness and his refusal to acknowledge that his search for it blights the lives of those around him mark him as a supreme egotist. Ransom, the truth-speaking outsider, as good as tells him so when he explains why Lavinia attempted to block the impending marriage: 'You needed a companion and used her as one. And threw her away when you chose another. It had to lead to something, and it led to this'. But his words fail to penetrate Ninian's all-encompassing self-love. Later, when Ninian proves to be as duplicitous as Lavinia, Ransom's choric comment sums up the extent of his brother's selfishness: 'people who have power respond simply. They know no minds but their own'.[20] This judgement is proved correct when Ransom dies. Although Ninian has given his word that he renounces all claim to Ransom's money, he does everything he can to wrest it from Lavinia and ultimately succeeds. The defeat of Lavinia and Hugo leaves the domestic order as it was; Ninian (the mighty) has fallen in everybody's estimation except his own, but this psychological difference alters nothing, for he remains firmly in power.

Ninian's patriarch functions as a secular surrogate for a jealous god. Selina regularly invokes the deity as a means of intimidating her wayward grandchildren.[21] And Ninian, of course, behaves like a capricious god, taking a daughter to wife and then discarding her when she has served her purpose. But when Ransom threatens to take Lavinia away, Ninian insists on paternal precedence: 'And *Father*? . . . Who is that to you now?'. His casual disregard for the way he has deformed her life only confirms Hugo's sense of his wilful omnipotence: 'I have never believed in God. I believe in him now. We have known he is a father. And I see that he is yours. There are the anger, jealousy, vaingloriousness, vengefulness, love, compassion, infinite power'. In fact, Ninian's behaviour warrants only some of the attributes in this catalogue, as there is little of love or compassion in it. His control of his dependants requires him not only to adopt the guise of a god-like figure but also to promote belief in a deity above himself, whom he can claim to represent. The atheist Selina puts the point with unflinching candour: 'They need to accept an All-seeing Eye. Or rather we need them to. No ordinary eye could embrace their purposes. We may as well depute what we can'.[22]

The panoptic eye is an instrument of control. It represents the rule of the father, and the entire domestic order falls within its purview. All dependants, but particularly children and servants, are surveyed. Strict orders are issued concerning access to various domestic spaces. Children belong primarily in the nursery and garden but are occasionally permitted to eat in the dining-room; access to the drawing-room is limited, while the library (father's inner sanctum) is a forbidden place, entered only when punishment is due. Children are rarely out of the sight of either a nurse or a governess. Under-servants, in turn, belong below stairs and must vacate their masters' rooms as soon as they have completed their duties; their activities and movements are patrolled by the rulers' representatives in the servants' quarters – primarily the head butler but also (for the maids) the cook. In *Manservant and Maidservant*, for example, Bullivant describes himself as Horace's 'deputy, authorised to carry out his task'; part of his role (like Ainger's in *The Mighty and their Fall*) is to socialize the under-servants and police their behaviour.[23] Compton-Burnett's novels also pay a good deal of subtle attention to the way that those in authority use a house's internal topography to institute a hierarchical order, marking out people's stations, controlling their where-abouts, restricting their movements in domestic spaces, and generally ensuring that surveillance remains as unbroken as possible. Children are perhaps most vulnerable in this respect; fathers demand that they always be watched, since they are thought to be naturally inclined to stray from the path of righteousness. In text after text, children seek to escape the all-seeing eye, which they explicitly identify with patriarchal power. Avery puts it most clearly in *Manservant and Maidservant*: 'Is Father gone now? . . . I don't want him to come here. He is always in all the places. I don't want him to come here where I sleep. I don't like to think he might look at me in the night'.[24]

Surveillance and the control of domestic space are crucial to the mainte-nance of order, but in Compton-Burnett's novels they merely buttress the control of discursive space, which is the pre-eminent instrument of those in power. The novels reveal the way that language is used either to socialize children or, whenever they seem recalcitrant, to bludgeon them into submission. Guardians exercise power by controlling access to language; they 'name' reality and forbid others to contest this 'naming' by enjoining them to silence. Consider the following exchange:

> 'Agnes and Hengist and Leah, lend me your ears. I come to bury something, not to praise it. The mistake your father has made will not live after him. I have come to end it with a word. It is a word you will hear in silence, with your eyes fixed on my face. Do not look at each other. Do not utter a syllable or a sound . . . Do you hear and understand?'
> There was silence.
> 'Should you not answer your grandmother?' said Miss Starkie, in a rather faint tone.
> 'She said we were not to speak,' said Leah.

Children's (public) speech is allowable only within certain contexts and parameters. As Selina says: 'you will accept what I say. You will not differ from me or voice thoughts of your own'.[25] Selina, Ninian's representative, grasps that those who control language control intersubjective space. She prevents her account of events from being challenged by imposing it on the children and preventing them from disputing it in the public sphere (they are not to *voice* whatever it is they might privately think). Nor is her statement that she has come to stifle speculation 'with a word' a casually chosen turn of phrase. Compton-Burnett's tyrants repeatedly employ this locution. Her novels thus disclose an acute understanding of the way that power is linguistically mediated. Although they do not collapse the economic basis of power into language, they show how social institutions such as the family are upheld by access to and control of discursive space.

The authority exercised by Compton-Burnett's tyrants is always directed at those who are subservient to them. Some succumb, others resist. Power is shown to be far from all-encompassing and is withstood in a variety of ways, including a more or less willing assimilation to the social order in the hope of preferment (servants), subversion through innuendo and parody of hegemonic discourses (children), and rejection through the refusal to conform to established codes of masculine behaviour (younger sons and brothers).

Consider the case of Percival in *The Mighty and their Fall*. He exists just on the edge of representation in this novel. Before he makes his first appearance, he is 'an unseen hand' from which Ainger takes a tray, and Ainger later describes him metonymically as 'a pair of hands'. His name, with its upper-class connotations, disturbs Selina, for whom he is interchangeable (as pairs of hands tend to be) with the serving boy who preceded him: 'Must we call him *Percival*?' said Selina. 'What about the name of the last boy?' Selina demands that Percival be renamed James. Percival is at first resentful and tries to resist this subordination of his identity to his professional function:

> 'I do not look for anything in you, James. The idea not having struck me. And is the hall your place? – And when I speak, I await reply.'
> 'You didn't speak to me.'
> 'Oh, there is this trouble with the name, Cook,' said Ainger, idly. 'He is one thing to himself and another to everyone else.'
> 'I am myself and no other person,' said James with a heat the words hardly seemed to warrant.
> 'And is it so much to be?' said Cook. 'That you claim it in the face of everything? The self you refer to is known as James, to those who are aware of it.'
> 'I am myself and not the last boy.'

Ainger and Cook, acting as the representatives below stairs of the rulers above stairs, seek to teach Percival his 'place' just as Bullivant and Mrs Selden do with George and Miriam in *Manservant and Maidservant*. As *The Mighty and their Fall* progresses, James comes to accept both his place and the name that denotes it, until by the novel's end he has been fully socialized into his role, not only performing his duties with alacrity but also taking pride in his subordinate status:

> 'He is born to be a slave,' said Ainger, who perhaps hardly opposed the tendency.
> 'To render service,' said Cook, glancing at James.
> 'I was not born to it,' said the latter, in honest admission. 'But I am one who learns.'
> 'No more trouble with the name, Cook. That is in the past.'
> '*James* is a usual name for a house servant,' said the new owner of it with fluency. 'And it saves inconvenience.'
> 'Saves whom?' said Ainger. 'Those who have the least?'
> 'They should not have any,' said James, in a grave tone.[26]

The servant's new values have been instilled in him from above. He has learned that within this social order he is an impostor as Percival but a valued member of the domestic economy as James. He has grasped, moreover, that Ainger's position is not impregnable; if he accepts his place (for now) and plays his cards right, he may usurp the head butler. As upstart

Percival, he is forbidden entry to the text, being visible only as a pair of hands whose body remains outside the door and outside representation; as obedient James, a boy who has embraced his social position, he enters the novel and is given licence to speak. This licence depends on James's acceptance of a hierarchical structure; it is because he has successfully assimilated himself to the social system that he may in the future expect preferment within it.

Compton-Burnett ruthlessly lampoons those who are in authority for their blindness to the lives of their dependants. The latter often undermine that authority (although they never overturn it in open revolt) by ridiculing their superiors' words. The following exchange is typical of her work:

> 'What can you want in this house that you do not have?'
> 'Well, ma'am, I suppose there are possibilities.'
> 'Well, that would be so in the case of a king.'
> 'That is a position I am not conversant with, ma'am. Gulfs have narrowed, but not to that extent.'
> There was some mirth, and Hollander's lips twitched, while Jocasta's continued grave.
> 'You are well housed and fed. And have reasonable time to yourself.'
> 'Is that the life of a king, ma'am? It is scarcely as it is imagined.'
> 'It would describe the life of most kings. Except that the amount of work they do is greater.'
> 'We hear of that, ma'am. There is less said about the amount of work they make.'

Jocasta's lack of awareness about the lives of her servants is matched by Eliza Heriot's lack of concern for their welfare. When the Heriots fear that they must retrench by moving from the main house to the lodge, she leaves Mrs Duff to deal with the necessary redundancies while disingenuously claiming that the servants 'must decide for themselves' and hoping 'they are not fair-weather friends'. For Eliza, the gap between servants and masters is unbridgeable; when Madeline observes that their servants 'have the same feelings as we have ourselves', she retorts that 'they have quite different ones'. It is this perceived difference, always coded as one of superiority/ inferiority, that permits those in charge to rule with such impunity.[27]

The treatment meted out to younger brothers, who occupy uneasy positions within the family, also indicates how economic strength underpins power. Younger brothers are vulnerable for various reasons: they are financially dependent on either their father or their eldest brother, since under primogeniture it is he who inherits; they are members of the family but if they remain with it are usually unproductive, perhaps helping on the estate but generally leading lives of leisure; they have no real authority and an indeterminate status. But because they stand in the margins of the domestic scene, they are in a position to mock the social order that subordinates them. They frequently do so by repudiating the masculine code represented by fathers and elder brothers.

Younger brothers such as Hugo (*The Mighty and their Fall*), Angus (*The Last and the First*), Mortimer (*Manservant and Maidservant*), and Walter (*A Heritage*) are all dandiacal figures; lacking the power and authority that is invested in their elder brothers, they rebel by rejecting patriarchal notions of masculinity. They are Wildean figures in manner and attitude: self-deprecating, languid, effete, and often self-consciously effeminate. Always quick with the kind of verbal riposte that has the flavour of the decadent 1890s about it, they constantly turn 'serious' matters into jokes. Witness Walter's response to his mother's query about his university debts: 'If I had paid them, they would not be bills, Mater. They would be receipts. And I put those in a drawer'.[28] Both Hugo and Mortimer emphasize that their personalities have been moulded by their position as younger sons. Hugo's adoptive father left him 'only just enough for [his] support'.[29] Mortimer, in turn, is financially dependent on Horace and explains his attempt to escape by way of marriage as an act of desperation: 'I was in someone else's power. You do not know what it is, never to earn any money'. All these figures are trapped in a dilemma: they desire the wealth and ease that masculine headship confers but despise the posturing that seems to be its necessary corollary. Their revolt takes the form of living off their brothers' money while rejecting their concept of manly behaviour. As Mortimer wryly observes, '[t]he words, "behave like a man", seem to have assumed the sense of behaving like a god'.[30] Younger brothers such as Hugo and Mortimer self-consciously stand back from society; cynical and jaded, they exude ennui. Their response to their lack of success in life's lottery is to adopt the pose of detached observer, to confront powerlessness by refusing to engage in the drama of social and domestic conflict, thereby turning life's numerous disappointments into spectacles of vicarious pleasure. As Mortimer puts it: 'I am content to live in other people's lives, content not to live at all'.[31]

Children stage a different form of revolt. Another vulnerable group, they target language, but their resistance is as oblique as that of servants and younger brothers. Language, as I have argued, functions as the primary means by which parents police the behaviour of their offspring in Compton-Burnett's novels. Children can do little about the control of domestic space and time in these texts; if they ignore injunctions about which rooms they are forbidden to enter, or disregard rules about their daily schedule, they signal disobedience and risk immediate punishment. Such a strategy is strewn with pitfalls. But language, which is a subtle weapon, can be turned against the authority figures that wield it so caustically. Children can re-quote portentous words in contexts that disclose their vapidity; can ask apparently innocent questions in order to expose sham values; can invert various common-sense maxims in order to challenge their subordination of the particular to the general; can act as licensed speakers of truth (like the fools of old), since their young age encourages adults to dismiss their talk as nonsense; and can make dramatic *sotto voce* asides to sympathetic siblings and complicit readers. In these ways they subvert the universalizing discourse beloved of those who rule them, demonstrating that the social order they represent as divinely ordained is culturally constructed. Any such demonstration is of course superbly ignored by those against whom it is aimed. Thus its truths hover at the edges of public knowledge, are both known and not known. It must be so if the fiction of late Victorian social and domestic respectability is to be sustained.

The networks of power that uphold social respectability are just barely in place in the pre-war world of Compton-Burnett's novels, for they are everywhere declining in scope and vitality. Her works can be seen as belated contributions to the 'Condition of England' question, as I have suggested, because they confront the problem of who will inherit England. Compton-Burnett's account of late Victorian and Edwardian society suggests that decay has set in because the old order – represented by the fathers – refuses to give way. In novel after novel closure is achieved when the forces of change are summarily defeated and stasis returns. This is almost never (*The Last and the First* is an exception) a synthesis in which old and new, or internal and external, can be united; it is precisely a return to the established regime after the threat to it has been seen off.

The most interesting novel from this point of view is *A Heritage and its History*. Simon Challoner's frustrations are apparent from the outset, since he makes no effort to hide his frustration at having to wait for his inheritance and therefore being unable to be its ruler in his prime. He directs his frustration at the stasis that is strangling the house and its inhabitants. The creeper, which he threatens to cut down when he is in command, symbolizes the oppressive social order against which he inveighs: 'Look at this room and its dinginess! It gets darker every day. It is the creeper smothering the house'. The implacable, unflappable Sir Edwin resists all Simon's pleas; everything will remain as it is. Simon is not alone in fearing that the family will 'go on and on in the same way'. Marcia virtually refuses to stay in the house because she perceives its petrifaction; to her the Challoner household is 'like some fossilised thing', and the social order it represents is for her an antiquated one that needs to be overthrown. But by the time Simon does inherit, the old order has effectively tamed him, for he concludes by upholding the structure of values that he initially strove to overthrow. When Deakin asks if the creeper is to be cut back, he is told to let it alone: '"We will give it a respite, Deakin," said Simon. "Encroachment seems to be its work. And we are so inured to the shadow, that we might be startled by the light"'.[32] The house's heritage has so encroached on Simon's life that he himself now prefers the desuetude of the regime he once abominated. Closure in this text is as pessimistic as in *The Mighty and their Fall*. Ainger, that novel's choric figure, concludes that '[t]he new generation cometh . . . and might as well be the old'.[33]

The Last and the First contains a curious remark made by Angus to his mother: 'You might be a figure in history, corrupted by power. It is what you are, except that you are not in history'.[34] This comment raises the question of what is meant by history. Angus imagines that for Eliza to be 'in history' she would have to be some sort of grand personage whose actions affect numerous lives. But Compton-Burnett's novels operate with a different conception of history; they explore in minute detail the day-to-day history of the lives of people in late Victorian and Edwardian upper-class households. Despite its resolute non-realism and consequent obliquity of approach, this is fiction as social history. It refuses the nostalgia identified by Elizabeth Bowen, disclosing the injustices suffered by various people under a relentlessly hierarchical social order. Compton-Burnett's lancinate style pierces the cloak of legitimacy in which her ruling classes shroud themselves and strips away the façade of respectability which shields their decaying houses. Wells's *Tono-Bungay*, which deals with the rapacious world replacing the country house estates, is equally contemptuous of the social order they represent: 'There in that great pile of Victorian architecture the landlords and the lawyers, the bishops, the railway men and the magnates of commerce go to and fro – in their incurable tradition of commercialized Bladesovery, of meretricious gentry and nobility sold for riches. . . . Respect it indeed! There's a certain paraphernalia of dignity, but whom does it deceive?'.[35] Feudal Bladesover never deceived Compton-Burnett. Her œuvre destroys the facade of propriety behind which the Victorian ruling class sheltered, offering an emphatic retort to the rhetorical question posed by Miles Mowbray: 'Now that I am about to lead a just and loyal life in a respected place, I will be left unmolested to do so. Have you anything to say?'.[36]

Henry Green

Any assessment of Henry Green's theory of fiction must be wary of lending it a spurious cohesiveness. The late theory should not simply be seen as the end-point that all the earlier work was somehow trying to approach. To take such a view is to impose a false teleology on Green's canon and to conceal its heterogeneity. Green's work discloses a persistent tension between Imagism (concretion, objectivity) and Symbolism (nuance, subjectivity).[37] The theory that Green elaborated in the early 1950s abandoned the Symbolist tendencies discernible in novels such as *Loving* (1945), *Back* (1946), and *Concluding* (1948). The novels on which I want to focus – *Caught* (1944), *Nothing* (1950), and *Doting* (1952) – curtail this lyricism in favour of a crisp, minimalist narrative mode in which the authorial presence is suppressed so that events can be portrayed impersonally. These texts clearly conform to the principles Green outlined in his late theoretical pronouncements. The modernism that informs Green's theory of fiction can be traced back to figures such as T. E. Hulme, Ezra Pound, and Wyndham Lewis. Hulme, for example, urged a classical revival that would repudiate Romantic excess. In an early essay he associated classicism with 'dry hardness' and 'accurate, precise and definite description'.[38] Later, under the influence of Wilhelm Worringer, he was to distinguish between vital (organic) and geometric (non-organic) art, but his language remained the same. Geometric art was 'austere' and 'bare'; it was an art of 'rigid lines and dead crystalline forms'.[39] These ideas were to influence Pound's Imagism, with its emphasis on direct treatment of objects and anti-didacticism, as well as Lewis's Vorticism, with its stress on externality and the visual imagination. For Lewis, stream-of-consciousness writing surrendered to T.S. Eliot's 'immense panorama of futility and anarchy', whereas Vorticism imposed artistic form on the chaos of contemporary history and thereby escaped it.[40] Tarr, Lewis's thinly disguised alter ego, declares that 'good art must have no inside'.[41] Hence Lewis's uncompromising battle-cry: 'Dogmatically, then, I am for the *Great Without*, for the external approach'.[42]

Green's theory of the novel and the texts he wrote in support of it belong to this modernist tradition. Although his style is inimitable, he shares both Lewis's satirical proclivities and his detached viewpoint, refusing to interpret characters' inner motivations and favouring an impersonal narrative mode. He justifies his rejection of omniscience on epistemological grounds. People do not learn about life by being 'told' about it by some 'demi-god' but by observing whether behaviour and speech are congruent or discrepant. In life, it is 'only by an aggregate of words over a period followed by an action, that we obtain . . . a glimmering of what is going on in someone, or even in ourselves'.[43] Like Lewis, Green rejects interiority; just as the former refuses to 'let the reader "into the minds of the characters"' and calls for 'a *visual* treatment', so the latter argues that human knowledge is gained by '*watching* the way people . . . behave'.[44] In his late works Green altogether cuts out an identifiable narrator, presenting events as though they are being witnessed by a *tabula rasa* that blankly registers what occurs. The more he limits authorial omniscience the more spoken language comes to the fore, until his style has been pared so close to the bone that it relies almost exclusively on dialogue. Showing is thus preferred to telling, for 'if you want to create life the one way *not* to set about it is by explanation'.[45] And this Flaubertian imperative goes hand in hand with Green's conviction that art should not be didactic, since 'narrative is not a medium for the proselytising of readers to the writer's personal point of view'.[46]

Two questions arise from this account of Green's theory. If he adopts an impersonal stance, can an authorial point of view be identified? And in what sense can one speak of Green, as I have been doing, as a critic of society? The answer lies in not confusing authorial detachment with authorial disinterestedness. There is a danger that an objectivist mode will be read as the corollary of a neutral attitude. The two should not be conflated. As Green himself notes, his impersonal approach is primarily a technical matter, which 'has nothing to do with the *theme* of [a writer's] work. We are all individuals and each writer has *something of his own to communicate*'.[47] The techniques that Green favours do not entail the abnegation of an authorial perspective. Far from it. As I shall argue below, although they tend to eschew *direct* commentary, interpretation or judgement, they nevertheless establish a critical stance *vis-à-vis* characters and events. *Caught*, for example, focuses on the Phony War and the Blitz, subtly undermining what has come to be known as the 'myth of the Blitz' by disclosing the unreliability of personal and collective memory. *Nothing* and *Doting*, in turn, the two texts that most fully exemplify Green's theory of fiction, reveal a pessimistic view of the post-war settlement and offer an oblique indictment of both the Labour Government and the rentier class that is declining under it. In all three novels the author refuses to take a bow, but, like Flaubert, although he is nowhere visible, he is everywhere present.[48]

If *Nothing* and *Doting* make extensive use of dialogue, then *Caught* exploits the principle of montage. *Caught* deals with the Blitz, evoking the tense uncertainties of the Phony War and the experience of bombardment from a fireman's perspective. It explores both personal and collective myth-making during the war and thus questions the validity of what Angus Calder has called the 'myth of the Blitz'.[49] The novel conveys a sense of personal and social dislocation in a variety of ways: it employs a complex time-scheme (reminiscent of Conrad's *Nostromo*), frequent changes of tense, heavy use of prolepsis and analepsis, abrupt pronominal shifts, and a cinematic technique that cuts swiftly from scene to scene.

Caught is divided into three sections. It begins in the country, describing Richard Roe's visits to Dy, his deceased wife's sister, and to his son

Christopher; it then shifts to London and to Roe's experiences in the Auxiliary Fire Service prior to the Blitz; it ends just after the Blitz has begun, with an emotionally and physically shattered Roe once more on leave in the country. This loose tripartite structure goes hand in hand with Green's inversion of a linear time-scheme. *Caught*'s opening thirty pages not only establish the atmosphere that will pervade the novel, one of anticipation and tension, but also mirror its characters' disrupted lives through their dislocations of normal chronology. The resultant fractured narrative mode enables Green, like Conrad, both to portray social disarray and to explore particular instances of confusion or dissimulation. The latter is perfectly exemplified by the discrepancy between Roe's nostalgic mourning of his wife and his making love to Hilly, for although these scenes are *narrated* some 100 pages apart from each other, they *occur* within a few days of each other. The contradictory nature of Roe's behaviour in these scenes places him as a character, although Green proffers no overt judgement of his protagonist; he seems more interested in exploring the way memory distorts the past under the pressures of imminent disaster. In *Caught,* the fear of death and the destruction of pre-war life leads characters to falsify the past. Thus the contrast between Roe's seduction of Hilly and his yearning for his wife is intensified when the reader realizes that his memories of the latter are unreliable. In an effort to escape the pressures of the present, Roe escapes into a comforting world of make-believe where his wife 'took him up to bed at all hours of the day, and lay all night murmuring to him in empty memory'. This is a distorting fantasy, for pre-war domestic life was in fact nothing like this: 'When she was alive, days at the office were long, evenings brief by such time as he got back from work. At that period, when his life lay ready to hand, he had not bothered, had taken the companionship of wife and baby for granted'.[50]

It is no accident that Roe's nostagia for a past life that never really existed takes place in the country. *Caught*'s opening sections make use of the country/ city contrast in order to undermine the pastoral life myth. The text suggests that pastoral life is defenceless against the coming war and that the memories it evokes are sentimental falsehoods.[51] Roe's private myth of a past life in the country is in fact the corollary of the public myth that rural England somehow represents the 'heart' of the country, that it embodies the values for which the nation fought the war and the virtues that enabled it to emerge victorious. This powerful myth was put to work in a variety of contexts during the war, perhaps most notably in Ministry of Information propaganda. Artefacts such as Frank Newbold's poster of a couple picnicking on a peaceful village green, which has the caption 'Your BRITAIN – fight for it now', or films such as the GPO Film Unit's *Britain at Bay* (1940), with its emphasis on the British countryside, are good examples. Newbold's image invites all observers to identify with the bucolic scene it evokes, and the caption attempts to conceal its class basis. His poster employs a strategy of incorporation, implying that the whole nation partakes of the lifestyle he evokes. This was far from true. The majority of servicemen who fought the war had no access to such arcadian pleasures, as the class conflicts precipitated by evacuation made abundantly clear. A greater measure of truth was unwittingly revealed in A. P. Waterfield's hapless poster (lambasted by *The Times*), which consisted of a white typeface on a black background and read: 'YOUR COURAGE, YOUR CHEERFULNESS, YOUR RESOLUTION, WILL BRING US VICTORY'.

Caught's undermining of Roe's leaves in the country, which hints that idealizations of pre-war life are illusory, is related to its portrayal of Roe's experiences in the city, since the text also questions the myth of a unified nation that overcame class conflicts for the duration of the war. Indeed, the account given of the tensions within the AFS suggests that Roe's individual distortion of the past is but a counterpart to the collective myth-making that surrounded the Blitz. Angus Calder has described in detail how the country's belief in a purposeful Home Front unity was gradually built up, arguing that the 'myth of the Blitz' evolved from a number of interrelated factors: the spontaneous accounts of those involved; historical fact; and various forms of propaganda, such as Churchill's speeches, the broadcasts of Priestley and Murrow, and the films of Humphrey Jennings. Calder suggests that the 'myth' of the Blitz 'should not be taken to be equivalent to "untruth", still less to "lies"' but that it should be acknowledged that, though partly true, it tends to conceal anything that might qualify it.[52]

Calder's findings are supported by Tom Harrisson's *Living Through the Blitz*, a Mass Observation report, and by Ian McLaine's *Ministry of Morale*, a study of the Ministry of Information.[53] Both authors claim that although the popular belief that there was unity and good morale is broadly accurate, numerous conflicts have been obscured. With Calder, they agree that there were crucial internal conflicts – such as middle-class resistance to evacuation, anti-Semitism, resentment of conscientious objectors, strikes – and that reactions to bombing included looting, hysteria, anti-war feeling, anger at local authorities for inefficiency and cowardice, cynicism over the fact that the better-off seemed to suffer less, and post-raid depression. Harrisson contends that at 'no time in World War II generally and in the Blitz particularly were British citizens united on anything'. Calder argues that after the outbreak of war 'class divisions in British society were demonstrated and exacerbated as at no time since the 1926 General Strike', and that during the summer of 1940 the national 'unity' invoked by Churchill and Priestley 'was provisional, conditional, and potentially fragile'.[54]

Caught has usually been read as a powerful evocation of the disruptions caused by war. It is certainly that. But in *Caught* Green also explodes the myth of the Blitz. In this novel the proximity to one another of different social classes does not lead to a bonding together that overcomes class conflict but leads to a grudging acceptance of the need to work together. Roe finds it hard to fit in with his fellow firemen and his snobbishness is in turn resented by them. When he tries to buy his way into favour by standing rounds of drinks the other auxiliaries simply take advantage of him. Failures to communicate are frequent, as are the misunderstandings caused by individuals' inability to 'read' one another in social situations. The entire conflict between Pye and Roe, which contributes to Pye's suicide, is itself exacerbated by their different class positions. Brought together because of the war, they are placed in a proximity with one another that leads to class conflict. Forced to work under Pye, Roe tries to ingratiate himself but is unable to bridge the class barrier that separates them. Pye, in turn, is placed in the anomalous, and for him unbearable, position of being at once Roe's social 'inferior' and his professional 'superior'. The view that the war brought people together is ironized throughout, for human contact is shown to be at best precarious, at worst absent. The suggestion that the war has in fact exacerbated existing social divisions is echoed throughout *Caught*. The war effort is shown to be impeded not only by an inefficient bureaucracy but also by rumour and petty struggles for power. Until the bombing begins, the AFS is rife with intrigue and gossip. The men come to believe that Christopher was abducted not by Pye's sister but by Pye himself, and this has disastrous consequences, for when Pye later gives shelter to a stray boy the two incidents are put together and he is suspected of paedophilia; Roe and Hilly speculate erroneously about other people's sexual relationships; the execrable Piper tries to curry favour with Pye's superior, Trant, by informing on Pye; Trant, thus disposed to be critical of his subordinate, tries to assert his authority over Pye; Pye, in turn, pricked on by Trant's vindictiveness, takes it out on the men under his command and mistakenly blames Roe for his difficulties. Most of the characters are either plotting against someone else or are suspected of doing so. Against the backdrop of these conflicts, various characters articulate the frustration and anger that the 'myth' of the Blitz has suppressed. Mary Howells expresses a popularly held view when she asserts that the 'dreadful war' is 'all on account of the rich, they started it for their own ends'; after the invasion of Norway, morale is shown to be extremely low, and anger at the firemen grows as civilians accuse them of trying to avoid army service; most damningly, perhaps, the war is shown to have provided careerists with a golden opportunity for advancement.[55]

Caught focuses primarily on Roe's personal experiences of the Blitz; both these and the context in which they are placed highlight the darker side of the events of 1939–41. To be sure, once the bombing begins the firemen fight the conflagration valiantly; Green in no way denies that there was bravery and self-sacrifice on the part of most of those who underwent the Blitz. He refuses, however, to treat the Blitz sentimentally, to side-step those aspects that do not quite match the popular picture of events. In so doing, he verifies Calder's claim that the myth of the Blitz comprises fact and fiction, and has thus become a kind of 'legend'.[56] In contrast to a propaganda film like Jennings's documentary *Fires Were Started* (1942), which portrays group unity in the face of fire, *Caught* refuses to suppress social conflict. In opposition to the documentary film's putative verisimilitude, the novel's cinematic narrative is chosen for its expressionist ability to convey the phantasmagoric unreality of the time, as Roe admits: '"The extraordinary thing is," he said, "that one's imagination is so literary. What will go on up there to-night in London, every night, is more like a film, or that's what it seems like at the time"'. *Caught* acknowledges the difficulty of accurately recounting the Blitz because it recognizes that it is already mediated by the visual and verbal story-telling of its participants, who construct the 'legend' as they live it in order to be able to survive their experience. The novel thus undercuts Roe's exaggerated account of the Blitz in a lengthy parenthetical aside that begins: 'It had not been like that at all'. Apart from this aside, however, the scene in which the Blitz is described is narrated by Roe; fittingly, in a novel that explores the unreliability of memory, Green concludes by concentrating on the problem of representing the past. Roe's awareness that he is distorting his experience of bombardment and fire-fighting allows Green to reveal the discrepancy between events and individuals' subsequent accounts of them and thus to hint at how a more serious,. collective misrepresentation of the Blitz could come to pass. Roe finally acknowledges the myth-making in which he has himself engaged: 'Yet I suppose it was not like that at all really. One changes everything after by going over it'.[57]

Whereas *Caught* deals with the Phony War and the Blitz explicitly, *Nothing* and *Doting* explore the late 1940s obliquely. Nevertheless, they are imbued with the flavour of the period. The late 1940s are inseparable from images of austerity, and these images are in turn bound up with the Labour Government of 1945–51, which introduced the National Health Service and a national insurance scheme, restructured the education system, and nationalized key industries. For non-socialists many of these changes were dismaying; they produced reactions that ran the gamut from fatalistic pessimism to outraged horror. Upper-middle-class writers such as Angela Thirkell, Nancy Mitford, Christopher Fry, Chetham Strode and Evelyn Waugh perceived the social changes heralded by the emerging welfare state as a threat to a whole way of life. Fear of social homogenization (seen as a levelling down), insecurity about the fate of the individual in a 'mass' society, concern about loss of privilege, and distrust of centralization, were frequently expressed anxieties. John Betjeman located his ideal Britain in a rural past in order to portray socialism as an urban dystopia:

> I have a Vision of The Future, chum,
> The workers' flats in fields of soya beans
> Tower up like silver pencils, score on score:
> And Surging Millions hear the Challenge come
> From microphones in communal canteens
> 'No Right! No Wrong! All's perfect, evermore.'[58]

In Waugh's *Brideshead Revisited* Ryder torments himself with a nightmare vision of archaeologists from the future concluding of post-war Britain that '[h]ere you see a people of advanced culture . . . overrun by a race of the lowest type'.[59] Parading his royalism in 'Aspirations of a Mugwump', Waugh played on Cold War rhetoric when he described 'the Attlee–Cripps regime' as one during which 'the kingdom seemed to be under enemy occupation'.[60] Though extreme, this statement did little more than articulate a far-reaching suspicion of the Labour Government's broadly redistributive social and economic policies. Even a socialist sympathizer like Stephen Spender explained that, for him, the welfare state 'was aptly symbolized by the Festival of Britain . . . with its look of cut-rate cheerfulness cast in concrete and beflagged'.[61]

Nothing and *Doting* are inseparable from this social and political climate. Both novels not only articulate the anxieties of a fast declining rentier class but also reproduce in formal terms the very austerity of which they complain. Green's last two novels represent the most complete expression of his external narrative mode and his dialogistic theory of fiction. In these texts the author is almost completely absent; keeping descriptions and commentary to a minimum, Green allows his characters to reveal themselves through their language, gestures, reactions, and silences. This technique, which earned plaudits from the French *nouveau romancier* Nathalie Sarraute, recalls her 'literature of suspicion' and its corollary – the 'sub-conversation'.[62] Like Sarraute, Green eschews interiority and explores the fissures between the said and the unsaid through a montage of scenes, externally observed behaviour and reported speech. He makes a creative virtue out of social and literary exhaustion by continuing to mine an all but empty seam. Utilizing a rigorously external mode, he moves from plenitude to privation (and here he approaches Beckett) and thus develops a minimalism that should be read not as a retreat into the aridity of mere technique but as an aesthetic choice that allows him to portray the enervation he perceives in post-war British society. The austerity of Green's late mode, in short, functions as the counterpart to the pessimism it conveys.

Although both *Nothing* and *Doting* are comedies of manners and display a light surface touch, they are nevertheless pessimistic books. The nothingness in *Party Going* (1938), a novel that bids farewell to the gaiety of the pre-war era, returns with a vengeance in Green's last two fictions. *Nothing* and *Doting* focus on characters who belong to the same kind of social set as that in *Party Going*, but who are now middle-aged and impoverished; the two novels explore their anxieties about loss of social position and their frustrations with welfare-state Britain. Although Green makes no attempt to 'reflect' the period after the manner of nineteenth-century realism, both texts clearly belong to the 1940s. A preoccupation with such issues as the decline of the rentier class, rationing, a distrust of centralization (nationalization), and the impossibility of maintaining the same standard of living as before the war, permeates both novels. References to economies abound. In *Nothing* John Pomfret and Jane Weatherby constantly fret about money, and their subsequent marriage is motivated as much by economic realities as by an emotional attachment. *Doting*'s Arthur Middleton has similar anxieties, worrying that he cannot afford to pay for a private hospital-room for his son. Disillusionment with the post-war dispensation is rife, Arthur attributing his depressions to 'the times', and John Pomfret perceiving the future in bleak terms, with 'every hope gone' and only 'endless work work work!' to look forward to. A fear that the post-war settlement is leading to a general levelling down haunts *Nothing*, just as it does the opening and closing pages of Waugh's *Brideshead Revisited*. The once exclusive hotel where the characters meet for their assignations now admits a different class of guest, much to the *maître d'hôtel*'s displeasure: '"Oh Mr. Pomfret sir,' he hissed, 'they are not your people, they are any peoples [sic] sir, they come here now like this, we do not know them Mr. Pomfret"'.[63]

In *Nothing* and *Doting* the fear of social homogenization cuts across the generational divide; both parents and children view the new social order with suspicion. The older generation is haunted by the impossibility of returning to the comforts of pre-war life. In *Nothing*, Philip remarks that 'one has to be sorry for parents. They had such a lot of money once and we've never seen what that was.' *Doting*'s Annabel, in turn, finds Arthur's generation 'melancholy', and this melancholia is well illustrated in an exchange between Diana and Arthur in which Diana wishes that they had 'gone somewhere further' in life. The older generation's sense that they have lost their opportunities is matched by the younger generation's sense that they do not have any. Green portrays Philip and Mary, for example, as dull, unimaginative creatures who deserve the society they shall inherit. Like *Brideshead Revisited*'s Hooper, they are less the products of the welfare state than its typical legatees. For Mary, who is 'sick of it all', everything is 'hopeless'. Her despair is directly bound up with resentment of nationalization and the growth of the public sector, which is perceived as an obstacle to the individual's realization of his or her professional goals:

> I mean now that the only jobs one can land, or the only ones within my reach, are state jobs, well I just can't move on, get promotion, arrive at the top where there's just the one person, you know. In the days there was more private industry one could change around but as I am, I'm no more than in a Grade which I drag about with me like a ball and chain if I apply for another Department.

And despite his own feeble protest that they are 'making this country a place fit to live in at last', Philip displays a similar lack of confidence in the future, expressing a pessimism that stands as an ironic comment on the optimism of the Labour Party's 1945 election manifesto, which was entitled 'Let Us Face the Future':

> 'Fifty two weeks in the year and we work fifty,' he muttered.
> 'And they say buy a new hat so you'll feel different,' she agreed.
> 'But we've got everything before us haven't we?' he moaned as if he were looking into his own grave.
> 'Year in year out,' she assented.
> 'Sometimes it seems hopeless,' he said and in his turn took on an appearance of obstinacy younger even than his years.[64]

Philip's despair admits of no remedy for the social ills he describes. Whereas the older generation casts longing glances back at the past, the younger generation cannot see beyond the harsh realities of the present. Ironically, however, the resentment of public-sector growth described here owed more to suspicion of welfare capitalism than to reality. David Coates has argued that perceptions of the 1945–51 Labour Government are misleading, since it 'had not created a socialist commonwealth, nor even taken a step in that direction. It had simply created a mixed economy in which the bulk of industry still lay in private hands, and the 6 years of its rule had only marginally altered the distribution of social power, privilege, wealth, income, opportunity and security.'[65]

Nothing and *Doting* are hardest on the older generation, portraying them as frivolous, egotistic and hypocritical. Obsessed with keeping up appearances at all cost, they routinely deceive one another and their own children, concealing their real motives behind a stream of duplicitous words. The oblique way in which *Nothing* conveys these dissimulations owes everything to the external narrative mode, as the following scene reveals. Philip has upstaged his mother at a party by announcing his engagement to Mary, a girl of whom his mother privately disapproves:

> Jane turned to John Pomfret, one hand pressed on the soft mound above her heart and hissed,
> 'Is this your doing? Did you know of it?'
> 'Good God good for them. First I've heard,' he said.

'Oh my dear,' she cried. 'I feel faint!'

... A naturally graceful woman, Mrs. Weatherby was superb while she crossed the room afloat between one tall mirror and the other, a look of infinite humility on her proud features. The occasion's shock and excitement had raised her complexion to an even brighter glow, a magnificent effulgence of what all felt she must feel at this promise of grandsons ... as Mrs. Weatherby took the young lady to her heart it must have seemed to most the finest thing they had ever seen, the epitome of how such moments should be, perfection in other words, the acme of manners, and memorable as being the flower, the blossoming of grace and their generation's ultimate instinct of how one should ideally behave.[66]

Lifting the veil with the carefully placed word 'hissed', Green exploits the discrepancies between Jane's public reaction, her private feelings, and the guests' mistaken reading of the situation. But the ebullience of Green's irony and the glee with which he skewers his victims should not distract the reader from the serious purpose behind such a scene. It not only reveals Jane Weatherby as a hypocrite and John Pomfret as a fool but also suggests a more pointed criticism of their 'generation', which is so obsessed with keeping up appearances and thereby concealing its social and economic decline that it has become blind to hypocrisy.

Once the novel has established Jane's opposition to the wedding between Philip and Mary, her plotting is more evident. Working for a *rapprochement* between herself and John Pomfret, she does everything in her power to prevent one marriage in order to secure another. And this too is a calculated decision, for the genteel poverty in which these representatives of the rentier class find themselves means that pre-war living standards are gone for ever. Jane's desire to marry John is thus motivated by financial considerations rather than amorous inclinations, as her oblique proposal makes manifestly clear: 'Two people live cheaper than one! They always have and will.'[67] The difference between pre-war comfort and post-war austerity could not be more pointed. Whereas *Party Going*'s Bright Young Things sought the fleeting pleasures of adventure and sexual bliss, now, approaching middle age in the becalmed 1940s, they seek only to retain the semblance of a smashed lifestyle through strategic acts of union.

It would be implausible to suggest that Green can be regarded as a 'committed' writer. His pronouncements against an overtly political literature are clear.[68] Yet Green also stressed the inseparability of the literary from the social. He declared in a wartime letter to Rosamond Lehmann that 'these times are an absolute gift to the writer. Everything is breaking up. A seed can lodge and sprout in any crack or fissure'.[69] Elsewhere he emphasized how important it was 'to write in the idiom of the time'.[70] His post-Flaubertian modernist mode accentuates style, technique, and purity of form, but its externalist Lewisian approach also enables him to explore fundamentally social issues in a crystalline idiom that he made his own. The separation of the social from the literary (rather like that other old chestnut, the distinction between form and content) is inapplicable to Green's and Compton-Burnett's work. The objectivist 'late modernism' developed by both novelists not only calls into question Amis's, Cooper's and Snow's reading of modernism as inescapably subjectivist but also disturbs the distinction between realism and experiment inaugurated by the early twentieth-century avant-garde.

Notes

1. C. P. Snow, 'Challenge to the Intellect', *Times Literary Supplement* (15 August 1958), p. vi.
2. Ivy Compton-Burnett, 'A Conversation', *The Art of I. Compton-Burnett: A Collection of Critical Essays*, ed. Charles Burkhart (London: Victor Gollancz, 1972), p. 27.
3. Maurice Cranston, 'The Writer in His Age', *London Magazine*, 4. 5 (May 1957), pp. 38–40, at p. 39.
4. For examples of the first tendency, see Walter Allen, 'Henry Green', *Penguin New Writing*, 25 (1945), pp. 144–55; Giorgio Melchiori, *The Tightrope Walkers: Studies of Mannerism in Modern English Literature* (London: Routledge and Kegan Paul, 1956); and John Russell, 'There It Is', *Kenyon Review*, 24. 2 (Winter 1964), pp. 433–65; for the second tendency, see Stephen A. Shapiro, 'Henry Green's *Back*: The Presence of the Past', *Critique*, 7 (1964), pp. 87–96; Kingsley Weatherhead, *A Reading of Henry Green* (Seattle: Washington University Press, 1961).
5. Henry Green, *Surviving: The Uncollected Writings of Henry Green*, ed. Matthew Yorke (London: Chatto and Windus, 1992), p. 247.
6. Michael North, *Henry Green and the Writing of his Generation* (Charlottesville: Virginia University Press, 1984), pp. 214–15.
7. Virginia Woolf, 'Mr. Bennett and Mrs. Brown', *The Captain's Death Bed and Other Essays* (New York: Harcourt Brace Jovanovitch, 1950), pp. 94–120.
8. Henry James, *Letters of Henry James*, Vol. 2, ed. Percy Lubbock (London: Macmillan, 1920), p. 384.
9. Ford Madox Ford, *Parade's End* (London: Penguin, 1990), p. 307.
10. Elizabeth Bowen, 'The Bend Back', *The Mulberry Tree: Writings of Elizabeth Bowen*, ed. Hermione Lee (London: Virago, 1986), pp. 57, 58.
11. Ivy Compton-Burnett, 'Interview with Michael Millgate', in Burkhart, *Art*, p. 43.
12. Burkhart, *Art*, p. 45.
13. H. G. Wells, *Tono-Bungay* (Harmondsworth: Penguin, 1946), p. 13.
14. Burkhart, *Art*, p. 46.
15. See, for example, Pamela Horn, *The Changing Countryside in Victorian and Edwardian England and Wales* (London: Athlone, 1984); G. E. Mingay (ed.), *The Vanishing Countryman* (London: Routledge, 1989).
16. See, for example, C. F. G. Masterman, *The Condition of England* (London: Methuen, 1909), pp. 29, 39, 190, 203; Ford Madox Ford, *The Good Soldier* (Harmondsworth: Penguin, 1981), pp. 59, 131–5, 153.
17. Oscar Wilde, *Complete Works of Oscar Wilde* (London: Collins, 1990), p. 332.
18. Ivy Compton-Burnett, *The Mighty and their Fall* (London: Virago, 1990), pp. 12, 15; *A Father and his Fate* (Oxford: Oxford University Press, 1984), p. 14; *The Last and the First* (Harmondsworth: Penguin, 1986), p. 107.
19. Compton-Burnett, *The Mighty*, p. 27.
20. Ibid., pp. 37, 110, 124.
21. Ibid., p. 18.
22. Ibid., pp. 132, 166, 61.
23. Ivy Compton-Burnett, *Manservant and Maidservant* (London: Victor Gollancz, 1951), p. 215. See in particular pp. 186, 210–11, 214–18.
24. Ibid., p. 55. See also Ivy Compton-Burnett, *A Heritage and its History* (London: Virago, 1992), p. 252.
25. Compton-Burnett, *The Mighty*, pp. 56, 11.
26. Ibid., pp. 20, 111, 183.
27. Ivy Compton-Burnett, *The Last and the First* (Harmondsworth: Penguin, 1986), pp. 104, 110, 111.

28. Compton-Burnett, *A Heritage*, p. 34.
29. Compton-Burnett, *The Mighty*, p. 49.
30. Compton-Burnett, *Manservant*, pp. 183, 182–3.
31. Ibid., p. 9.
32. Compton-Burnett, *A Heritage*, pp. 21, 74, 216, 251.
33. Compton-Burnett, *The Mighty*, p. 184.
34. Compton-Burnett, *Last*, p. 87.
35. Wells, *Tono-Bungay*, p. 372.
36. Compton-Burnett, *A Father*, p. 201.
37. For Imagism, see Ezra Pound, 'A Few Don'ts by an Imagiste', *Imagist Poetry*, ed. Peter Jones (London: Penguin, 1988), pp. 130–4; for this aspect of Symbolism, see Mallarmé's description of poetry as 'une série de déchiffrements' in *Oeuvres Complètes* (Tours: Éditions Gallimard, 1945), p. 869, or Verlaine's claim that he seeks 'rien que la Nuance!', in 'Art Poétique', *Oeuvres Complètes*, Vol. 1 (Paris: Albert Messein, 1919). Also significant here is Pound's distinction between 'phanopoeia', in which 'we find the greatest drive toward utter precision of word', and 'melopoeia', in which 'we find a contrary current, a force tending often to lull, or to distract the reader from the exact sense of the language'. See Ezra Pound, 'How to Read', *Literary Essays of Ezra Pound*, ed. T. S. Eliot (London: Faber and Faber, 1954), p. 26.
38. T. E. Hulme, *Speculations: Essays on Humanism and the Philosophy of Art*, ed. Herbert Read (London: Routledge and Kegan Paul, 1987), pp. 126, 132.
39. Ibid., pp. 96, 87.
40. T. S. Eliot, 'Ulysses, Order and Myth', *A Modernist Reader: Modernism in England 1910–1930*, ed. Peter Faulkner (London: Batsford, 1986), p. 103.
41. Wyndham Lewis, *Tarr* (London: Penguin, 1982), p. 312.
42. Wyndham Lewis, *Time and Western Man* (London: Chatto and Windus, 1927), p. 159.
43. Green, *Surviving*, pp. 139, 141.
44. Wyndham Lewis, *Satire and Fiction* (London: Arthur, 1930), p. 46; Green, *Surviving*, p. 139.
45. Green, *Surviving*, p. 137.
46. Henry Green, 'The English Novel of the Future', *Contact*, 1 (August 1950), pp. 21–4, at pp. 23, 24.
47. Green, *Surviving*, p. 142.
48. For a helpful discussion of the way Green's rhetorical strategies provide clues to the author's stance, see Donald Taylor, 'Catalytic Rhetoric: Henry Green's Theory of the Modern Novel', *Criticism*, 7. 1 (Winter 1965), pp. 81–99.
49. Angus Calder, *The Myth of the Blitz* (London: Cape, 1991). For a different kind of discussion of the distortions of memory in *Caught*, see Rod Mengham, *The Idiom of the Time: The Writings of Henry Green* (Cambridge: Cambridge University Press, 1982).
50. Henry Green, *Caught* (London: Harvill, 1991), p. 30.
51. Ibid., pp. 6–7.
52. Calder, *Myth*, p. xiii.
53. Tom Harrisson, *Living Through the Blitz* (London: Collins, 1976); Ian McLaine, *Ministry of Morale: Home Front Morale and the Ministry of Information in World War Two* (London: George Allen and Unwin, 1974).
54. Harrisson, *Living*, p. 15; Calder, *Myth*, pp. 59, 90.
55. Green, *Caught*, pp. 114, 136, 155, 108.
56. Calder, *Myth*, p. 2.
57. Green, *Caught*, pp. 175, 177, 180.
58. John Betjeman, 'The Planster's Vision', *Collected Poems* (London: John Murray, 1970), p. 128.

59. Evelyn Waugh, *Brideshead Revisited* (Boston: Little, Brown, 1945), p. 7.
60. Evelyn Waugh, 'Aspirations of a Mugwump', *Spectator* (2 October 1959), p. 435.
61. Stephen Spender, *The Thirties and After: Poetry, Politics, People, 1933–75* (London: Macmillan, 1978), p. 99.
62. Sarraute wrote appreciatively of both Compton-Burnett and Green. See Nathalie Sarraute, *Tropisms; and The Era of Suspicion*, trans. Maria Jolas (London: Calder, 1963).
63. Henry Green, *Nothing, Doting, and Blindness* (London: Picador, 1979), pp. 182, 12, 13.
64. Ibid., pp. 42, 282, 259, 43, 44, 45.
65. David Coates, *The Labour Party and the Struggle for Socialism* (London: Cambridge University Press, 1975), p. 163.
66. Green, *Nothing*, pp. 78–9.
67. Ibid., p. 147.
68. See Green, *Surviving*, p. 247; Green, 'English Novel', p. 24.
69. Rosamond Lehmann, 'An Absolute Gift', *Times Literary Supplement* (6 August 1954), p. xli.
70. Green, *Surviving*, p. 97.

3

Politics and History in the Caribbean

In the late 1940s and early 1950s a group of aspiring writers emigrated from various parts of the Caribbean to Britain. Many of them became successful novelists – Wilson Harris, John Hearne, George Lamming, Roger Mais, V.S. Naipaul, Orlando Patterson, Vic Reid, Andrew Salkey, and Sam Selvon all produced significant work during the period that followed. Most accounts of post-war British fiction make no mention of them.[1] They are discussed in books on Caribbean writing but are not seen as part of the country's literary and cultural *milieu*. Why the neglect? Could it be because most of these novelists write from an explicitly anti-colonialist perspective and seek to explore the effects of imperialism on the countries of their origin, thereby raising political questions that many in Britain would prefer to pass over in silence? To engage with the work of Caribbean-born writers is necessarily to confront the history of imperialism and to face Britain's role in implementing it. Easier by far to sideline these issues.

The struggle to elaborate a language of one's own lies at the heart of Caribbean writing. Most novelists seek to overthrow the centuries-old inculcation of metropolitan European values that sanction relations of dominance between colonizer and colonized by instituting and upholding rigid dichotomies between 'centre' and 'margin'. The realm of cultural production becomes a key site of historical and political contestation in this situation; conflict arises not only over accounts of past and present but also over the literary modes by which oppositional accounts should be mediated. Hence the numerous discussions of Creolization, syncretism, catalysis, Negritude, and indigenous forms.[2] Caribbean writers explored these questions in great detail.[3] Most of the contributors to these debates were acutely aware of a twin danger: on the one hand, they sought to avoid complicity with the aesthetic values of the culture that had oppressed the Caribbean for 3 centuries, and on the other hand, they strove to avoid a naive 'authenticity'. They were aware, moreover, of the multiple cultural traditions at work in the Caribbean and sought poetic or novelistic forms that could articulate this diverse heritage. In this context, discussion of realism was inevitable. John La Rose was adamant that aesthetic ties to Western culture must be severed, since they upheld the very hierarchy that Caribbean writers should be dismantling: 'If we do not break our tete-a-tete with Europe, and this self-abasement to a certain kind of form which we have inherited through the language, we cannot explore all these possibilities'.[4] Wilson Harris, whose syncretic work has explored these possibilities for many years, argued that realism was 'a dead-end' for Caribbean writers and should be replaced by a transformative imagistic art conceived as 'an extraordinary drama of consciousness whose figurative meaning lies beyond its *de facto* historical climate'.[5]

George Lamming and V.S. Naipaul have both confronted the problem of novelistic form. But their respective attitudes to European culture and to their tasks as writers could not be more different. Consider the following passage from Naipaul:

> The great societies that produced the great novels of the past have cracked. Writing has become more private and more privately glamorous. The novel as a form no longer carries conviction. Experimentation, not aimed at the real difficulties, has corrupted response; and there is a great confusion in the minds of readers and writers about the purpose of the novel. The novelist, like the painter, no longer recognizes his interpretive function; he seeks to go beyond it; and his audience diminishes. And so the world we inhabit, which is always new, goes by unexamined, made ordinary by the camera, unmeditated on; and there is no one to awaken the sense of true wonder. That is perhaps a fair definition of the novelist's purpose in all ages.[6]

Naipaul's conception of the novelist's function is apolitical; he is to interpret society and meditate upon it in order to create 'true wonder'. He writes elsewhere that the 'problems of Commonwealth writing are really no more than the problems of writing'.[7] Literature is consistently kept separate from the political realm in Naipaul's conception of it; although it may deal with political topics, this is incidental to the writer's function. Thus he considers Achebe's view, which is shared by Lamming, that literature may be a 'political weapon' to be an 'alarming suggestion . . . of our time'.[8] Naipaul's own works fit perfectly into a European tradition of writing, often being praised for their Augustan poise and the pellucid quality of their prose.[9] Lamming, in contrast, sees himself as an oppositional writer whose task is to challenge the discourses that have enslaved the minds and lives of the Caribbean peoples:

> I am a direct descendant of slaves, too near to the actual enterprise to believe that its echoes are over with the reign of emancipation. Moreover, I am a direct descendant of Prospero worshipping in the same temple of endeavour, using his legacy of language – not to curse our meeting – but to push it further, reminding the descendants of both sides that what's done is done, and can only be seen as a soil from which other gifts, or the same gift endowed with different meanings, may grow towards a future which is colonised by our acts in this moment, but which must always remain open.

For Lamming the struggle over discourse is central to the destruction of the centre/margin hierarchy and the legends that sustain it. The myth of white supremacy by which Prospero enslaved Caliban cannot be destroyed 'until we christen Language afresh' and show it to be 'the product of human endeavour'.[10] Lamming's writing thus inverts the hierarchy of national and political values inaugurated by the binary thinking that informs imperialist politics.

I have chosen to write on Naipaul and Lamming because the contrast between them is instructive. Alone of the Caribbean-born novelists, Naipaul has gained wide acceptance in Britain, and this fact is perhaps not unrelated to the deeply critical attitude he displays to the region of his birth. Lamming, in contrast, focuses on Caribbean history in order to form a critique of both imperialism and decolonization as well as to expose the material oppression suffered by the majority of the population and to help heal the fractured consciousness he and they share. Naipaul and Lamming both explore the history of the Caribbean, but their readings of it differ. Naipaul's novels frequently display a hostility to the region of his birth, which manifests itself not just in his satire but in his implicit assumption about its culpability for its historical predicament and its congenital incapacity for regeneration. Lamming takes as his point of departure the hierarchy inculcated in both colonizer and colonized by the Prospero/Caliban relationship, seeking to understand its corrosive consequences and to break free from its mind-forged manacles.

V. S. Naipaul

The desire to escape the Caribbean pervades Naipaul's writing from the outset. Looking back on his youthful ambitions, in *The Enigma of Arrival* (1987), Naipaul observes that the scholarship that took him to England represented 'not a wish so much to go to Oxford as a wish to get out of Trinidad and see the great world and make myself a writer'.[11] Naipaul has frequently emphasized the effect that exile has had on his situation as a writer, employing it as a kind of key to his aesthetic stance and characteristic subject matter. Consider this comment: 'It came to me that the great novelists wrote about highly organized societies. I had no such society; I couldn't share the assumptions of the writers; I didn't see my world reflected in theirs. My colonial world was more mixed and secondhand, and more restricted'.[12] The claims advanced here are familiar to Naipaul readers: European writers of the past belonged to a stable society and had a literary tradition on which they could draw; Naipaul, in contrast, is in exile from a fractured society, which constrains the individual's perspective and denies him a literary context within which to work.[13] Two consequences follow from this self-perception. Firstly, Naipaul turns his negative view of the Caribbean into his subject-matter: 'The new politics, the curious reliance of men on institutions they were yet working to undermine, the simplicity of beliefs and the hideous simplicity of actions, the corruption of causes, half-made societies that seemed doomed to remain half-made: these were the things that began to preoccupy me'.[14] Secondly, he distances himself from the societies about which he writes by utilizing narrative strategies that allow him to adopt the stance of outsider. Rob Nixon has analysed Naipaul's professed objectivity in detail, showing how it functions as the means by which the writer can elevate himself above the societies he examines and how it results in a condemnation of non-Western societies that is far from being ideology-free.[15] Nixon's first-rate analysis focuses on Naipaul's non-fiction, but his insights are equally relevant to the novels. Naipaul's evocations of the Caribbean, perhaps with the exception of *A House for Mr. Biswas*, tend to be presented from an external vantage-point. In novels like *The Mimic Men* and *A Bend in the River*, for instance, he creates first-person narrators who present themselves as external observers.[16] This spectating, objectifying stance, so long a *topos* of European writing about non-occidental societies, accords with the position Naipaul adopts on his travels. The experience of travel, he notes, permitted him 'to be [him]self, to be what [he] had always been, a looker'.[17]

What are the implications of this detached mode? I shall argue that much of Naipaul's fiction is complicit with orientalist stereotypes.[18] Naipaul, I suggest, views the West Indies and Africa as places that lack history and are caught' in regressive cyclical patterns that permit no development. He portrays Caribbean societies as half-finished, fractured, and unproductive, thereby at least acknowledging the colonial legacy; but he represents Africa (and he frequently relies on the homogenizing singular) as belonging to the sphere of ahistorical nature. His fiction inverts Aristotle's distinction between the universal and the particular and thus confirms Hegel's interpretation of history. For Aristotle literature deals with the timeless, the general, and the universal; history with the time-bound, the arbitrary, and the accidental. In Hegel's *Lectures on the Philosophy of History*, the problem 'is to develop a "plot" for history, and it is this endeavour which is stated in the doctrine of inevitable progress'.[19] For Hegel, however, history can only begin when a people becomes self-conscious. Africa remains outside the historical process because it is trapped in the realm of nature. Africa, Hegel claims, 'is no historical part of the World; it has no movement or development to exhibit . . . What we properly understand by Africa, is the Unhistorical, Undeveloped Spirit, still involved in the conditions of mere nature'.[20] In Naipaul's novels, the histories of the Caribbean and Africa conform to broad patterns that, far from being contingent on the Aristotelian model, prove to be relatively fixed, allowing little possibility of escape from their predetermined trajectories.

The Mimic Men, a novel that explores post-colonial politics in the Caribbean through the memoirs of Ralph Singh, a defeated politician, brings many of these issues to the fore. Singh is initially a faceless narrator whose name and identity are not revealed until a third of the book has passed. He is a variant on Conrad's hollow men; like Kurtz, he is a man of many talents who can play a number of different roles.[21] When boys, he and his school-mates were all 'natural impersonators', and this skill later enables him to select a character for himself as though he were merely trying on a suit.[22] He is hardly the trustworthy narrator whose *apercus* are to be taken at face value. A mimic *par excellence*, who becomes a post-colonial politician by accident, he is in part the target of Naipaul's satire. What complicates matters, however, is that a good deal of Singh's retrospective analysis not only sounds like authorial commentary but also resembles Naipaul's own views as expressed elsewhere. The various roles Singh plays cannot easily be conflated, and there is a degree of slippage in the way the older figure represents his former selves such that the fine line between reminiscer and protagonist cannot easily be drawn. These caveats apart, a loose distinction can be drawn between the stoical figure who reflects on the significance of his life and the benighted agent who lived it. The older Singh offers an auto-critique through which he not only dissects his younger self but also lambastes the society that produced him. This experienced narrator, a man putatively freed of illusions, assesses his individual actions against a social background that is found to be wanting. The criticisms Singh makes of himself are not *qua* individual, but *qua* member of a particular society. His sense of deracination, and his desire to escape, stem alike from his conviction that it is his *society* that is to blame for his political naivety and his cultural disaffection. Thus he presents his younger self – the self he criticizes in his retrospective narration – as the product of a haphazard, sterile environment.

West Indian society is, in Singh's portrayal, separated from the metropolitan centre it admires but can never match, is a source of disorder, and is characterized by self-alienation:

> We lack order. Above all, we lack power, and we do not understand that we lack power. We mistake words and the acclamation of words for power; as soon as our bluff is called we are lost. . . . Our transitional or makeshift societies do not cushion us. There are no universities or City houses to refresh us and absorb us after the heat of battle. For those who lose, and nearly everyone in the end loses, there is only one course: flight.[23]

The fictional Caribbean island described here is a half-made place that can provide no support for political life, leaving those who fail to transform it socially and economically – a failure the narrative implies is inevitable – to undergo the privations of placelessness. The use of the second-person plural, furthermore, serves to widen the scope of this particular indictment by implicitly embracing the West Indies as a whole.

The identification of Isabella (Naipaul's imaginary island) with the Caribbean is later made more explicit: 'There, in Liege in a traffic jam, on the snow slopes of the Laurentians, was the true, pure world. We, here on our island, handling books printed in this world, and using its goods, had been abandoned and forgotten. We pretended to be real, we mimic men of the New World, one unknown corner of it, with all its reminders of the corruption that came so quickly to the new'.[24] The assumptions embedded in these words rely on a series of binary oppositions: true/false; real/unreal; pure/tainted; creative/imitative; known/unknown. They serve to establish a distinction between centre and periphery and to legitimize the superiority of the former over the latter. Europe and North America represent the possibility of an existence unfettered by the encumbrances of post-colonial conflicts. The Caribbean, in contrast, is obsequiously mimetic; it has no internal, self-created substantiality and can only deceive itself that it provides the conditions for meaningful life. It is represented, in a figure taken from colonial writing, as an uninscribed place that is 'unknown' and 'new', descriptive terms that might perplex the autochthonous peoples who inhabited the region long before the imperialist enterprise got under way.

Isabella is conceived as a derivative society that can generate no history of its own, a failure predetermined by its colonial status. Singh, like *The Mystic Masseur*'s Ganesh, acts as a metonym for Isabella, and Isabella functions as a metonym for the West Indies. Singh and Ganesh are 'types' who figure their country's contradictions; as *The Mystic Masseur*'s narrator remarks, 'the history of Ganesh is, in a way, the history of our times'.[25] Isabella, in turn, embodies the region as a whole; it is an imagined place because this enables Naipaul to synthesize his knowledge of the Caribbean and to suggest that his fictional construct symbolizes the entire area. The consequences of such typification – whether it takes place at the level of character or country – are always the same: generality displaces particularity. The overview can point to common features only by abstracting them from the determinate conditions that produced them, and the holistic account thereby achieved pays little attention to all-important detail and specificity. Naipaul's metonymic mode has precisely this consequence. *The Mimic Men* moves swiftly from part to whole, leaving the impression that Singh can stand for Isabella, and that Isabella can stand for the West Indies.

Such substitutions accord with the text's account of history, which it describes as the product of general patterns rather than retrospectively identifiable contingencies and socio-economic factors. The book assigns a 'plot' to history, thereby inverting Aristotle. But it is a double inversion, for the 'plot' that *The Mimic Men*'s narrator identifies is one of undoing rather than making, and therefore provokes obloquy, not approbation. Singh's analysis of his participation in post-colonial Isabellan politics returns again and again to his conviction that events fall into preordained cycles and that actions are doomed to be repeated: 'My career is by no means unusual. It falls into the pattern'. His account is consistently stoical; as he looks back on a foreshortened political life, he justifies his fate to himself by presenting it as part of a rotation in which he is an unwitting cog:

> For I find I have indeed been describing the youth and early manhood of a leader of some sort, a politician, or at least a disturber. I have established his isolation, his complex hurt and particular frenzy. And I believe I have also established, perhaps in this proclaimed frivolity, this lack of judgement and balance, the deep feeling of irrelevance and intrusion, his unsuitability for the role into which he was drawn, and his inevitable failure. From playacting to disorder: it is the pattern.

This is an Arnoldian account. The young Singh, like *Culture and Anarchy*'s populace, is unfit to participate in government because he lacks the requisite judiciousness. He nurses the grievances that will lead him to overturn the existing socio-political order but has nothing to put in its place. He is a frenzied agitator whose entry into the public sphere must lead to chaos, since it is part of 'the pattern'. As he says elsewhere: 'We zestfully abolished an order; we never defined our purpose. And it has happened in twenty countries'.[26]

Singh's recurrent stress on post-colonial patterns and cycles lends the events he describes an air of inevitability, encouraging them to be seen as part of a historical plot that is fixed, not contingent. Of the 'political awakening' in Isabella he remarks: 'It has happened in twenty countries. I don't want to exaggerate our achievement. Sooner or later, with or without us, something similar would have occurred'. Of the subsequent backlash he comments: 'It has happened in twenty places, twenty countries, islands, colonies, territories ... I cannot see our predicament as unique'. This perceived lack of uniqueness justifies Singh in the suppression of historical particulars: 'I will not linger on the details of our movement'. The details are irrelevant because they could reveal no clear programme and no coherent ideology:

> What did we talk about? We were, of course, of the left. We were socialist. We stood for the dignity of the working man. We stood for the dignity of distress. We stood for the dignity of our island, the dignity of our indignity. Borrowed

phrases! Left-wing, right-wing: did it matter? Did we believe in the abolition of private property? Was it relevant to the violation which was our subject? We spoke as honest men. But we used borrowed phrases which were part of the escape from thought, from that reality we wanted people to see but could ourselves now scarcely face. We enthroned indignity and distress. We went no further.

A passage such as this illustrates Singh's distrust of post-colonial politics. The casual aside 'of course' signals the superficiality of the commitment to socialism; the assumption that the difference between right-wing and left-wing politics is unimportant suggests a thoughtlessness on the part of the political protagonists; the emphasis on borrowed terminology and modes of analysis implies not only that there is a radical disjunction between Europe and the Caribbean but also that the latter is incapable of independent thought and action. There is, on the one hand, a desire for 'authenticity' here, for a society untarnished by the depredations of imperialism; but, on the other hand, the rhetoric rejects the possibility either of productive interchange between colonizer and colonized or of the subversion of their hierarchical relationship. Thus both cultural purity and cultural hybridity are presented as equally unattainable and equally objectionable.

Singh's account of his political failure relies on the belief that his society is irremediably sterile. His party's inability to hold on to power and to push through any lasting political changes can be explained by the fact that 'in a society like ours, fragmented, inorganic, no link between man and the landscape, a society not held together by common interests, there was no true internal source of power, and . . . no power was real which did not come from the outside'.[27] What is 'real' in this text always lies elsewhere, and the narrator once again invokes this contrast, opposing a faith in organic community (over there) to a mistrust of fractured disaccord (over here). The only solution is to escape, and Singh effects this literally, by choosing exile, and, metaphorically, by purging himself of his experiences through writing.

Writing is placed in opposition to politics. It enables Singh to reveal the bitter truth of his political life and to suggest that this truth holds for post-colonial societies in general. It also permits him to exorcise the past. Through writing, he not only orders perceived chaos into patterns that serve to extenuate his behaviour but also frees himself from the pain of political struggle: 'No more words for me, except these I write, and in them the politician, chapman in causes, will be suppressed as far as possible'. His words are to be literary, not political. He can write 'with composure' because he has seen through the illusions that spurred him on, and precisely because these were *political* illusions his narrative will eschew the language of ideology. Thus '[t]hese are not . . . political memoirs'. Except that of course they are. Singh's words return again and again to the specific political actions in which he participated. Moreover, he can only make sense of them by arguing that they were doomed to fail because of the nature of post-colonial societies and by contending that the only way to avoid such failure is to abandon politics altogether. Thus the literary words with which Singh seeks to transcend the conflicts he describes bear a massive political charge: they urge an essentialist account of Caribbean history.[28]

This account inverts Aristotle. *The Mimic Men* collapses the particular and the contingent into the general and the predetermined. There is no materialist sense here of the way that economic and social forces constrain human political activity but at the same time provide the conditions in which it must take place and which it may transform. *The Mimic Men* posits instead a fragmented and denatured region, which is ruled by impersonal forces that push it into atavistic cycles and make a mock of human agency. Its emphasis on 'type' with reference to character and on 'pattern' with reference to nation fixes the 'plot' of history in a way that, paradoxically, denies historicity to the region by treating it as innately disordered. From this plot there can be no escape, as it is in the *nature* of post-colonial societies to repeat, interminably, the actions that doom them to anarchy. The novel denies the specificity that would foreground the differences between Caribbean states and thus show that, for all their shared characteristics, they have histories of their own, have developed in particular ways, and are heterogeneous in nature.

Does Naipaul offer a similarly negative reading of Africa? *The Mimic Men* may provide a clue. Ralph Singh makes a cryptic comment early in that novel, describing his community as 'an intermediate race, the genes passive, capable of disappearing in two generations into any of the three races of men'. The reference to three races remains unexplained until old Deschamp-neufs outlines a theory that seems to accord with Singh's views, dividing 'nations into the short-visioned, like the Africans, who remained in a state of nature; the long-visioned, like Indians and Chinese, obsessed with thoughts of eternity; and the medium-visioned, like himself'. Deschampneufs mimics Hegel here: he identifies the 'African' with 'nature' and thus places the entire continent outside the realm of history.[29]

This conception of a monolithic Africa pervades *A Bend in the River* (1979), a novel in which the first-person narrator's assumptions are never questioned. Salim's stance is, throughout, that of the detached observer who looks from a distance. He finds it hard to see history in a country that he primarily interprets through its landscape. Africa, which attracts words such as 'pure' and 'real' to it with revealing frequency, is primarily associated with vegetation. Since the latter is primordial, the mode of existence it facilitates is deemed to be unchanging. This is how the President's plans are described: 'He was creating modern Africa. He was creating a miracle that would astound the rest of the world. He was by-passing real Africa, the difficult Africa of bush and villages, and creating something that would match any-thing that existed in other countries'.[30] A metonymic strategy similar to that in *The Mimic Men* here constructs a model of Africa's culture on the basis of its geographical features. Modernity belongs exclusively to Europe – while the role of imperialism in its production is occluded – and is super-imposed onto a world that cannot take its imprint. Africa is portrayed as part of a Hegelian realm of nature on which history, to adapt Prospero, can never stick.

The way *A Bend in the River* describes social and political change is startlingly disingenuous. Consider the following passage:

> I couldn't help thinking how lucky Ferdinand was, how easy it had been made for him. You took a boy out of the bush and you taught him to read and write; you levelled the bush and built a polytechnic and you sent him there. It seemed as easy as that, if you came late to the world and found ready-made those things that other countries and peoples had taken so long to arrive at – writing, printing,

universities, books, knowledge. . . . Ferdinand, starting from nothing, had with one step made himself free, and was ready to race ahead of us.

The paternalism underlying these words is silent about the history of exploitation that antedates the 'luck' which will give Ferdinand certain advantages in his society only at the price of severe cultural dislocation. But something more like dominion is at work in the language of taking, levelling, and building. What sanctions such language is the assumption that the person being remodelled exists in the pre-cultural domain of nature. Ferdinand, prior to his extraction from 'the bush', is perceived to be outside the realm of culture. The bush stands in opposition to the civilization that teaches literacy, the acquirement of which signals the historical void that preceded it. Ferdinand is a *tabula rasa* who awaits inscription. But the concern with how he is to be inscribed discloses the post-imperial anxieties informing this text. His very belatedness, it transpires, gives him an unfair advantage, for he can passively receive what others have striven for and then threaten to supersede them. The dissemination of knowledge must therefore be controlled from the 'centre' if this supersession is to be staved off. Indar, employing an Arnoldian turn of phrase, clarifies the novel's paternalism: 'You see why my outfit is needed. Unless we can get them thinking, and give them real ideas instead of just politics and principles, these young men will keep our world in turmoil for the next half century'. He later completes the metonymic circle when he explains why his 'outfit' lacks faith in the social and political changes being implemented: '"We don't believe – well, because of this". And Indar waved at the fishermen's village, the bush, the moonlit river'.[31]

Frantz Fanon writes that 'Black Africa is looked on as a region that is inert, brutal, uncivilized – in a word, savage'.[32] The problem with novels such as *A Bend in the River* and essays like 'A New King for the Congo' lies not with their censure of politics in certain countries but with the form this censure takes. It denies such countries a historical past that precedes the arrival of the colonists because it conceives history as predicated on literacy.[33] It treats them as interchangeable because what they share – an essential Africanness – is more significant than what differentiates them. It portrays Africa as a timeless, homogeneous entity whose social characteristics are to be explained and interpreted in terms of its geographical features, since it posits a clear homology between forms of landscape and types of community. But neither the landscape nor the society it apparently gives rise to are conceived in a historical light. The essentialism that equates 'Africa' with 'the bush' and then portrays the latter as sempiternal *produces* a monolithic account of 'post-colonial society' that, by virtue of its own presuppositions, must not only ignore concrete details but also explain all political violations in terms of atavism. Naipaul's persistent identification of reprehensible political acts with *African* politics and with the *African* cast of mind, is pernicious. This form of identification pervades 'A New King for the Congo': the new administrators fear 'to be returned from the sweet corruptions of Kinshasa to the older corruption of the bush, to be returned to Africa'; bribes are required on the 'African steamer' that 'is run on African lines'; disappointment with social change may 'at any time be converted into a wish to wipe out and undo, an African nihilism, the rage of primitive men coming to themselves and finding that they have been fooled and affronted'. Nurture, on this view, will not stick on recalcitrant nature: 'The bush works; the bush has always been self-sufficient. The administration, now the court, is something imposed, something unconnected with the true life of the country. The ideas of responsibility, the state and creativity are ideas brought by the visitor; they do not correspond, for all the mimicry of language, to African aspirations'.[34]

Naipaul's assessment of complex post-colonial societies relies on a simple nature/culture dichotomy. Civilization is imported from elsewhere but has no lasting effects. The binary opposition between primitivism and culture associates the latter with certain forms of technology and social organization but views the former as belonging to an unchanging, preconscious realm. It is in fact the relative recency of civilization (when seen in epochal terms) that guarantees its culture, for the ability not only to distinguish between present and past but also to conceive the present as fundamentally different from the past signals the Hegelian entry into self-awareness and historicity. For Hegel, we remember, Africa lacked self-consciousness and was thus 'enveloped in the dark mantle of Night'.[35] Naipaul's rhetoric echoes this judgement: change in Africa takes place on the surface, leaving the continent's essence – 'the vacancy of river and forest, the hut in the brown yard, the dugout' – absolutely unaltered.[36] It is here that George Lamming's indictment of complicity with such orientalist stereotypes is right on target: 'West Indians, on the whole, still have to learn that Africa existed – not simply as desert, river and malaria – but as a home where men were alive and engaged in a human struggle with nature'.[37]

The Enigma of Arrival (1987), which is something of a cross between autobiography and fiction, reverts to the intersecting problems of history, politics, and writing in a way that casts light on Naipaul's views. It explains how he arrived at his early view of history thus: 'I hardly knew our own community; of other communities I knew even less. I had no idea of history – it was hard to attach something as grand as history to our island. . . . So that almost everything I read about history and other societies had an abstract quality'. History is what takes place elsewhere, in lands big enough to be worthy of its weightiness. Abstraction, however, also provides a way of evading a sense of inferiority, since it can allow the individual to ignore the conditions of his present life in the expectation that it will eventually be left behind: 'All my life, from the moment I had become self-aware, had been devoted to study, study of the abstract sort I have tried to give some idea of. And then this idea of abstract study had been converted into an idea of a literary life in another country. . . . My real life, my literary life, was to be elsewhere'.[38]

The Enigma of Arrival explores the split between literature and society inherent in Naipaul's early conception of writing. It analyses the colonization of his mind, a colonization that led him to reject Trinidad as unworthy of literary treatment, to affect a metropolitan manner, and to adopt a Eurocentric aesthetic. His self-alienation results in a separation of 'man' from 'writer', and the latter, adopting 'abstract attitudes' to the experiences of the former, exacts an appalling form of self-censorship. In particular, the young literary aspirant refuses to confront his colour and the problem of race prejudice: 'Racial diminution formed no part of the material of the kind of writer I was setting out to be. Thinking of myself as a writer, I was hiding my experience from myself; hiding myself from my experience'. Naipaul's account of how he overcame this self-division entails a critique of the colonial education that produced him and the mode of perception it fostered. His education had taught him that culture belongs to and is exemplified by Europe and that he can only approach its Parnassus by conforming to its ideals. The inculcation of a European aesthetic forces him to deny his experience and leads to an apparently disinterested mode of perception. But the abstract approach inherent in this writing ensures that the young Naipaul, who does not really look, cannot really see: 'I took everything I saw for granted. I thought I knew it all already, like a bright student'. Naipaul's teleological account of his development achieves closure when he grasps that he must be true to his experience: 'I defined myself, and saw that my subject was not my sensibility, my inward development, but the worlds I contained within myself, the worlds I lived in'.[39] It is at this point that man and writer can merge.

The Enigma of Arrival marks something of a departure for Naipaul, because it problematizes the role of perception. Whereas in earlier works he had observed from a detached standpoint and had implied that this spectating stance guaranteed objectivity, in *Enigma* he emphasizes the validity of different ways of looking and acknowledges that perception depends on education, background, and personality.[40] Despite this acknowledgement, however, Naipaul's hard-won victory over his cultural schizophrenia proves to be more ambiguous than his account of it allows. *Enigma* posits a clear link between the overcoming of self-alienation and true vision. Whereas the tyro traffics in clichés, the mature writer sees truly. Most importantly, he claims to be able to acknowledge the reality of Caribbean life as well as its historicity.[41] But this recognition of historicity rarely finds its way into the novels Naipaul presents as the outcome of his reintegration as man and writer. As I have argued, his novels continue to employ strategies that distance the author from his material, to observe as though from outside, and to treat history as somehow fixed in advance. Naipaul may have made the Caribbean his subject, but his satiric mode ensures that he predominantly treats it from an external, and implicitly superior, vantage point.[42]

The Caribbean, then, is portrayed by Naipaul as a homogeneous region filled with inorganic, fragmented and unproductive societies that can only mimic the metropolis from which they are disssevered, and thus can generate no meaningful history of its own. Africa's forms of social organization can be read off from its geographical features; it is locked into the realm of nature, which is atavistic and threatens to plunge its people into a nihilist whirlwind. Naipaul's predilection for a detached stance produces an allochronic discourse that not only posits a distinction between the knowing subject and the known object but also establishes a conceptual difference between the time of the observer (the historical present) and that of the observed (the dim and distant past). Johannes Fabian has analysed the operation of this discourse in anthropological writing, arguing that it consigns the society being studied to the realm of pre-history and thus institutes a centre/margin opposition that values the observer's culture and forms of knowledge over those he studies.[43] The detached stance favoured by Naipaul is inseparable not only from his reading of the Caribbean and Africa as imitative places but also from his choice of language and narrative mode, since both distance him from the worlds he describes. Naipaul's limpid, measured prose, I would argue, not only constructs the Caribbean and Africa as objects of study to be assessed in a monological, rather than a dialogical, manner but also signals its own elevated status as language, since it displays the eloquence that it denies to almost all its native characters. Eloquence, Eric Cheyfitz argues, functions as the means by which the colonizer establishes the symbolic mastery that his material power underpins. Prospero's power has no meaning unless there is an 'other' over which he can wield it. His admission that Caliban cannot be missed because he 'serves in offices / That profit us', refers as much to the physical tasks carried out by the slave as to his symbolic role as corroborator of Prospero's superiority: Caliban confirms the hierarchy of power.[44] The native characters portrayed via Naipaul's detached narrators function in this way. Whereas they are unable to put their fractured historical experience together, Naipaul casts himself in the role of the eloquent orator capable of providing the necessary totalizing perspective. His eloquence attests his honorary membership of the 'centre' while their inarticulacy consigns them to the 'margin' whose very function, in this economy, is to reflect the mastery and superiority of the 'centre' back to it.

George Lamming

Caliban is Prospero's creation, acknowledged by him as his 'thing of darkness' in *The Tempest*'s final act. It is the arrivants who have brought Caliban into being, awakening him to the self-consciousness that language bestows. Caliban does not dispute the truth of this narrative. He rages instead against its implications for his subsequent life on the island, for Prospero's apparently disinterested gift of language carries with it a hierarchical conception of their respective roles. The Europeans have endowed Caliban's 'purposes / with words that made them known', but this munificence only confirms their power over him, since it insists that his self-knowledge is their bequest.[45] Caliban's entry into the realm of intersubjectivity is thus predicated not on reciprocity but on the subtle exercise of power. The language he has been taught brings him to a consciousness of self that immediately places him as other, for it has already inscribed him as a slave.

Whereas Caliban sees language as a curse, George Lamming considers it to be the indispensable means by which the discourses of colonialism can be challenged and transformed. The double heritage conferred by the Prospero/Caliban encounter is for Lamming paradigmatic of the post-colonial situation. The writer cannot disavow the historical past but must contest the account of it offered by those whose economic and cultural interests it serves. This account presents colonialism as producing a divinely ordained, symbiotic socio-economic order whose benefits were shared by all and whose purpose was to civilize the benighted natives, a *topos* already at work in *The Tempest*.[46] Lamming argues that the hierarchical relationship sanctioned by the play is, within its terms, unalterable. Caliban is fixed in his role as a slave because his 'nature' resists the imprint of 'nurture'. The imperialist enterprise has been built on various versions of this assumption, and, for Lamming, liberation from its subjugation of the mind entails not only a re-examination of the region's history along the lines set out by writers such as C.L.R. James and Walter Rodney, who focus on the labour, lives, and struggles of the colonized, but also a transformation of the Prospero/Caliban relationship that enables the latter to break free from the confines in which it traps him. The past must be rediscovered and rewritten, and Caliban must be able to redefine himself in his own terms, to make Prospero's language his own and thereby release himself into a new mode of being. For Lamming, because 'it is the function of the writer to return a society to itself', he sees Caribbean novelists as 'the major historians of the feeling of [their] people'.[47]

I want to focus primarily on the representation of history in Lamming's first four novels (they comprise a loose tetralogy) in order to show how his engagement with it, which differs so markedly from Naipaul's, traces the process of liberation from the political upheavals of the late 1930s to the decolonization of the 1950s, in an attempt to forge the conscience of his region. The first four novels that Lamming wrote – *In the Castle of My Skin* (1953), *The Emigrants* (1954), *Of Age and Innocence* (1958), and *Season of Adventure* (1960) – explore Caribbean history from the 1930s to the late 1950s. *Castle* is a *Bildungsroman* that traces a boy's development from childhood to early manhood, concentrating on his growing awareness of imperialism and his gradual awakening to the history and politics of the region; *The Emigrants* focuses on the disturbing experiences and subsequent disillusionment of a disparate group of West Indians who move to England in search of a better life; *Of Age* follows the return of four characters to the island of San Cristobal, which is on the eve of independence, and explores the emergence of a complex and fragile political *démarche*; *Season*, finally, describes San Cristobal several years later, at a time when the first republic is about to fall, suggesting that political emancipation will fail if its concern with race leads it to neglect the issues of class and the psycho-social legacy of colonialism.

In the Castle of My Skin has become something of a Caribbean classic. Its portrayal of the gradual awakening to political consciousness of an intelligent boy who barely comprehends the events that overtake his village enables Lamming to explore the gap between lived experience and theoretical critique. Set in the 1930s and culminating with the riots that later paved the way for post-war decolonization, the novel stays firmly within the mind-set of villagers who confront colonialism in their daily lives but lack the analytic tools to dissect its mode of operation. This allows Lamming to portray a society that is on the brink of political awareness by the novel's end and to show how it was formerly all but coerced into quiescence. Although the novel focuses on the development of the boy G., it presents him as one figure in a thoroughly social landscape. The village is in certain respects more of a central character than G. himself, for the community, conceived as the repository not just of collective wisdom but also of social weakness, becomes the novel's main protagonist. Its stoicism, commitment to a Christian ethic that promises spiritual riches in an afterlife, lack of formal education, and overriding respect for the white landlord, is communicated through the choric figures of Ma and Pa. These characteristics enable the villagers to survive psychologically but prevent them from mounting any kind of offensive against the political order that they have been taught to see as immutable and divinely ordained.

A large part of Lamming's evocation of Barbadian village life in the 1930s focuses on the educational underpinning of imperialism. It is significant that both Trumper and G., the two characters who are able to leave Barbados, have very different perceptions of it. Trumper's education is the product of his experience of working in the United States, which brings him into contact with black activists, who politicize him. G.'s schooling, in contrast, is institutional and takes place under colonial auspices. It offers him the chance to rise out of his social class and to escape to a putatively better reality abroad but teaches him nothing about the historical background to his community's poverty. Education separates an emergent bourgeois class from its origins in the villages and from those who are intellectually and materially left behind. Neither Trumper's nor G.'s other childhood friends go on to the High School after they complete their elementary education, and it is this further instruction that acts as 'the instrument that tore and kept [them] apart'.[48] But although G.'s education ensures that he is, by the novel's end, poised to enter a world of privilege, it has prevented him from seeing colonialism as anything other than a benevolent form of social administration. It is Trumper, whose formal schooling has been of limited duration, who brings the tidings from elsewhere that stir G. into incipient political consciousness, which he realizes must be proved by experience: 'Trumper made his own experience, the discovery of a race, a people, seem like a revelation. It was nothing I had known, and it didn't seem I could know it till I had lived it'.[49]

Lamming has written extensively about the role that schools played in inculcating imperial attitudes in the colonies: 'It had made us pupils to its language, baptized us in the same religion, until Empire ceased to be a dirty word and seemed to bear little relation to those forms of domination we now call imperialist'.[50] His words are carefully chosen here; England was for a long time viewed as a benevolent parent and its heritage was seen as a common one. Empire was, in the minds of many, associated not with dominion and exploitation but with guardianship and reciprocity. *In the Castle of My Skin* reveals how the education system instilled such beliefs in the minds of its pupils. The gala day at the village school sparks off a communal reverie that shows how deeply ingrained they are:

> There were more flags now, the school was bigger and the children more clever. They could take and give orders, and parade for the inspector. And they understood the meaning of big words, but nothing had really changed. The flags were the same colour. It was a queen in their time. Now it was a king. But the throne was the same. Good old England and old Little England. . . . Three hundred years, more than the memory could hold, Big England had met and held Little England and Little England like a sensible child accepted . . . Barbados or Little England was the oldest and purest of England's children, and may it always be so. . . . Little England remained steadfast and constant to Big England. . . . Indeed, it was God's doing.[51]

The thinly concealed irony is the silent narrator's, but his superior perspective is *post factum* and belongs to one who has a political understanding of what he describes. It is a perspective denied to all his characters except Trumper in the novel's closing pages, for the text portrays not a radicalized communal consciousness but a pre-revolutionary state of mind which has been mentally colonized with some success.

This colonization discloses itself through the villagers' self-alienation, the headmaster's anguished desire to fulfil his masters' expectations, and in the community's belief that the only meaningful life lies outside of Barbados. The hierarchy of values that conceives Barbados as a child in perpetual need of guidance produces a racial inferiority complex so deep that self-alienation is rarely far from the surface. It is manifested primarily in an internalized racism that turns the community against itself in abject fulfilment of the colonizers' expectations:

> The image of the enemy, and the enemy was My People. My people are lowdown nigger people. My people don't like to see their people get on. The language of the overseer. The language of the civil servant. The myth had eaten through their consciousness like moths through the pages of ageing documents. Not taking chances with you people, my people. They always let you down. Make others say we're not responsible, we've no sense of duty. That's what the low-down nigger people do to us, their people. Then the others say we've no sense of duty. Like children under the threat of hell fire they accepted instinctively that the others, meaning the white, were superior, yet there was always the fear of realizing that it might be true. This world of the others' imagined perfection hung like a dead weight over their energy. If the low-down nigger people weren't what they are, the others couldn't say anything about us. Suspicion, distrust, hostility. These operated in every decision. You never can tell with my people. It was the language of the overseer, the language of the lawyers and doctors who had returned stamped like an envelope with what they called the culture of the Mother Country.[52]

A passage such as this discloses the internalization of Prospero's values. The language of self-hatred is inculcated by the overseer, who is the colonizer's representative, and by the salaried bourgeoisie, who have escaped the villages by virtue of an education that reinforces the margin/centre opposition. Anger is displaced away from the cause of suffering (a carefully administered colonial system) and onto its victims; the latter are thus thought to merit the low opinion held of them by the whites and to deserve being placed in a subordinate position. But those West Indians who hold such a view, though they may be beneficiaries of upward social mobility, cannot escape the fact that it remains to some extent a self-perception. They can only maintain it by turning what is in fact a deep-rooted self-hatred into hatred of others; such displacement ensures that it is always some other individual or some other group that behaves in the way that then justifies the negative view. But racism is not known for making such nice distinctions, thus any West Indian who speaks contemptuously of 'my people' must at some level recognize himself in the picture being drawn; however hard he tries to distance himself from it, he knows it is a group portrait. The resultant oscillation between self-recognition and denial produces the racial schizophrenia that Lamming sees as one of colonialism's most lasting features. The enemy (my people) is always within the frame, never outside it.

The novel records the gradual movement away from such disastrous self-perceptions. For all her dignity, Ma remains the spokeswoman for the old view, sympathizing with the landlord's parental responsibilities to the villagers and mourning the disrespect they show him when they start to revolt against the social order. But other villagers, G., and Trumper, grow in political awareness as they realize that the education they have been given has not only suppressed enormous chunks of history but also conceived it in terms of a providential design that acts to sustain the imperialist project. The shoemaker is one of the first to hint at this aspect of Barbadian education: ' "But if you look good," said the shoemaker, "if you remember good, you'll never remember that they ever tell us 'bout Marcus Garvey. They never even tell us that they wus a place where he live call Africa" '.[53] G. and his friends, in turn, start to question the account of history the school has provided when they hear about slavery, in which they initially disbelieve but which they eventually come to see as historical truth. This disturbs them at first because it turns upside-down their perception of the social order and their place within it. The naturalization of history that their education has ensured means that they neither see an alternative to colonial society nor yet seek one. As the young Trumper puts it: 'I don't ever get the feelin' whatever I say that anythin' could change so. An' I won't like it, 'cause 'tis so much more easy this way, everybody sort of steady an' know what they want to do an' so on. I like that'.[54]

Trumper's desire for change overcomes his need of stability when he gains a consciousness of his people not as 'the enemy' to be execrated but as the 'Negro race' to which he belongs and which, as Lamming writes elsewhere, is not to be conceived as an essence but as 'a profound and unique historical experience'.[55] The boys' initial passivity is inseparable from their inability to conceive of an alternative to the only social order they know. This inability, in turn, is closely linked to the language available to them to formulate their experience of colonialism. On the one side, they are granted an education that does not begin to address the history of their region from their perspective, and, on the other side, they daily witness their mothers' stoic Christianity and their fathers' aimless disgruntlement. This means that the villagers' sense of injustice lies deep in their experience but remains politically inchoate since the discourse required to turn experience into critique is unavailable:

> We had talked and talked and talked. We had talked a lot of nonsense, perhaps. But anyone would forgive us. . . . We weren't ashamed. Perhaps we would do better if we had good big words like the educated people. But we didn't. We had to say something was like something else, and whatever we said didn't convey all that we felt. We wouldn't dare tell anybody what we had talked about. People who were sure of what they were saying and who had the right words to use could do that. They could talk to others. And even if they didn't feel what they were saying, it didn't matter. They had the right words. Language was a kind of passport. You could go where you like if you had a clean record. You could say what you like if you know how to say it.[56]

Language is here conceived not only as the means by which reality is named and thereby known but also as a powerful instrument of communication. Having 'the right words' ensures that what is felt can be conveyed, and gives the confidence that facilitates intercourse. The boys' volubility attests the need to translate experience and feeling into speech, however inadequate, but their insistence that they would not repeat their words to others signals their fear of linguistic inadequacy. Yet their self-deprecation is only half-right, as Lamming subtly suggests; their dismissal of their reliance on simile is unfounded, for example, since Lamming's own writing is abundantly metaphorical and pays tribute throughout to the rhythms and stratagems of vernacular speech.

Language is a double-edged sword, however. It enables knowledge and communication but is also a weapon. *In the Castle of My Skin* is ambiguous about this second aspect of language; it is unclear whether the language that education confers leads to a liberation of hitherto unarticulated grievances or whether it culminates in their repression. The passage cited above goes on to describe language as a tool that can slaughter feelings until 'you didn't have to feel at all', and here language functions as a barrier to self-knowledge.[57] This ambivalence about language is of crucial importance to Lamming's work. Lamming considers that 'the education of feeling must be at the heart of any struggle for liberation', and sees his novels as contributions to that struggle.[58] The question, clearly, is what kind of education is to take place; will it kill feeling by casting it in imposed linguistic forms or will it teach feeling to think by transforming it into the articulacy of self-knowledge? The boys fear that G. will choose the former path. His articulacy is a threat, leading them to designate him a future politician or lawyer, professions they despise: ' " 'Tis the same thing by a different name," Bob said, " 'tis the same thing since they both equal to blasted liar" '.[59] But G. refuses this comfortable option. The first-person narrative implies that he is to become a writer who has chosen the other path, using language as the means by which historical self-knowledge can be attained.

It is here that history emerges as a contested terrain. Lamming's account of Walter Rodney's work provides a clue to his own concern with history. Rodney, Lamming argues, 'believed that history was a way of ordering knowledge which could become an active part of the consciousness of an uncertified mass of ordinary people and which could be used as an instrument of social change'. Rodney did not view history as an ideologically neutral practice predicated on the historian's disengaged stance; he conceived it as the recovery from below of a buried past in the service of social critique. His task was not to engage in debates with scholars who thought of Caribbean history in terms of ruling groups' policies and conflicts, but to remap the entire field, to bring about a paradigm shift in the discipline, by writing a history from below that focused on the labour, the daily lives and the struggles of those whose hands had transformed the land and made it economically viable. Thus Rodney shows that 'the history of humanizing this landscape is primarily the history of those hands'; his 'was the task of excavating and reaffirming that particular history'.[60]

Lamming's imaginative reconstructions of history in novelistic form are similar in spirit to Rodney's historical excavations. Caribbean fiction, he observes, 'has served as a way of restoring these lives – this world of men and women from down below – to a proper order of attention: to make their reality the supreme concern of the total society'. But this is no anthropological exercise produced from some implicitly superior vantage point, the writer splitting himself off from the world he describes; it is an exploration in which the writer recognizes 'that this world, in spite of its long history of deprivation, represented the womb from which he himself had sprung'.[61] There is thus a double aspect to such writing: it seeks not only to return a people to their heritage but also to overcome the novelist's self-alienation.

Lamming's first four novels recreate aspects of Caribbean history from the 1930s to the 1950s that colonialism has suppressed. But this act of empirical retrieval, though valuable, is of limited use if it does not simultaneously transform the conception of history that produced such suppression. If one part of Lamming's purpose is to write fiction from below in order to affirm the important historical role played by the vast majority of the Caribbean population, then another part is to shatter the assumptions that led to the need for such an affirmation. Thus his novels not only explore the past from an anti-colonial perspective but also focus on his characters' gradually changing perceptions of what constitutes history. The boys in *Castle*, as might be expected, initially see history as the study of kings and queens and the important events they apparently caused to happen. Moreover, history, as in Naipaul's work, is what takes place elsewhere. Since they have been taught that England did the Caribbean a big favour in deigning to notice and succour it, they are in no position to see their own region and lives as historically significant. When they first hear about slavery they dismiss it: 'they weren't told anything about that. They had read about the Battle of Hastings and William the Conqueror. That happened so many hundred years ago. And slavery was thousands of years before that. It was too far back for anyone to worry about teaching it as history'.[62] History for them consists of wars and conquests that take place in Europe but not in the Caribbean. But since history is about altering the course of events, is about making things happen, the boys can also glimpse in it the possibility of changing their own circumstances. After the headmaster has beaten their friend, they fantasize about challenging his 'power and authority':

> *Fourth Boy:* We going to make hist'ry. I always want to make some hist'ry.
> *Second Boy:* Me too. I read 'bout all those who been making hist'ry. William the Conqueror an' Richard an' all these. I read how they make hist'ry, an' I say to myself 'tis time I make some too.
> *First Boy:* We going to make hist'ry by Foster Fence. Let's make hist'ry.[63]

This is a key moment, for the idea of making 'hist'ry by Foster Fence' suggests that the local landscape can be a site of historically significant acts. But for this to be the case the boys have to free themselves not only from the hierarchy of centre and margin but also from their fetishization of grand events. They need to see history as the product of socially-grounded human practices that have been shaped and constrained in various ways and which, although not generally of cataclysmic importance, nevertheless comprise the contexts of their past and present lives. As Lamming puts it: '[E]verybody is history, everybody is a maker of history. I don't think the educational system – certainly the one that I came through – allowed this to get through to the consciousness of people. Most people do not believe that they are history'.[64] The adult Trumper recognizes this, insisting that the colonial view of history can never lead to this new understanding: 'An' when you see what I tellin' you an' you become a Negro, act as you should an' don't ask Hist'ry why you is what you then see yourself to be, 'cause Hist'ry ain't got no answers. You ain't a thing till you know it, an' that's why you an' none o' you on this island is a Negro yet'.[65]

By the time of *The Emigrants*, traditional history's lack of answers produces psychological trauma. The African Azi, for example, writes about history's arbitrariness and its inability to explain oppressive social relations.[66] *Of Age and Innocence* takes this one step further, focusing on the attempt by local political activists to bring about independence and thereby to overthrow such relations. *Of Age* grows directly out of the experiences canvassed in *The Emigrants*. The latter depicts West Indian emigration to England as a journey to an expectation that is never fulfilled. The emigrants' disillusionment with the 'mother country' and its promise of a shared heritage stems from the suspicion with which they are treated by English people, the social conflicts they witness, and their gradual realization that Britain is no imperium but a small island in seemingly terminal political decline. The power and prestige that can be sustained at a distance collapse with proximity; this collapse leads many to rethink the history of their region and to wish to return in order to change its present political structures.[67]

Shephard's attempt to wrest power from the English by bringing about a coalition between San Cristobal's Indians, Chinese, and Blacks is part of this rethinking and desire for change. But his political activism also functions as the public counterpart of a private battle to redefine the self. The country's struggle for independence is the analogue to Shephard's search for a post-colonial identity that will reverse the hierarchical relation between Prospero and Caliban. Shephard's political epiphany occurs when he realizes that he 'had always lived in the shadow of a meaning which others had placed on [his] presence in the world, and [he] had played no part at all in making that meaning, like a chair which is wholly at the mercy of the idea guiding the hand of the man who builds it'. This meaning exists prior to any relation with the other who defines him; his subject position, like Caliban's, is always already inscribed in the discourse that names him. Shephard's rejection of this subject position leads him to redefine his identity and to reverse the trajectory of the colonial gaze: 'they are really frightened that the order of privilege which is an essential part of their conception of themselves can be revalued, redistributed, or even abolished completely. They are terrified of becoming like the chair which is defenceless against the idea of chair. I am the one who now sees them, not they me'.[68]

Season of Adventure effectively moves this story one step further. Political emancipation has been achieved, but the process of decolonization is proving to be more complex than many had imagined. The first post-independence republic is about to fall, amid various recriminations, most notably its failure to break free from American influence and its inability to confront the class conflicts that the preoccupation with race had previously concealed. The political reorganization of San Cristobal turns out to be little more than a first step, which not only leaves a range of unresolved conflicts but also creates a host of new social divisions by conferring education, authority, and status on some groups at the expense of others. The question that the novel confronts is what can be done to go beyond a political emancipation that has had so little effect on people's self-conceptions and their social relations with one another. Powell, the most politicized of the men from the *tonelle*, raises this issue in the novel's opening pages when he ridicules Crim for having hoped that Independence would improve society and ' "change everythin' that confuse" ': ' "Change my arse," he shouted, "is Independence what it is? One day in July you say you want to be that there thing, an' one day in a next July the law say all right, from now you's what you askin' for. What change that can change? Might as well call your dog a cat an' hope to hear him mew. Is only words an' names what don' signify nothin'" '. For Powell, freedom cannot be granted, for the very act of conferral ensures that at a deeper level the hierarchy of power that it ostensibly shatters remains intact. As long as one country's 'liberation' is controlled by another, it cannot be free: 'If ever I give you freedom, Crim, then all your future is mine, 'cause whatever you do in freedom name is what I make happen'.[69]

Season offers the two paths taken by Powell and Fola as alternatives. Powell is so politically sensitive that he interprets almost everything as an affront either to himself or to his people; his racialist rage is destructive, for he can only curse his meeting with Prospero. Fola, who is a miscegenetic child, initially denies her Afro-Caribbean background but is given the opportunity to acknowledge her suppressed past by the Ceremony of Souls; her 'backward glance' is liberating, for it shows her that her personal history is inseparable from 'the contagious blackmail of slavery working a crime on every skin that comes too thick with colour'.[70] Powell's brooding pessimism drives him to assassinate the republic's president and thereby to precipitate a national crisis. But the Ceremony of Souls shakes Fola's 'disenchantment with the future' and makes her 'alive to the passion which would let her give new meanings to the past; alive to the power which ordered her to choose some future for herself'.[71] Fola's awakening to the possibility of a different future is crucial, but it leaves Powell, and everything that Powell symbolizes, out of account. It is with this problem that *Season* grapples, and its intractability is what makes the novel so bleak. For Powell, though he disappears from the text, haunts its every page, as the 'Author's Note' that interrupts the narrative makes clear:

> I believe deep in my bones that the mad impulse which drove Powell to his criminal defeat was largely my doing. I will not have this explained away by talk about environment; nor can I allow my own moral infirmity to be transferred to a foreign conscience, labelled imperialist. I shall go beyond my grave in the knowledge that I am responsible for what happened to my brother.

Whereas others see Powell either as a man 'crippled' by a pure notion of 'freedom as an absolute', or as 'a man for whom nostalgia was an absolute', Lamming sees him as the victim of an educational divide that separated the author from Powell forever: 'It had earned me a privilege which now shut Powell and the whole *tonelle* right out of my future. . . . Instinctively I attached myself to that new privilege; and in spite of all my effort, I am not free of its embrace even to this day'.[72]

Season figures Lamming's struggle with his conscience through Chiki, the Cambridge-educated artist who by the novel's end is no longer able to paint, since he cannot do justice to the experience and needs articulated by the drums of the *tonelle*. Baako, the future president, confronts Chiki with the aesthetic imperative that has always motivated Lamming's writing: 'if politics is the art of the possible, then your work should be an attempt to show the individual situation illuminated by all the possibilities which keep pushing it always towards a destiny, a destiny which remains open'.[73] In *Season*, the openness of this destiny is signalled by Powell and Fola, children of a double-heritage that in one case leads to despair and in the other to the possibility of regeneration.[74] So *Season* remains both open-ended and ambivalent: Powell's trauma permeates the book, and Fola's self-discovery is in an embryonic stage. The second republic, effectively brought into being with American approval, must confront all the economic, racial, social, and psychological problems that brought down the first one.[75] The new president, echoing Powell's more violently expressed words, has already told Chiki that Independence is but a first step, 'a freedom . . . to make the abortive life you've known more liveable' but that 'trying to be alive in a state of freedom' is the real problem. He reverts to this issue in his first broadcast, focusing on the new state's desperate need to forge an inclusive political language that will confront class divisions and therefore seek to embrace the entire nation.[76] But the novel suggests that the prognosis is not good.

Lamming, as we have seen, differs markedly from Naipaul. His work does not attempt to offer a surface realism but aims to educate the feeling by destroying appearances: 'The novel does not only depict aspects of social reality. It explodes it. It ploughs it up. There are writers who take an easy short cut and go around photographing the absurdities that appear on the social landscape; but they have no plough'.[77] Could Lamming have Naipaul in mind here, as the editors of *Conversations* suggest? He had earlier lambasted Naipaul, describing his work as 'castrated satire' and criticizing him for being 'ashamed of his cultural background'.[78] Certainly their respective approaches to writing could hardly be further apart. Whereas one embroils himself in the conflicts of the Caribbean, the other stands back from them, adopting a detached, aloof stance. Naipaul has written that 'auto-biography can distort' but 'fiction never lies: it reveals the writer totally'.[79] If this is so, then the novels of Lamming and Naipaul reveal how closely they conform to two of the three stages elaborated by Fanon in his account of colonial writing. Fanon's tripartite schema fell into three historical phases: firstly, assimilation of the colonizer's culture; secondly, awareness of the discrepancy between colonizer and colonized but inability to move beyond reminiscence and nostalgia; thirdly, revolt against the colonizer and development of a fighting, national literature. Naipaul's work, I suggest, belongs to the second phase, which in Fanon's words 'is dominated by humour and allegory' but 'is symptomatic of a period of distress and difficulty'. Lamming's writing, in contrast, belongs to the third phase, which is oriented to the political and psychological overthrow of colonialism.[80] His work thus remains true to *The Emigrants*' imperative: 'But you remember: every word you use can be a weapon turned against the enemy or inward on yourself, and to live comfortably with the enemy within you is the most criminal of all betrayals'.[81]

Notes

1. For this deafening silence, see Bryan Appleyard, *The Pleasures of Peace: Art and Imagination in Post-war Britain* (London: Faber and Faber, 1989); Bernard Bergonzi, *The Situation of the Novel* (London: Macmillan, 1970); Malcolm Bradbury (ed.), *The Novel Today: Contemporary Writers on Modern Fiction* (Manchester: Manchester University Press, 1977); Malcolm Bradbury and David Palmer (eds), *The Contemporary English Novel* (New York: Holmes and Meier, 1980); Frederick R. Karl, *A Reader's Guide to the Contemporary English Novel* (London: Thames and Hudson, 1972); Stuart Laing, 'Novels and the Novel', *Society and Literature, 1945–1970*, ed. Alan Sinfield (London: Methuen, 1983); David Lodge, *The Novelist at the Crossroads* (London: Routledge and Kegan Paul, 1971); Rubin Rabinovitz, *The Reaction against Experiment in the English Novel, 1950–1960* (New York: Columbia University Press, 1967).
2. See Aimé Césaire, *Cahier d'un Retour du Pays Natale* (Paris: Présence Africaine, 1971); Wilson Harris, *The Womb of Space: The Cross-Cultural Imagination* (Westport, Connecticut: Greenwood, 1983); Leopold Sedar Senghor, *Selected Poems of Leopold Sedar Senghor*, ed. Abiola Irele (New York: Cambridge University Press, 1977); Denis Williams, *Image and Idea in the Arts of Guyana* (Georgetown, Guyana: Natural History and Arts Council, 1969).
3. See Ann Walmsley, *The Caribbean Artists Movement, 1966–72: A Literary and Cultural History* (London: Beacon, 1992).
4. Quoted in Walmsley, *Caribbean*, p. 172.
5. Wilson Harris, 'History, Fable and Myth in the Caribbean and Guianas', *Caribbean Quarterly*, 16. 2 (June 1970), pp. 1–32, at pp. 21, 26.
6. V. S. Naipaul, 'Conrad's Darkness', *The Return of Eva Peron* (London: Penguin, 1988), p. 218.
7. V. S. Naipaul, 'Images', *Critical Perspectives on V. S. Naipaul*, ed. Robert D. Hamner (London: Heinemann, 1979), pp. 26–9, at p. 28.
8. Ibid., p. 28.
9. See, for example, Peter Hughes, *V. S. Naipaul* (London: Routledge, 1983).
10. George Lamming, *The Pleasures of Exile* (Ann Arbor: University of Michigan Press, 1992), pp. 15, 118–19.
11. V. S. Naipaul, *The Enigma of Arrival* (London: Penguin, 1987), p. 106.
12. V. S. Naipaul, *Eva Peron*, p. 205.
13. Naipaul reiterates this position time and again. See 'Jasmine' and 'Without a Place', in Hamner, *Critical Perspectives*, pp. 16–22; 39–47.
14. V.S. Naipaul, *Eva Peron*, p. 207.
15. Rob Nixon, *London Calling: V. S. Naipaul, Postcolonial Mandarin* (Oxford: Oxford University Press, 1992).
16. V. S. Naipaul, *The Mimic Men* (London: Penguin, 1969), pp. 11, 132; *A Bend in the River* (London: Penguin, 1980), pp. 21–2.
17. V. S. Naipaul, *Finding the Centre* (London: Penguin, 1988), p. 11.
18. I am indebted in what follows to those critics who have argued along similar lines. See, in particular, Nixon, *London*; Angus Richmond, 'Naipaul: The Mimic Man', *Race and Class*, 24. 2 (Autumn 1982), pp. 125–37; A. Sivanandan, 'The Enigma of the Colonised: Reflections on Naipaul's Arrival', *Race and Class*, 32. 1 (1990), pp. 33–43.
19. George Dennis O'Brien, *Hegel on Reason and History: A Contemporary Interpretation* (Chicago: Chicago University Press, 1975), p. 146.
20. G. W. F. Hegel, *Lectures on the Philosophy of History*, trans. J. Sibree (London: Dell and Daldy, 1872), p. 95.
21. Joseph Conrad, *Heart of Darkness* (New York: Signet, 1950), p. 151.

22. Naipaul, *Mimic*, pp. 134, 20.
23. Ibid., p. 8.
24. Ibid., p. 146.
25. V. S. Naipaul, *The Mystic Masseur* (London: Penguin, 1964), p. 18.
26. Naipaul, *Mimic*, pp. 8, 184, 198.
27. Ibid., p. 206.
28. Ibid., pp. 10, 8, 7–8.
29. Ibid., pp. 57, 172.
30. Naipaul, *A Bend*, pp. 41, 108.
31. Ibid., pp. 109–10, 129, 146. Compare Arnold: 'Only it must be *real* thought and *real* beauty; *real* sweetness and *real* light.' *Culture and Anarchy*, ed. J. Dover Wilson (Cambridge: Cambridge University Press, 1988), p. 69.
32. Frantz Fanon, *The Wretched of the Earth*, trans. Constance Farrington (London: Penguin, 1969), p. 130.
33. Thus Naipaul writes: 'Beyond . . . people's memories was *undated time, historical darkness*. Out of that darkness (extending to place as well as to time) we had all come.' *Finding the Centre*, p. 51, emphasis added.
34. V. S. Naipaul, 'A New King for the Congo: Mobutu and the Nihilism of Africa', in Naipaul, *Return*, pp. 172, 176, 187, 195.
35. Hegel, *Lectures*, p. 95.
36. Naipaul, *Return*, p. 196.
37. Lamming, *The Pleasures of Exile*, p. 155.
38. Naipaul, *Enigma* , pp. 131–2, 108.
39. Ibid., pp. 111, 117, 134, 135.
40. Ibid., pp. 11, 22, 23, 49, 58, 80, 170, 172, 176, 200.
41. Ibid., pp. 126, 136, 142.
42. Rob Nixon sees this as an imperialist perspective. Nixon, *London*, p. 32.
43. Johannes Fabian, *Time and the Other: How Anthropology Makes its Object* (N. Y. Guildford: Columbia University Press, 1983).
44. Eric Cheyfitz, *The Poetics of Imperialism: Translation and Colonization from The Tempest to Tarzan* (Oxford: Oxford University Press, 1991), p. 84.
45. Shakespeare, *The Tempest*, ed. Stephen Orgel (Oxford: Oxford University Press, 1987), 1. ii. 355–7.
46. For a description of such accounts, see Peter Fryer, *Black People in the British Empire: An Introduction* (London: Pluto, 1988), pp. 71–2. Prospero's references to providence are at 1. ii. 60–3 and 1. ii. 159.
47. George Lamming, *Conversations: Essays, Addresses and Interviews, 1953–1990*, ed. Richard Drayton and Andaiye (London: Karia, 1992), p. 81.
48. George Lamming, *In the Castle of My Skin* (Harlow: Longman, 1987), p. 208.
49. Ibid., p. 290.
50. Lamming, *Conversations*, p. 188.
51. Lamming, *Castle*, p. 29.
52. Ibid., pp. 18–19.
53. Ibid., p. 96.
54. Ibid., pp. 62, 136.
55. Ibid., p. 287; Lamming, *Conversations*, p. 162.
56. Lamming, *Castle*, pp. 145–6.
57. Ibid., p. 146.
58. Lamming, *Conversations*, pp. 28–9.
59. Lamming, *Castle*, p. 150.
60. Lamming, *Conversations*, pp. 273, 274.
61. Ibid., p. 48.
62. Lamming, *Castle*, p. 50.
63. Ibid., p. 40.

64. Lamming, *Conversations*, p. 291.
65. Lamming, *Castle*, p. 290.
66. George Lamming, *The Emigrants* (London: Allison and Busby, 1980), pp. 206–7.
67. The link between the two novels is made explicit in George Lamming, *Of Age and Innocence* (London: Allison and Busby, 1981), p. 168.
68. Ibid., pp. 203, 205.
69. George Lamming, *Season of Adventure* (London: Allison and Busby, 1979), pp. 17, 18–19.
70. Ibid., pp. 120, 94.
71. Ibid., pp. 247, 246.
72. Ibid., pp. 332, 330, 331.
73. Ibid., p. 324.
74. Powell is the narrator's 'half-brother by a different mother' and Fola is the child of a 'double fatherhood'. Lamming, *Season*, pp. 331, 343.
75. For the subtle references to American influence, see Lamming, *Season*, pp. 352–7. Does Lamming perhaps have *Nostromo*'s emphasis on American power in mind here? See Joseph Conrad, *Nostromo*, (Harmondsworth: Penguin, 1979), pp. 399, 400, 414.
76. Lamming, *Season*, pp. 362–3.
77. Lamming, *Conversations*, p. 29.
78. Lamming, *Pleasures*, p. 225.
79. Naipaul, *Return*, p. 67.
80. Fanon, *Wretched*, p. 179.
81. Lamming, *Emigrants*, p. 101.

4

After Socialist Realism

Trotsky claims that 'artistic creation is always a complicated turning inside out of old forms, under the influence of new stimuli which lie outside of art'.[1] This view, though entirely in keeping with Marxist thought, was for many years a maverick one. Engels and Chernyshevsky established a close link between Marxism and realism in the nineteenth century, and this link was codified in 1934 when the first congress of the Soviet Writers' Union accepted the party's imposition of Socialist Realism as the most appropriate form for creative writing. Socialist Realism was supposed to be popular, to display a mature ideology, and to follow the party line.[2] Stalin's emphasis on the writer's role as an engineer of human souls meant that Socialist Realism was soon associated with 'progressive' depictions of reality that were to disclose its revolutionary potential.[3] In practice, its plots quickly degenerated into descriptions of the emergence from the people of a central protagonist who was politically educated by the party and subsequently performed heroic feats on its behalf.[4]

Even where such schematic writing was not treated very seriously, realism held pride of place in Marxist aesthetics. Lukács, for example, devoted most of his career to 'critical' realists such as Balzac, Thomas Mann, Rolland, and Tolstoy. His account of realism emphasized that the novelist's task was to depict typical characters in typical circumstances, portray social totality, and penetrate the surfaces of collective human life in order to disclose the dialectical unity of essence and appearance.[5] His unbending commitment to these precepts meant that he could see little value in modernism, which he attacked as an uncritical capitulation to the disorder of modern capitalist life. Brecht, one of Lukács's main targets, responded by pointing out that Lukács's conception of realism was ahistorical. Since it took little account of how society had changed, it promoted an art-form that belonged to a bygone era. Against Lukács's insistence that modernist art failed to confront the social realities of capitalism, Brecht contended that new techniques were necessary because these realities were so unlike those depicted in nineteenth-century realist novels. Echoing Trotsky, he declared: 'New problems appear and demand new methods. Reality changes; in order to represent it, modes of representation must also change'. For Brecht, Lukács's account of realism was formalist because his criteria were purely literary; realism, he argued, should be 'wide and political, sovereign over all conventions'.[6]

The conflict between Lukács and Brecht over realism is pertinent to the post-war work of John Berger and Doris Lessing for two reasons: first, because their early writing explicitly belongs to a realist tradition that is socialist and not, say, liberal humanist; secondly, because their respective departures from a fairly narrow conception of realism to more experimental modes is clarified by Brecht's defence of a non-conventional realism. This is particularly true of Berger. During the 1950s, he championed realism against abstract art, and his account of the former, despite much twisting and turning, was often hard to distinguish from Socialist Realism. Realism was, in Berger's view, driven not only by the impulse to represent the world with fidelity but also by the desire to challenge exploitative social relations. But Berger's enormous respect for the modernist art of Cézanne, Picasso, and Léger meant that a narrow commitment to realism was always going to prove hard to sustain. He quickly adopted a Brechtian approach to the problem of realism, arguing that 'its methods and aims are always changing' and claiming that, whereas realism always pointed to some hitherto undisclosed aspect of reality, formalism offered technical breakthroughs that were only internally significant.[7] Berger's increasingly modernist approach to realism went hand in hand with his growing discomfort with orthodox Marxism, which ultimately led him to a conception of art that drew on the young, Hegelian Lukács, Heidegger, and Benjamin. His own fiction went from the broad realism of *A Painter of Our Time* (1958), to the early experimentation of *The Foot of Clive* (1962) and *Corker's Freedom* (1964), to the Cubist-inspired, dialectical form of *G.* (1972) and then, in the *Into Their Labours* trilogy (1979, 1983, 1990), to a traditional story-telling mode.

Lessing's career has been more explosive. Like Berger, she was initially a realist and socialist. Realism, she declared, was 'the highest form of prose writing; higher than and out of the reach of any comparison with expressionism, impressionism, symbolism, naturalism, or any other ism'. She defended realism as the literary mode best suited to left-wing preoccupations, stressed her faith in 'the class analysis of society and therefore of art', and promoted *engagement*.[8] By the 1960s, however, Lessing had become disillusioned with politics and had moved a long way from her early socialist beliefs. Her concern with the rapidly changing nature of the post-war world led her to conclude that realism was unable to represent contemporary reality, which was daily becoming 'wilder, more fantastic, incredible'.[9] The subsequent implosion of realism in novels such as *The Golden Notebook* (1962), *Landlocked* (1965), *The Four-Gated City* (1969), and *Memoirs of a Survivor* (1975) is inseparable from her abandonment of the socialism that had been the driving force of her realism. As she put it in an interview: 'I must have been mad – I'm not just talking about being a Communist; I mean thinking that politics comes up with answers to social problems, which it manifestly doesn't do'.[10] Lessing's crisis of socialist belief resulted in the fissuring of nineteenth-century forms into an experimental realism and into fantasy, apocalypse, science fiction, and myth.

John Berger

Berger's early art criticism and the novel that emerged from it (*A Painter of our Time*) belong in a Cold War context. His aggressive championing of a socially committed art was symptomatic of the Old Left at that time. Raymond Williams points out that because the idea of commitment had been under attack during this period, many of its supporters felt vulnerable and defensive.[11] Moreover, the backlash against communism, neatly captured in the title of Richard Crossman's *The God That Failed*, gathered force in the 1950s, throwing much of the socialist movement into disarray.[12] It was not until the New Left took off in 1957 that those socialists who had become disillusioned with Soviet communism found a political movement which they could wholeheartedly support. Most of Berger's early art criticism thus falls victim to the rigid dichotomies of the Cold War period. The polarization between Moscow and Washington led numerous socialists into intellectual difficulties, as they struggled to fit their beliefs to the Procrustean theories promulgated by a frequently doctrinaire Marxism.

As art critic for the *New Statesman*, Berger sought to outline a Marxist view of art that avoided the sterility of Socialist Realism on the one hand and the superficiality of much abstract painting on the other. He argued that serious art must be oriented to human emancipation, and attacked artistic tendencies that eschewed referentiality. Post-war abstract art was in his view bankrupt. Whereas the modernism of the early twentieth century had led to 'important technical and aesthetic discoveries', the contemporary avant-garde was unable to work its sense of crisis into its art and thus revealed only 'the desperation of despair'. Having failed to generate a meaningful subject matter, it had reduced art to the question of form. For Berger, art's aesthetic dimension had to be primarily oriented to the social domain. Conventional art criticism, in his view, was formalist; it ignored art's social significance by insisting on the primacy of an autonomous aesthetic realm. Berger, in contrast, argued that great art offered 'the possibility of an increase, an improvement' because it encouraged people 'to know and claim their social rights'.[13]

Berger's critique of abstract art was doctrinaire. It disclosed an untenable distinction between form and content, an insufficiently theorized account of the differences between 'progressive' and 'decadent' art, and a suspicion that art, whatever its orientation, was in any case escapist and therefore politically irresponsible. Because his conception of Marxist aesthetics required him to defend realism, he was all but forced to argue that non-representational art was *per se* incapable of being socially relevant. This meant that he not only failed to do justice to the complexity of abstract art but also ignored the historical context in which it was being produced. A further problem, identified by Richard Wollheim in a perceptive article on Berger's art criticism, concerned the status of realism in his theory. Wollheim pointed out that Berger's account of realism was imprecise and in need of closer argumentation, that he was unable to justify his claim that art produced a form of knowledge, and that his faith in its political effectiveness rested less on the art object than on the attitude or stance of the viewer. How art taught individuals to demand their social rights remained obscure.[14]

Berger was to move away from his initial commitment to realism, but

'Problems of Socialist Art' (1961) illustrates how difficult it was to do so. Two incompatible discourses compete with one another in this essay. Berger's goal is to argue against Socialist Realism by suggesting that contemporary painters cannot ignore the revolution in art instigated by modernism. Modernist art, he suggests, shows life as a contradictory totality and as a process; it thereby clears a path for truly dialectical painting. Contemporary socialist art should seek to extend these modernist experiments. But this position, as Berger is aware, goes against the dictates of Socialist Realism. Thus he ties himself in knots in an attempt to forestall the inevitable criticisms. In phrases worthy of a Zhdanov he reminds his readers 'that the Marxist–Leninist theory of the origins, nature and use of art is fundamentally correct; that today revisionism as applied to the arts is a disruptive and dangerous influence, leading to petty bourgeois cynicism and triviality . . . that the Soviet achievement in the arts is unique and of the greatest significance'.[15]

A Painter of Our Time explores these conflicts. It signals its historical provenance in two ways: published in 1958, it was written at the height of socialist soul-searching in the wake of Khrushchev's 'secret' speech, the invasion of Hungary, and unrest in Poland; set in the years 1952–6, it steps back into Cold War days, exploring many of the conflicts that led to the later emergence of the New Left. The novel focuses on the legacy of modernism and the fraught relationship between art and politics. Its main narrative consists of an exiled Hungarian artist's journal, which the narrator designates a 'Portrait of the Artist as an Emigré'.[16] The idea that the contemporary artist is an émigré is developed in some detail. Whereas Janos Lavin is portrayed as an émigré because he is cut off from the political tradition to which he gives allegiance, English painters are seen as the voluntary victims of an internal exile because their predominantly abstract art has no social purpose.

Lavin is no unrecognized genius; he is depicted as a good painter, but one who is racked with guilt over his failure to contribute to the struggle for socialism in post-war Hungary and his inability to meld his politics with his art. Two questions torment him. Can one create a political art that does not degenerate into propaganda? Does a dedication to the life of art represent a betrayal of one's political commitments? As a young man, he was an activist, but whereas his friends remained in Hungary to fight for socialism he 'never went back to the front' but 'slipped away to paint'. Lavin's language suggests desertion, and the anxiety that art is of little value when compared with politics haunts his journal: 'I have made myself doubly an émigré. I have not returned to our country. And I have chosen to spend my life on my art, instead of on immediate objectives. Thus I am a spectator watching what I might have participated in'.[17] Lavin's self-critique turns on a distinction between activity (politics) and passivity (art); it is because he has devoted himself to painting that he has not 'participated' in the political events of the day.

The tension between the demands of art and politics, which comprises the novel's central problematic, remains unresolved. But it is revealing that Berger is, in this text, unable to conceive of politics and art as anything other than two opposed terms. *A Painter* discloses a basic distrust of the aesthetic realm. Lavin's attempt to forge a committed art is compromised from the outset, since politics always assumes primacy over painting in his thinking.

His pursuit of a political art is persistently undermined by his prior conviction – never clearly voiced – that dedication to art, however *engagé* it might be, conceals an escape from 'real' politics. Moreover, the novel never defines Lavin's politics with any precision and remains vague about how he proposes to create a committed art. The problems that Wollheim identified in Berger's art criticism resurface here, as the following diary entry indicates:

> All of these men were militant: militant to the point of being prepared to die for what they believed in. Delacroix believed in his *petite sensation;* Van Gogh in his 'Humanity, humanity, and again humanity.' They fought for their various visions and most of their militant energy was concerned with fighting the difficulties of realising their vision, of finding the visual forms that would turn their hunches into facts. Each of their different visions, however, sprang from the same kind of conviction; they each knew that life could be better, richer, juster, truer than it was.[18]

A passage such as this points to Berger's difficulties. It is framed by two political statements, which the enclosed words do little to support. Berger's desire to assert a clear link between the value of art and the struggle for justice leads him to account for these painters' quality in terms of their implicit social stance. But he is able to articulate this leftist aesthetic only by papering over the cracks of a contradiction. The bulk of the passage admits that art possesses a dimension, difficult though it may be to capture, that cannot be explained in political language. Yet the writer's desire to equate artistic value with social critique leads him to frame his commentary with a political rhetoric that the rest of the passage cannot uphold.

The tension between art's plastic qualities and its social function is everywhere evident in *A Painter*. Lavin paraphrases Berger's position in *Permanent Red* when he argues that true art 'communicates and so extends consciousness of what is possible', although he cannot articulate how it does so.[19] At the very moment that he gains public recognition for his painting, he chooses to return to Hungary in order to take part in the uprising of 1956. But this return only reveals the dubiety of Berger's claim that the contemporary artist is forced to be an émigré. For Lavin's homecoming, which symbolizes his return to 'active' politics, allows him to overcome his émigré status only at the cost of his ceasing to be an artist. The novel's initial premise that significant art implicitly depends on some form of *engagement* is inverted; art is shown to be so completely severed from the social realm that it must be abandoned if the artist is to fulfil his political obligations. The aim of articulating how art and politics may productively inform one another lies in tatters, leaving the reader with an unanswered question: has Lavin, by renouncing art in favour of politics, solved his dilemma in the same way that Alexander 'solved' the Gordian knot?

Berger was unable fully to escape the straitjacket of political correctness in *A Painter*. Both *The Foot of Clive* (1962) and *Corker's Freedom* (1964) represented attempts to break free from a stultifying realism by combining detailed naturalism with an experimental approach to the rendition of interiority. *Corker's Freedom*, which is more successful in this respect than *The Foot of Clive*, turns on the dissonance between the externals of social life and the internal revolt against the resultant limitation of human potential. The novel explores its central characters' alienation from the world of work and from each other. The ritualized working relationship between Corker, the

63-year-old owner of an employment agency, and Alec, his young assistant, prevents them from establishing any genuine contact with each other. The interior narratives of both protagonists are set against their public actions, disclosing the discrepancy between their innermost longings and their conventional behaviour. Alec awaits the untoward events that disrupt the daily routine, since these 'challenge it' and thereby 'allow him to feel a closer connection between daily life and his being alive'.[20] Corker, in turn, fantasizes about escape, dreaming of a life in which he could be free of crushing domestic responsibilities and the meaninglessness of his habitual existence.

The single day during which the novel's action takes place represents a watershed for Corker. His refusal to go on living as he has done requires him to articulate the resentments that have hitherto remained unacknowledged. His 'break' is only made possible when he becomes fully conscious of his frustration and communicates it to others. The rambling talk he gives in the church hall is significant because he wants not only to make his private epiphany public but also to invite his auditors to reflect on its relevance to their own pinched lives. But Corker's utopian desire for a 'world where we could all be ourselves' meets with incomprehension, since his audience displays a deep-rooted pessimism: 'Life, they say, is like this. . . . It is a hard job to maintain any position. The forces against you are so strong that you have only to glance away for a second for everything to revert to its inhospitable, inert, winter state'.[21]

Corker's escape attempt meets with disaster. He loses all means of material support through a series of accidents, and by the novel's end is a down-and-out scavenging for meals. The text remains ambivalent about his actions. Corker, like Janos Lavin, has confronted the compromises inherent in his habitual life and has sought to undo them. But he has been guilty of hubris. He has overestimated his own powers and failed to see how easily the individual can be broken. The novel does not judge Corker. It grants him respect for his protest but suggests that he is a political innocent whose belief in personal solutions to social and economic problems is inadequate.

The search for a narrative mode that could not only offer a form of social critique but also articulate Berger's sense of Cubism's revolutionary potential was to find its clearest expression in *G*. In this novel Berger jettisons a narrowly conceived realism and turns to Cubism in the way he had urged in 'Problems of Socialist Art'. For Berger, Cubism's multiple viewpoints evoked the complex nature of reality and emphasized process. Cubism suggested that human understanding is made, and thus opened up the question of how it is made. Its shattering of the single perspective focused attention on the interaction between artist and object, revealing that the 'world-as-it-is is more than pure objective fact, it includes consciousness'.[22] Because, in Berger's view, Cubism replaced the metaphor of the mirror with that of the diagram, it encouraged him to reject his earlier espousal of a simple representational aesthetic in favour of a self-reflexive realism that took modernist insights as its point of departure.[23] Its polyvalence also led him away from a doctrinaire Marxism, as is suggested by essays such as 'Sekher Ahmet and the Forest' and 'The Secretary of Death', which reveal the influence of Heidegger and the young Lukács. Berger refers in 'Sekher

Ahmet' to Lukács's conception of the novel as the form 'born of a yearning for what now lay beyond the horizon', and combines this with Heidegger's claim that 'thought approaches the distant; but the distant also approaches thought'.[24] These ideas are linked still more closely in 'The Secretary', which suggests that the novel's tenses 'are those of the future or the conditional' because novels 'are about Becoming'.[25] On this view, individuals project their activity into the future, for it is in the future that their utopian aspirations will bear fruit. That Berger could never have expressed himself thus in the 1950s only reveals how far beyond orthodox Marxism he had now moved.

G. represents Berger's attempt to develop a nuanced account of history within the form of fiction. Central to his writing is the belief that the responsible individual should be self-critical as well as critical of the society she or he seeks to alter. This dual perspective explains why *G.* quotes the following passage from Collingwood: 'All history is contemporary history: not in the ordinary sense of the word where contemporary history means the history of the comparatively recent past, but in the strict sense: the consciousness of one's own activity as one actually performs it. History is thus the self-knowledge of the living mind'.[26]

A utopian impulse is discernible in *G.*, but the text refuses to offer falsely optimistic hopes for the future. The novel does not so much propose a different form of social life as disclose the need for a critical attitude to any given present. The text's utopianism is hinted at when Laura explains what *G.* means to her: 'She wants with her baby to start an alternative world, to propose from his new-born life a new way of living'.[27] *G.* has already been associated with Garibaldi, and this passage, which alludes to the hopes inspired by Christ's birth, identifies him as a nexus of revolutionary possibilities. But the novel immediately warns that although emancipatory hopes are centred on G. they may be dashed, for the opening words of the next section explain that Laura did not succeed in her goal. G. will in fact prove to be a curious kind of revolutionary, and his last acts are of fairly minor significance, since they do little more than symbolize his identification with a collective/political struggle rather than a personal/sexual one. To a certain degree, then, *G.* focuses on its main protagonist and invites the reader to do likewise. But the text also treats this figure with disdain and marginalizes him in diverse ways. The novel cannot in fact be understood if G. either occupies centre stage or is conceived in psychological terms. He is clearly not a 'realistic' character: he remains 'the boy' until a third of the book has unfolded; he is denied a proper name; his status as a literary construct is stressed through allusions to Don Juan, Garibaldi, Christ, and Satan. His role is ambiguous throughout, and he tends to be portrayed as an intertextual cipher. The novel thus rings the changes on the Lukácsian conception of the 'type' as 'a nexus of the social and individual', suggesting that character can no longer bear this totalizing burden.[28] But although *G.*'s modernist style undermines the nineteenth-century approach to character, its aim is not to erase human agency. It is to suggest, rather, that although the individual's scope has been reduced in the twentieth century he or she is still obliged to participate in political life. Whereas the view of the individual as history's puppet has become a postmodern commonplace, Berger, far from acceding to it, suggests that the 'puppet' can still give its 'master' a few hard knocks.

G. is both cipher and agent because, whereas in local terms he is an actor on history's stage, in global terms he is acted upon by a historical stage that dwarfs him.

This dialectic receives structural support. The novel's four sections correspond, as David James has noted, to different periods in G.'s life, but they also exhibit other structural parallels.[29] The first section, which introduces G. and prefigures the text's main concerns, stands apart from the other three sections. The latter share two features: each contains a turbulent historical episode where G. confronts a dispossessed crowd in relation to which he must take a stance; each contains discussions or enactments of historical moments that have little direct bearing on the events being narrated. Section 2 features the 'I Fatti di Maggio 1898' Milan uprising, together with a discussion of Boer colonialism and an account of the 'Great Amaxosa Delusion'; section 3 includes the flight of Chavez and the crowd at Brig, as well as the analysis of 'A Situation of Women'; section 4 contains the Trieste riot of 1914, together with a description of the Young Bosnians and an account of the Battle of Auvers Ridge. Each of the historical tableaux in these sections illuminates different kinds of injustice: class, sexual, and national oppression.

This associative and montage-like structure, which establishes unexpected connections between areas of political life that initially appear to be disparate, aims to provide a paradigmatic rather than syntagmatic view of the historical period under consideration. Structurally, *G.* utilizes the argument of Berger's 'The Moment of Cubism' essay, synthesizing its insights as follows: 'Never again will a single story be told as though it were the only one.'[30] Although it is only in *G.* that Berger makes formal use of this view, incorporating it into the very structure of his text, it is already present in his thinking in *A Painter of Our Time*, for in that text Lavin observes: 'What eyes Cubism has given us! Never again can we make a painting of a single view. We now have a visual dialectic'.[31] Both statements help to explain *G.*'s structure and narrative mode. Written out of a conviction that the single view cannot do justice to the complexity of reality, the novel rejects conventional realism by incorporating clashing viewpoints into its narrative fabric in order to create 'dynamic relationships and processes instead of appearances fixed to one position and one moment'.[32] The novel's narrator explains his technique thus: 'I have little sense of unfolding time. The relations which I perceive between things – and these often include causal and historical relations – tend to form in my mind a complex synchronic pattern. I see fields where others see chapters'. Writing 'in the spirit of a geometrician', a phrase that recalls the Vorticists as much as the Cubists, Berger constructs a syntagmatic picture of *fin-de-siècle* Europe, creating a post-war version of the spatial form that artists of that time were themselves elaborating.[33]

The narrator's claim that he has small appreciation of 'unfolding time' is disingenuous. It would be more accurate to say that, like the Vorticists and Cubists, he has reservations about *presenting* events as they unfold in time. *G.*'s structure has less to do with its author's sense of time *per se* than with the aesthetic implications of alternative narrative modes. The linear telling of stories implies a kind of formal order and cohesion that the text disavows. Linear narrative begins and ends at a distinct point in time and because it is in this sense teleological often lends its conclusion an air of inevitability. Berger is himself committed to a teleological conception of human life, but his aim is to escape the bonds of determinism and to avoid prejudging the outcome of the struggles he describes: 'The writer's desire to finish is fatal to the truth. The End unifies. Unity must be established in another way'.[34]

The novel's 'Cubist' dimension comes to the fore here, since it has important consequences for the novel's explorations of time and language, the twin issues that lie at the heart of its attempt to elaborate a non-linear, non-deterministic narrative mode. The text distinguishes between the completed past and the still unfolding present in order to emphasize that while the former is unalterable the latter is open to transformation. The attempt by hegemonic groups to make existing social relations appear natural is to make them appear inevitable. G. treats such naturalizing discourses as political givens, choosing to focus on their temporal consequences: 'Every ruling minority needs to numb and, if possible, to kill the time-sense of those whom it exploits by proposing a continuous present'.[35] The novel challenges this politically charged temporal continuity by oscillating between present-tense and past-tense narration. Moments of revolutionary promise tend to be narrated in the present tense, whereas scenes of oppression tend to be narrated in the past tense. The consequence of this is that present-tense scenes sparkle with drama and hope; as each episode unfolds before the reader in all its immediacy, its outcome is unknown, and the success or failure of the action being described remains an open question. The past-tense scenes, by contrast, are lifeless; they imply defeat, not only because they represent courses of action that failed but also because of the flat tone in which they are recounted.

The text adopts a similarly self-reflexive approach to language. When explaining his narrative mode, the narrator comments that he does not 'wish to become a prisoner of the nominal, believing that things are what [he] name[s] them', and his fear of nominalism pervades G. Throughout the text the narrator announces that he cannot convey his meaning because the nuances of human experience constantly elude language. Thus G.'s disgust at the scene with the two horses cannot be evoked: 'It is beyond me to create a name for this revulsion: the ones I can think up all simplify'. Description in general is portrayed as a form of distortion because it entails a falsifying selection of 'both the facts and the words describing them'. All that the narrator sees amazes him 'by its particularity', leaving him unsure 'how . . . to convey such uniqueness?'.[36]

Now this kind of writing has a sceptical postmodernist air, but in fact the text's obsession with the uniqueness of experience discloses a concern with the difficulties of evoking the concrete details of people's lives rather than a full-scale epistemological scepticism. Refusing to be defeated by such difficulties, G. elaborates and defends alternative cognitive modes in its attempt to do justice to the political reality of oppressed groups. Its lapses into silence are not admissions of defeat but attempts to find alternative ways to communicate. Berger has long been concerned with different modes of perception, as the titles of his books – *About Looking, Ways of Seeing, Another Way of Telling* – suggest. He sets up in G. an interaction between two different ways of knowing: a linguistic one that produces a factual historical discourse, and a visual one that relies on the apparently unmediated witness of sight.

The novel's account of the Milan rising of 6–9 May 1898 provides an instructive example of how the text's concern with time and language informs these two discourses. The episode reconstructs a riot in which the poor turned against the government. According to official figures, eighty rioters were killed and 450 were wounded, largely as a result of General Bava-Beccaris's decision to fire cannon and grapeshot into an unarmed crowd.[37] The scene is initially narrated in the present tense, when events seem so full of promise; once it has ended in disaster, however, the consequences of the defeat, with their air of finality, are described in the past tense. The conclusion to the scene, which first foregrounds sight and then seeks to authorize what has silently been witnessed by an appeal to historical evidence, illustrates the operation of the two cognitive modes I have described. The crowd, initially suspicious of the well-dressed G., ceases to be hostile to him when it realizes that he cannot speak Italian. In the riot that ensues he is adopted as a mascot because it is hoped that his inability to comprehend words will enable him the better to bear witness to deeds. Untrammelled sight will supersede tainted words: 'If the boy cannot understand their language, he is immune to the hypocrisy of deception of words and thus can be the pure witness of their actions'. In what follows, the young G. empathizes with the pain of the workers' plight despite being unable to understand the precise nature of their grievances. And when a worker is shot, the narrative breaks down, signalling its awareness of language's inability to evoke suffering:

> Write anything. Truth or untruth, it is unimportant. Speak but speak with tenderness, for that is all that you can do that may help a little. Build a barricade of words, no matter what they mean. Speak so that he can be aware of your presence. Speak so that he knows that you are there not feeling his pain. Say anything for his pain is larger than any distinction you can make between truth and untruth.[38]

It is hard to respond to such writing, but I suggest that this passage does not imply a thorough-going scepticism about language's referential function. The crowd is less suspicious of language *per se* than of the ways it can be employed to distort the truth. It grasps, moreover, that language is one of the most powerful weapons its rulers have. It is for this reason that it makes an appeal to unmediated sight, challenging G. to deny what his own eyes reveal to him. The narrator's wordless anguish, in turn, is an acknowledgement of the unbridgeable gap between actual pain and any vocabulary that could be used to describe it.

An awareness of language's limitations is a key feature of *G.*, but the text does not undermine language altogether. Although the narrator empathizes with the crowd's suspicion of language, his own, more disengaged, stance should not be confused with theirs. Sympathetic and involved though he is, he nevertheless stands apart from the events he is recounting. Indeed, the text's faith in language's referential function is disclosed by its reliance on a second cognitive mode – an authoritative historical discourse. Language is at key moments in the novel stripped of all its rhetorical artfulness – although this resort to 'plainness' is itself a rhetorical manœuvre – in an attempt to let the facts speak for themselves. For example, Umberto's fulsome description of the 15-kilometre tunnel that he sees as 'a marvel of science' is interrupted by a parenthetic omniscient interjection: '(The St Gothard tunnel was opened in 1882. Eight hundred men lost their lives in its construction)'. The imaginative account of the Milan workers' poverty is interrupted in a similar way: '(The eldest of these girls earns less than 10d a day)'. The conclusion to the Milan riot relies heavily on this kind of historical evidence for its rhetorical power. When the narrative breaks down because it cannot describe the killing of the workers, a flat summation of the scene follows:

> Between 6 May, when martial law was declared in Milan, and 9 May one hundred workers were killed and four hundred and fifty wounded. Those four days marked the end of a phase of Italian history. Socialist leaders began to lay more and more stress on parliamentary democracy and all attempts at direct revolutionary action – or revolutionary defence – were abandoned. Simultaneously the ruling class adopted new tactics towards the workers and the peasantry; crude repression gave way to political manipulation. For the next twenty years in Italy – as in most of the rest of Europe – the spectre of revolution was banished from men's minds.[39]

A passage such as this testifies to Berger's faith in the possibility of historical knowledge. The account of the Milan uprising does not break down because events are unknowable, as the confident use of the preterite tense and the precise, statistical language make clear; it breaks down because it cannot do justice to the irreducibly particular quality of individual experience. Berger is not a historian; he is a novelist. He tries, in a text like *G.*, to evoke the texture of human experience, while at the same time placing this evocation in a carefully researched historical context. Turning again and again to the facts of history, Berger suggests that they resonate with a power that, when liberated – paradoxically, it seems – by the writer's words, speaks for itself. But this is neither a positivist historicism, which denies the interpreter's perspective, nor a naive faith in historical omniscience, which denies that there are gaps in the historical record. The text's multiple viewpoints and self-reflexive view of language make sure of this. It is, rather, an attempt to use the novel form to create a visceral response in the reader and to emphasize the writer's hermeneutic obligation to aim for historical veracity.

I want now, in concluding this discussion of *G.*, to turn briefly to the motif of the crowd, which runs through the novel and clarifies the significance of *G.*'s final actions. Three crowd scenes ('I Fatti' in Milan, the flight of Chavez at Brig, and the riot in Trieste) function as indices of *G.*'s self-understanding. Each of these three crowds represents the hopes of an oppressed class, and in each scene G. is asked to define himself *vis-à-vis* the suffering that confronts him. The novel establishes its view of the crowd as an exploited body and invites identification with its plight in its opening pages. In a long passage the crowd is described as needing 'to overthrow the order which has defined and distinguished between the possible and the impossible at its expense, for generation after generation'. Such a crowd challenges the individual who is not of it, leaving him either to see 'the promise of mankind' there or to 'fear it absolutely'.[40] Whereas for members of the ruling class, such as Umberto, proletarian crowds are redolent of the mob to be feared, for Berger they are the corporeal manifestation of a political 'return of the repressed' – their poverty, anger, and sheer size signify the scale of the injustices that have been perpetrated against them.

It is no coincidence that *G.*'s conception of such crowds' demands for social justice stands in marked contrast to the Italian futurists' celebration of violent and irrational carnival. Given that the events of the novel's concluding section coincide with the activities of the futurists, its emphasis on self-examination and collective struggle can be seen as a rejection of Marinetti's proto-Fascist glorification of war ('the world's only hygiene') and his uncritical modernolatry ('We will sing of great crowds excited by work, by pleasure, and by riot').[41] In contrast to Marinetti's idealization of the proletariat, the three crowds in *G.* are linked through their poverty and disenfranchised status. They testify to a continuity of oppression, which the text evokes through its focus on that 'eternal present' (a denial of the possibility of change) imposed on the working class by those in power. *G.*'s realization that this interminable present must be shattered leads to his incipient understanding of himself as a historical being in the Collingwoodian sense that the novel earlier proposes.[42] Whereas in Milan he is a spectator, and in Brig an outsider, in Trieste he abandons his detached individualist stance and becomes a participant and leader. The meaning of his participation can only be understood in relation to the novel's concern with time and its Heideggerian stress on the individual's need to project himself into an open future that moves to meet him. For in Trieste, *G.*, like those who are forced to live under the sign of an eternal present, feels as though he is imprisoned by time: 'He had come to the point of feeling condemned to live even the present in the past tense'.[43] *G.*'s desire to defeat this sense of a future determined in advance leads him to reject his earlier apolitical stance. His involvement in the Trieste riot, which the text portrays as a parallel to that in Milan, represents the payment of his debt to the workers slaughtered in 1898, since he now enters historical time and recognizes the necessity of collective political action.

By the time Berger wrote *G.*, neither his socialist politics nor his conception of art could be circumscribed by Marxism. He has himself acknowledged this. In *Pig Earth* (1980) he wonders if a conclusive social revolution will ever take place and suggests that 'the peasant experience of survival may well be better adapted to this long and harsh perspective than the continually reformed, disappointed, impatient progressive hope of an ultimate victory'.[44] And in an interview with *Marxism Today* he claims to be 'a bad Marxist' because he has 'an aversion to political power whatever its form' and is intuitively 'always with those who live under that power'.[45] Berger's Marxism has shifted ground, becoming less deterministic and more open-ended, but it still attests his utopian faith in human agency: 'Each of us comes into the world with her or his unique possibility – which is an aim. . . . The job of our lives is to become – day by day, year by year – more conscious of that aim so that it can at last be realised'.[46]

Doris Lessing

Doris Lessing's novels trace a circular path that begins and ends with realism, taking a detour through the terrain of science fiction, apocalypse, and mythopoesis. Lessing, like Berger, was in the 1950s a socialist who considered politics and aesthetics to be inextricable. In an early manifesto, 'The Small Personal Voice', she described the nineteenth-century realists as her literary masters but situated herself in the socialist tradition, emphasizing her faith in class analysis and political art. Realism was indispensable to this committed conception of literature. In Lessing's view the European realists of the previous century shared a humanist outlook that enabled them, despite their political differences, to see society as a whole and to portray its diverse features in totalizing works of art. But the post-war novelist confronts the splintering of humanism into a plethora of competing and mutually incompatible discourses. Post-war literature reveals 'a confusion of standards and the uncertainty of values'; it portrays the individual either as an isolated monad unable to relate to others or as a social being who lacks uniqueness. Both portrayals capitulate to the problems facing the writer, who should try to balance human beings' irreducible individuality against their unavoidably social nature: 'The point of rest should be the writer's recognition of man, the responsible individual, voluntarily submitting his will to the collective, but never finally; and insisting on making his own personal and private judgements before every act of submission'.[47]

The careful phrasing of this statement hints at the internal conflict between artistic freedom and political duty that also marked Berger's work in the 1950s. It is characteristic of socialist writers emerging from the pre-Khrushchev era of icy dictates as to the nature of art and the function of the artist. Lessing never espoused Socialist Realism, but her defence of realism was strongly influenced by Marxism. Lorna Sage observes that her faith in it implied not just belief in 'a tradition and a cluster of stylistic strategies inherited from the nineteenth century' but 'a set of values, an ideology' that conceived it as a 'radical and in some sort revolutionary' literary mode.[48] Lessing's aesthetics were neither mechanistic nor doctrinaire; her commitment to realism's aim of portraying the relations between individual and society was informed by a socialist humanist understanding of social relations.

'The Small Personal Voice' reads as a strikingly optimistic piece, despite its awareness of the various challenges to the communication between writer and reader lurking in the near background. By the early 1960s, however, optimism was in rapid retreat. Lessing's disillusionment with Marxism grew apace, and her faith in realism's capacity to represent post-war social and technological change diminished. One of Lessing's primary concerns, particularly in the early fiction, had been to portray society dialectically. *Children of Violence* (a five-novel saga) was supposed to be 'a study of the individual conscience in its relations with the collective'.[49] *The Golden Notebook* dealt with 'the individual in relation to his society', and criticized human beings' tendency to atomize social life, a theme derived from Marxism, which 'looks at things as a whole and in relation to each other'.[50] But neither *The Golden Notebook* nor *The Four-Gated City* (the fifth and final volume of *Children*) could be contained by realist conventions. In both cases, the attempt to evoke contemporary society panoramically in a totalizing, unifying vision turned into a record of fragmentation, psychological breakdown, cultural collapse, and despair.

Lessing's faith in realism had begun to unravel in the 1960s. Before she embarked on *The Four-Gated City* she already knew that she would consider it 'a lie' because 'you can't get life into it . . . no matter how hard you try'. She repeatedly claimed that *The Golden Notebook*'s structure and themes were meant to comment on the impossibility of telling truth in the form of realism. The 'Free Women' envelope to the latter text functioned as a way of expressing her 'sense of despair about writing a conventional novel'.[51] By the time she wrote *Shikasta*, the first volume of her space fiction series *Canopus in Argos: Archives*, she had abandoned the attempt to confront contemporary social problems and had embraced Sufi mysticism. But, for Lessing, *Shikasta* represented a genuine breakthrough. She was convinced that the chaos of the post-war world could no longer be represented in conventional forms. Science fiction enabled her to act on her conviction that 'novelists every-where are breaking the bonds of the realistic novel because what we all see around us becomes daily wilder, more fantastic, incredible'.[52] Whereas novels like *The Golden Notebook*, *The Four-Gated City*, *Briefing for a Descent Into Hell* (1971), and *The Memoirs of a Survivor* (1974) disclosed a gradual shift away from realism, *Shikasta* signalled a fundamental break with the literary form that in her view legitimized the common-sense perceptions of reality she had largely rejected.

   The Golden Notebook is central to Lessing's œuvre. It documents Lessing's disenchantment with and subsequent rejection of Marxism. The loss of faith in politics had a direct effect on the novel's structure; the text not only reveals the dissolution of the Marxist metanarrative but also enacts the latter's collapse through its fractured form. An attempt to portray contemporary Britain panoramically, 'the way Tolstoy did it for Russia, Stendhal for France', it mutates into an account of social and individual breakdown.[53] In her first spoken words Anna Wulf observes that 'everything's cracking up', and the rest of the novel exhaustively describes the various manifestations of this implosion: the alienation of people from themselves and from one another; an all-pervasive sense of *anomie*; the ineffectuality of the individual in the face of world-scale problems such as poverty, exploitation, famine, and war; the atomization of social life; gender conflict; class struggle; and personal psychosis. Anna sees the events of the post-war period as 'a record of war, murder, chaos, misery'.[54] She herself functions as a microcosm of society, and her internal conflicts are homologous to the reality of the world in which she lives.

   The Golden Notebook's structure is complex. Two interrelated issues underpin it: firstly, the dramatization of Lessing's conviction that society has become so fragmented that the realist novel cannot contain it; secondly, the investigation of Marxism's dissolution as a secular 'world-mind' or 'world ethic'. The novel disrupts the coherence of realist narrative thematically and structurally. Anna writes in four diaries; each corresponds to a different aspect of her life: 'a black notebook, which is to do with Anna Wulf the writer; a red notebook, concerned with politics; a yellow notebook, in which I make stories out of my experience; and a blue notebook which tries to be a diary'. The notebooks attest Anna's inability to make her life cohere into a whole. Without them everything would be 'a scramble' or 'a mess' or 'chaos'.[55] They reveal the contradictory nature of Anna's practice. They protect her from a collapse into madness but suggest that this protection requires her to fictionalize her experience in a way that distorts it. Her private fictional reconstructions of her life (Mashopi, and *The Shadow of the Third*) fail to escape the evasions, nostalgia, and fatalism that she deplores in her published novel, *Frontiers of War*. 'Free Women', which surrounds the chaos of the four notebooks, initially appears to be the unadorned truth about her life but turns out to be a novel within a novel, written by Anna herself. It is another reworking of the material that comprises the notebooks. It quickly becomes apparent, moreover, that 'Free Women' is a parody; its ironic title, banal summaries at the head of each chapter, conventional structure, naturalistic dialogues, and flat tone reveal it to be a critique of realist fiction.

The Golden Notebook is a metafictional work constructed out of the unstable interaction between its constituent parts – notebooks and frame. It not only explores the multiplicity of interpretations to which Anna's experience gives rise but also forbids any simple resolution of them. Because the text is divided into five framing chapters, four notebooks, and the 'Golden Notebook', it disrupts perspective, linear chronology, and authorial omniscience. Every chapter of 'Free Women' is followed by the four notebooks, and each of these five segments deals with the same time-period from a different viewpoint. The complex reality thereby portrayed remains labile and inconclusive. When Anna eventually acknowledges her fractured psyche, she is enabled to overcome her creative impasse but only in order to produce *The Golden Notebook*, a recursive text that contains both the orderly (realist) parodic frame ('Free Women') and the disorderly notebooks. Her writing thus dramatizes, but fails to resolve, the conflicts that have haunted her.

Three of the novel's conflicts are of particular interest: the loss of faith in Marxism, which leads to a growing awareness of Freud's death instinct; the alienation of the individual from herself and from others; the problem of writing in the post-war period. Anna is in danger of slipping into madness for a variety of reasons, but her disillusionment with communism is a key factor. The collapse of this 'world ethic', which had given her life meaning and purpose, has cut the ground from beneath her feet. Socialism, she tells Tommy, has 'ceased to be a moral force'. Communism has become a nightmare: 'I wouldn't organise revolutions. . . . Because now we know what happens to revolutionary groups – we'd be murdering each other inside five years'. The difficulty Anna has in accepting this is compounded by her fellow communists' blind resistance to her questioning. Why is it that communists cannot 'admit that the great dream has faded and the truth is something else'?[56]

The Golden Notebook portrays Marx and Freud as counterparts. One proposed a way of healing social divisions; the other offered a way of healing individual distress. Anna's rejection of communism leads her into psychoanalysis with the slyly named Mrs Marks (Mother Sugar). But Mrs Marks's Jungian approach to psychoanalysis fails. Anna rejects her reactionary views and ahistorical interpretations of her experiences. She considers Mother Sugar's universalization of her (Anna's) experience to be another form of denial, which parallels those of former communists as much as her own fictional ones: 'I don't want to be told when I wake up, terrified by a dream of total annihilation, because of the H-bomb exploding, that people felt that way about the cross-bow. It isn't true. There is something new in the world. . . . I want to be able to separate in myself what is old and cyclic, the recurring history, the myth, from what is new'. Mother Sugar's version of psychoanalysis conceals the historicity of human life and thus denies the fragmented and potentially cataclysmic nature of contemporary social reality. Psychoanalysis anaesthetizes reality, just like the fiction in her own notebooks and the self-parodying humour of confused communists: 'all the pain, and the killing and the violence is safely held in the story and it can't hurt me'.[57]

The violence that Anna fears leads her from Marx to Freud. She is the representative of 'a hundred different people living now, in various parts of the world, talking and crying out and questioning' and her inner torment reflects a general crisis of belief. Her particular crisis turns on her loss of faith in the communist utopia. Michael pinpoints the issue: 'Do you realise, Anna, that when you and Molly talk of leaving the Party, the suggestion always is that leaving it will lead you straight into some morass of moral turpitude'.[58] This is only partly right. It is Anna's personal ideals that are forcing her to leave the Party, which she sees as corrupt, theoretically flawed, and complicit with gross crimes against basic human rights. What she fears is that the Party's inability to account for the horrors of twentieth-century life means that she will have to confront them herself.

Anna's apprehension of what she will later identify as Marxism's fatal blind spot is prefigured by Paul in the Mashopi pigeon-shooting episode. Paul's epiphany reveals to him a malevolence in nature, which exposes the gulf between communist idealism and the horrors of human life:

> 'Comrade Willi, would you not say that there is some principle at work not yet admitted to your philosophy? Some principle of destruction?'
> Willi said, in exactly the tone we had all expected: 'There is no need to look any further than the philosophy of the class struggle,' and as if he'd pressed a button, Jimmy, Paul and I burst out into one of the fits of irrepressible laughter that Willi never joined.[59]

Willi, whose response will later be duplicated by Anna's English communist friends, cannot really consider Paul's question but, like a pre-programmed machine, rejects it out of hand. Despite its apparent sophistication, Willi's Marxism is doctrinaire, and his humourlessness, like Anton Hesse's in *Children of Violence*, marks his scientific Marxism as deficient. Anna shares Paul's presentiment that socialism ignores this principle of destruction at its peril; thus her disillusionment with Willi and the disintegration of their relationship prefigure her later defection from the Party.

The spectre that haunts Paul is remarkably close to Freud's vision of the death instinct in *Civilisation and its Discontents*. In that pessimistic late work Freud disputes Marx's analysis of society's pathologies on the grounds that it depends on an untenable account of human nature. Whereas Marx claims that alienated labour 'estranges from man his own body, as well as external nature and his spiritual essence, his *human* being', Freud posits innate aggressiveness, arguing that it is 'an original, self-subsisting instinctual disposition in man'. For Freud, the Marxist view of human nature is 'an untenable illusion'. Neither private property nor capitalist economic relations have corrupted human nature, for aggressiveness 'reigned almost without limit in primitive times'; whatever path civilization takes, 'this indestructible feature of human nature will follow it there'.[60]

The struggle between civilization and the death instinct that threatens to destroy it is enacted in Anna's mind when her faith in the Marxist dream dissolves. Having left the Party, she opens herself up to the death instinct, which she names 'the principle of joy-in-destruction', in order to confront its pervasive presence at the centre of the chaos from which she is in flight. She tells Molly that the 'truth is something else' than the 'great dream' of communism, and she tells Mother Sugar what it is: 'It seems to me that ever since I can remember anything the real thing that has been happening in the world was death and destruction. It seems to me it is stronger than life.' And in the last 'Blue Notebook' she identifies the destructive principle with its ultimate manifestation – war: 'last night I had known, finally, that the truth for our time was war, the immanence of war'.[61]

Alienation is the second dominant conflict in *The Golden Notebook*. The text urges resistance to self-division, and Anna rejects communism in part because it has neglected the humanist aspects of Marx's early thought:

> Alienation. Being split. It's the moral side, so to speak, of the communist message. And suddenly you shrug your shoulders and say because the mechanical basis of our lives is getting complicated, we must be content to not even try to understand things as a whole? . . . But humanism stands for the whole person, the whole individual, striving to become as conscious and responsible about everything in the universe. But now you sit there, quite calmly, and as a humanist you say that due to the complexity of scientific achievement the human being must never expect to be whole, he must always be fragmented.

Alienation, in Marx's *Economic and Philosophic Manuscripts*, takes three forms: from labour, from self, from others. Anna identifies all three. People 'work and despise their work'; they 'refuse[ ] emotion because at the end of every emotion are property, money, power'; they 'love but know that it's a half-love or a twisted love'.[62] Central to the novel are alienation from others, which is disclosed through its numerous failed relationships, and alienation from the self, which is revealed through denial, role-playing, and self-parody.

Marion and Tommy illustrate how people preserve a measure of sanity by refusing to face reality. They both avoid breakdowns by denying their emotions and hiding from conflicts. Tommy 'heals' himself through an act of self-mutilation. Molly realizes to her horror that Tommy's physical blindness permits him to evade reality and thus enables him to be 'all in one piece for the first time in his life'. This wholeness is of course illusory; Anna sees Tommy as 'a sort of zombie' and reflects that a vital part of his personality has been permanently shattered. Marion, in turn, can free herself from the pain of being Richard's neglected partner only by turning to drink. Other characters display their lack of identity by adopting stylized roles that they can discard at will. People 'decide to be this or that' but 'it's as if it's a sort of dance – they might just as well do the opposite with equal conviction'.[63] Such characters engage in exaggerated acts of self-parody, accentuating their alienation through role-playing. In each case, the self-division between the private, tormented self and the public, apparently untroubled persona is made apparent.

Self-alienation is most acute for the novel's women. Lessing depicts this self-alienation as the product of sexual oppression. *The Golden Notebook*, which is set in the mid-1950s, portrays the social conflicts and internal questioning of a group of women living just before the second wave of feminism took off. The book has been attacked for its regressive representations of women as passive victims, its ahistorical account of gender relations, and its emphasis on the centrality of the male/female couple. Elizabeth Wilson, for example, writes that in the 1960s she admired both Lessing and de Beauvoir but 'noticed neither their political isolation (as women), nor their contempt for lesbianism, nor their romanticism when it came to sexuality'. She concludes that much of what Lessing says in *The Golden Notebook* was in fact 'the antithesis of women's liberation', for it sanctioned the attitudes that 1960s feminists 'were in revolt *against*'.[64] These criticisms indicate that *The Golden Notebook* can be read neither as a feminist tract that offers panaceas for gender conflict nor as an uncontested account of women's experiences at that historical juncture.

The novel's central women characters are portrayed as figures who have internalized male perceptions of women as well as the gender hierarchy that these perceptions sustain. They trust neither their emotions nor their analyses of their relationships with men. Their oppression is revealed by their inability to break free from the men who circumscribe their scope for living. Ella, for example, is passive in her relationship with Paul; she is willing to be defined by him and prepared to be dependent on him. As their affair develops, she slowly subsides into a dream-world; her personality is sapped, her intellect undermined, and her autonomy destroyed. It eventually occurs to her that Paul's 'arms had slowly, over the years, shut out everyone else'. But Ella is complicit with this disempowerment. She considers that 'real men' (several times invoked in the novel, and usually accompanied by homophobic denigrations of homosexuals) should somehow encompass women.[65] Thus her passivity is inseparable from her readiness to adopt a subordinate position and her concomitant refusal to think for herself. At the start of their relationship she 'drifted along on a soft tide of not-thinking'. Her relationship with Paul gives her life meaning and her identity shape. Feeling herself 'a real woman at last', she 'let herself go into Paul's love for her, and did not think'.[66]

Ella is Anna's alter-ego: 'I, Anna, see Ella. Who is of course, Anna. But that is the point, for she is not'. Ella is less Anna's double than a fictional other onto whom she displaces her conflicts in an attempt to resolve them. Ella's complicity with her own oppression is thus in part Anna's as well. Like Ella, Anna frequently splits herself into two people. Unable to resolve her political dilemmas, she divides herself into 'the dry, wise, ironical political woman' and 'the Party fanatic who sounds, literally, quite maniacal'. And in her relationship with Michael (which doubles Ella's with Paul) she suffers two further forms of self-division, separating her role as Janet's mother from that of Michael's partner, and keeping her love for the latter distinct from her critical intellect. This self-division is crippling. The two things that keep Anna sane whenever mental collapse threatens are her relationship with her daughter and her rational mind, yet her lover undermines both. Michael not only makes it difficult for Anna to be both mother and partner but also dislikes 'the critical and thinking Anna'. Anna's eventual recognition of her complicity with this negation of entire aspects of her selfhood leads her to an incipient feminist consciousness:

> Paul gave birth to Ella, the naive Ella. He destroyed in her the knowing, doubting, sophisticated Ella and again and again he put her intelligence to sleep, and with her willing connivance, so that she floated darkly on her love for him, on her naivety. . . . Now, when I am drawn to a man, I can assess the depth of a possible relationship with him by the degree to which the naive Anna is created in me.[67]

Anna's grasp of the power struggle in heterosexual relationships, which is caused in part by the hierarchical nature of gender relations, results in the beginnings of a feminist awareness. She is still locked firmly into a world where male/female relations take precedence over all others. Her despair at communism, in turn, leads to a rejection of politics *per se*, never taking her from Marxist analysis of class to feminist analysis of gender. As Adrienne Rich has argued, *The Golden Notebook*'s women 'have no real centre to their lives apart from trying to relate to men and to male politics'. For Rich, the novel's greatest weakness lies in its 'failure to envisage any kind of political bonding of women', and this aspect of it reveals that it had only partially broken free of a male-centred analysis of women's experience in the 1950s.[68]

The third conflict that torments Anna concerns the problem of writing in the post-war world. Anna's writing block is related to her sense of self-alienation but cannot be explained by it alone. To do so is to prejudge the issue by seeing it as an individual rather than a social matter. Yet Anna's refusal to write stems from her reservations about the authenticity of writing when the world is confronted by pressing social problems. She fears that society has become so chaotic that it is unrepresentable and that the writer escapes from reality to the consolations of art. Her socialism, however tenuous it has become, has left her with a politicized view of aesthetics. But her continuing belief in committed art is at odds with her loss of faith in politics; she upholds an artistic practice that is predicated on the assumption that society can be altered, but since her confidence in this assumption has been shattered her writing is effectively devoid of content.

Anna cannot write because 'the world is so chaotic, art is irrelevant'. Mother Sugar predictably interprets this in terms of personal neuroses, but Anna insists that their aetiology is social. Her analyst refuses to understand that she 'can't pick up a newspaper without what's in it seeming so overwhelmingly terrible that nothing [she] could write would seem to have any point at all'. She is paralysed, like Berger's Janos Lavin, by the thought that the intellectual's failure to participate directly in practical politics means that she has abandoned politics altogether. She explains to Saul that she is unable to write because as soon as she starts she imagines the objections of various freedom fighters from all over the world who ask 'why aren't you doing something about us, instead of wasting your time scribbling?'.[69] To sit scribbling seems an admission of defeat, an acknowledgement of the writer's impotence and art's irrelevance.

It is not just literature that is inadequate; language itself seems to be failing. *The Golden Notebook* is obsessed with what Anna sees as 'the thinning of language against the density of our experience'. Language and reality float apart, leaving the former helpless to evoke a world seen to be on the point of disintegration. The result is an existential anguish not dissimilar to the nausea experienced by Sartre's Roquentin. Anna reads her diary entries and finds herself 'increasingly afflicted by vertigo'. Words turn into 'a series of meaningless sounds, like nursery talk'; they can no longer evoke reality, for as she writes they 'detach themselves from the page and slide away, as if they had detached themselves from their own meaning'. Afflicted by this linguistic vertigo, Anna considers abandoning language altogether: 'real experience can't be described. I think, bitterly, that a row of asterisks, like an old-fashioned novel, might be better. Or a symbol of some kind, a circle perhaps, or a square. Anything at all, but not words'.[70]

Anna's concern with literary form is the corollary of her anxiety about language. She operates with such a strict distinction between 'truth' and 'fiction' that she can always convict the latter of falsifying reality. Thus she is caught between her desire to capture the truth, to portray contemporary life with the utmost fidelity, and her awareness that literature can never be an exact reproduction of the real. Anna's inability to accept this paradox paralyses her. On one side, she sees well-constructed, journalistic novels that are forms of sociological reportage; they are worthy but dull, flat in tone, and limited in scope. On the other side, she sees nihilist works, such as her own *Frontiers of War*. She longs for 'a book powered with an intellectual or moral passion strong enough to create order, to create a new way of looking at life', yet admits that she is herself 'too diffused' to write one. Her refusal of both nihilist and committed writing embroils her in a contradiction: 'And so this is the paradox: I, Anna, reject my own "unhealthy" art; but reject "healthy" art when I see it'.[71] Her refusal to submit to the despair of nihilism attests her utopianism, but her mistrust of a public art not driven by a private vision leaves her in a literary limbo. Anna cannot write because she cannot see how to encompass the chaos of the post-war world, because she considers art to be irrelevant to the problems she discerns, and because she cannot find an adequate narrative mode for her most pressing concerns. *The Golden Notebook* is in large part an account of its central protagonist's realization that truth and fiction are not polar opposites and that although art cannot reflect reality it can evoke it. Anna breaks out of the impasse in which she has been mired when she understands that she cannot capture the truth but can only disclose it. *The Golden Notebook* is the medium through which this message is communicated. It not only makes the chaos of Anna's private life a metonym for the disorder of the world, but also turns the fragmentation of life into the order of art by employing an artificial structure, which hints at the arbitrariness of structure in the absence of teleology, and a framing envelope, which parodies its own 'control' over the material it encases.

The trajectory of the novel's two narratives thus suggests that Anna moves towards a gradual resolution of her difficulties. Both the Anna of the notebooks and the Anna of 'Free Women' heal themselves by confronting their psychic and social conflicts. Anna overcomes her sense of self-division when she throws off her doubles and reintegrates her diverse selves into one personality. Having overcome self-division, the two Annas are able to effect a *rapprochement* with society. In the notebooks Anna defeats the will-to-destruction inside herself and gives her private outpourings a public forum. In 'Free Women' she undergoes a similar breakdown but decides to give up writing and to take up non-revolutionary politics and welfare work.

What remains is *The Golden Notebook* itself. The novel's metafictional structure ensures that the reader is given a triple-focus on the events it portrays. It offers two parallel versions of Anna's experience (the notebooks and the frame, 'Free Women') but creates a metacommentary on both versions by exposing the process through which they came into being. It is this metacommentary, which exists in the interstices of the two narratives, that comes to dominate *The Golden Notebook*. Lessing, the puppeteer pulling Anna's strings, provides two accounts of reality that evoke both parody and nihilism, the two impulses she and Anna most fear, but overcomes them by playing them off against one another. The novel's evocation of chaos is not smoothed over and rendered manageable, as in the ironic frame, but placed centre-stage. At the same time, it is held in check by the text's highly patterned structure, which thereby manages to portray the crises of belief characteristic of post-war life without succumbing to them. *The Golden Notebook*'s structure is crucial to its success. A major part of the novel's impact depends on the reader's perception of the discrepancy between Anna's apparent silence, her persistent claims that she cannot write, and the mass of words she is daily churning out. Lessing creates a character who articulates the aesthetic and political questions that plague the author herself but that would prevent her from writing if she allowed them to paralyse her. Anna's private, hidden, and disordered outpourings thus become Lessing's public, open, and ordered art-work. Anna is blocked, but writes voraciously; she is publicly silent but privately clamorous. Through the text's ingenious construction, this contradiction becomes the paradox of Lessing's 'wordless statement' – a book that is an account of why it could not be written, says what it cannot say, and evokes political despair without giving in to it.

The Golden Notebook attests Lessing's conviction that contemporary reality could no longer be contained by realist forms. But her departure from realism involves less a break in language and style than in form and content. She continues to employ a discursive narrative mode, revealing a marked preference for telling rather than showing. Her innovations are either structural, as in *The Golden Notebook*, or generic, as in the *Canopus in Argos* series, where she developed a form of science fiction that she called space fiction. Lessing's mistrust of realism, in other words, did not take her in the direction of modernism, as it did Berger when he wrote *G*. In fact, Lessing seems positively to distrust the mandarin style and preciosity of much modernist writing. She believes in simplicity and directness, which she associates with accuracy and truth, but is suspicious of highly wrought language. She remarks of her own work: 'I don't *polish* it – that would be the entirely wrong word, because in a way I roughen it; I try to get it simple, clear, which for me is the same as getting it right'.[72] Lessing's break with realism thus bypasses modernism altogether. Her challenge to the conventional novel lies in her subject-matter rather than in her style. She does not experiment at the level of the word or the sentence but transforms content and structure. The surface of her writing remains fairly constant, although in some novels (*The Summer Before the Dark*, *Memoirs of a Survivor*) she achieves a greater lyricism.

The Golden Notebook remains a landmark transitional text in Lessing's œuvre. The novels written prior to it are conventionally realist, exhibiting omniscient narration, linear chronology, unaffected language, naturalistic characters, and detailed social observation. *Landlocked*, the fourth volume of *Children of Violence*, marks a first step beyond realism. It abandons omniscience, uses a character as a central consciousness, and includes a fragmented diary towards the end. By the time of *The Four-Gated City* realism has collapsed into apocalypse, myth, and a form of science fiction. But it would be a mistake to infer from this that Lessing rejected realism altogether. Realism, rather, could no longer encompass all her concerns and needed to be stretched into new shapes. Lessing thus developed a kind of experimental realism through which she discovered new fictional terrains. At the same time she continued to write conventional novels in the old style. The innovative novels such as *A Briefing for a Descent Into Hell, Memoirs of a Survivor,* and *Canopus in Argos* need to be set alongside *The Summer Before the Dark, The Diaries of Jane Somers,* and *The Good Terrorist.*

These caveats apart, the period between 1962 and 1974 was certainly marked by Lessing's frustration with realism's limitations. This, in turn, was inseparable from her disillusionment with Marxism and her fear of nuclear apocalypse. *The Four-Gated City* ends with the destruction of the earth; *Memoirs* describes the breakdown of civilization and concludes with a passage into another realm of existence; *Briefing* warns of the world's imminent doom; by the time of *Shikasta* Lessing has turned her back on the earth, portraying it as a space colony. Fabulation, she clearly thought, was better equipped than realism to evoke her apocalyptic fears. In *The Four-Gated City*, for example, socialist politics and communal life are given even shorter shrift than in *The Golden Notebook.* The pointlessness of politics is disclosed through the futile figure of Phoebe Coldridge, whose lifetime of work on behalf of the Labour Party proves fruitless, and the impotence of community is signalled by the dissolution of the Coldridge household. Whereas social and political action are presented as sterile, individual development is offered as a solution to humankind's problems. Lessing, having despaired of political solutions to such problems as nuclear stockpiles and pollution, posits a strange evolutionary schema that goes far beyond Darwin. In a curious mix of R.D. Laing and Idries Shah (her Sufi mentor), individuals break down into one another, dissolving the naturalistic bonds of character, and either progress to a healthier psychic state or develop extra-sensory capabilities. Lynda literally 'sees' that the earth is being poisoned, thus enabling some of the Coldridges to flee the ensuing ruin. By novel's end, civilization has been destroyed, and hope lies with Joseph Batts, a mutant who possesses similar visionary abilities. Rationalism and socialist critique have been left far behind.

Lessing's distrust of rationalism is forcefully expressed in *Memoirs*, whose anonymous narrator observes:

> As for our thoughts, our intellectual apparatus, our rationalisms and our logics and our deductions and so on, it can be said with absolute certainty that dogs and cats and monkeys cannot make a rocket to fly to the moon or weave artificial dress materials out of the by-products of petroleum, but as we sit in the ruins of this variety of intelligence, it is hard to give it much value: I suppose we are undervaluing it now as we over-valued it then. It will have to find its place: I believe a pretty low place, at that.

In *Memoirs*, as civilization crumbles and the attempt to combat its collapse meets with failure, the real world retreats and the parallel world that the narrator has accidentally discovered begins to take over. This mystical realm enables her to see into the past and offers an escape from the gradual disintegration of the world she observes from the safety of her window. When society finally degenerates into anarchy the narrator and her group of refugees pass 'out of this collapsed little world into another order of world altogether'.[73]

Martin Green suggests that *Memoirs* shows 'Lessing saying goodbye to the novel form' and moving 'into a legendary and emblematic land, away from people, cities, and actuality'.[74] But the path Lessing has followed does not evince quite such a smooth progression as this. She did indeed lose faith in realism, largely because of her disillusionment with the Marxism and rationalism that for her fundamentally informed it. Because she perceived such a close link between realism and socialism, the crisis of representation that her novels enact should be explained by reference to her disenchantment with revolutionary politics. Lessing's abandonment of realism was temporary, however; it did not conclude her career as a realist novelist but represents a hiatus in it. Even though she moved away from realism in order to explore other forms, her subsequent re-examination of it leads her not to reject realism entirely but to return to it when it seems useful and to extend it in various ways. Ruth Whittacker is surely right when she notes that critics are tempted 'to give a spurious cohesion to [Lessing's] fiction, to suggest that she moves steadily from realism to fabulation, as if one excluded the other'.[75] But these two modes are not mutually exclusive. Lessing's experimental realism proves the point.

Berger's and Lessing's work provides two quite different post-war responses to a realism conceived in relation to the Marxist tradition. Whereas Berger develops a modernist-inspired dialectical fiction that draws on Brecht's non-conventional view of realism, Lessing disrupts realist narrative modes from within and turns to other genres in her search for ways to mediate contemporary social life. Berger does not abandon Marxism; he broadens his conception of it so that it can accommodate both his political commitments and his belief in 'the "mystery" of art'.[76] Lessing rejects Marxism; she releases herself into a wider scope, exploring realism's limitations by focusing on those areas of human experience that it cannot easily evoke. For Lessing the certainties of a narrowly conceived rationalism need to be questioned. This conviction leads her to alternate among or to fuse forms as diverse as realism, fantasy, science fiction, apocalypse, and myth. Refusing to be restricted to any single novelistic mode, Lessing elaborates an experimental realism that moves freely among a rich diversity of imaginative realms. Berger's work, in contrast, suggests that for him the Marxist approach to writing is still broadly right – literature should portray social conditions in order to disclose their contradictions and thus to suggest that other ways of life are potentially embedded in them.

Notes

1. Leon Trotsky, *Trotsky on Literature and Art*, ed. Paul N. Siegel (New York: Pathfinder, 1970), p. 37.
2. See Geoffrey Hosking, *Beyond Socialist Realism: Soviet Fiction since Ivan Denisovich* (London: Granada, 1980), p. 3.
3. See Nicholas Luker (ed.), *An Anthology of the Classics of Socialist Realism* (Ann Arbor: Ardis, 1988), p. 19.
4. Hosking, *Beyond*, p. 6.
5. See Georg Lukács, 'Art and Objective Truth' and 'Narrate or Describe?', *Writer and Critic*, ed. and trans. Arthur Kahn (London: Merlin, 1970), pp. 25–60 and pp. 110–48; Georg Lukács, 'Realism in the Balance', *Aesthetics and Politics: Debates between Bloch, Lukács, Brecht, Benjamin, Adorno*, ed. and trans. Ronald Taylor (London: Verso, 1980), pp. 28–60.
6. Bertolt Brecht, 'Brecht against Lukács', *Aesthetics*, pp. 68–85, at p. 82.
7. John Berger, *Permanent Red* (London: Writers and Readers Publishing Cooperative, 1979), p. 208.
8. Doris Lessing, 'The Small Personal Voice', *A Small Personal Voice: Essays, Reviews, Interviews*, ed. Paul Shlueter (New York: Alfred A. Knopf, 1974), pp. 4, 3.
9. Doris Lessing, *Re: Colonized Planet 5, Shikasta* (London: Cape, 1979), p. ix.
10. Doris Lessing, 'Profile', *New Review*, 1. 8 (November 1974), pp. 17–23, at p. 20.
11. Raymond Williams, 'The Writer: Commitment and Alignment', *Resources of Hope: Culture, Democracy, Socialism*, ed. Robin Gable (London: Verso, 1989), pp. 77–87.
12. R. H. S. Crossman (ed.), *The God that Failed: Six Studies in Communism* (London: Bantam, 1965). For good accounts of communism and socialism in Britain in the post-war period, see John Callaghan, *Socialism in Britain since 1884* (Oxford: Basil Blackwell, 1990); F. S. Northedge and Audrey Wells, *Britain and Soviet Communism: The Impact of a Revolution* (London: Macmillan, 1982).
13. Berger, *Permanent*, pp. 213, 17, 15.
14. Richard Wollheim, 'The Sectarian Imagination: On John Berger's Criticism', *Encounter*, 16. 6 (June 1961), pp. 47–53.
15. John Berger, 'Problems of Socialist Art', *Labour Monthly* (March 1961), pp. 135–43, and *Labour Monthly* (April 1961), pp. 179–86, at p. 186.
16. John Berger, *A Painter of Our Time* (New York: Simon and Schuster, 1959), p. 16.
17. Ibid., pp. 102, 93.
18. Ibid., p. 177.
19. Ibid., p. 180. Berger makes the same point in *Permanent Red*, p. 17.
20. John Berger, *Corker's Freedom* (London: Writers and Readers Publishing Cooperative, 1979), p. 10.
21. Ibid., pp. 191, 206.
22. John Berger, *Ways of Seeing* (London: BBC and Penguin, 1983), p. 11.
23. John Berger, 'The Moment of Cubism', *The Moment of Cubism and Other Essays* (London: Weidenfeld and Nicolson, 1969).
24. John Berger, 'Sekher Ahmet and the Forest', *About Looking* (New York: Pantheon, 1980), p. 83.
25. John Berger, 'The Secretary of Death', *The White Bird: Writings*, ed. Lloyd Spencer (London: Chatto and Windus, 1985), p. 241.
26. John Berger, *G.* (London: Chatto and Windus, 1985), p. 54.
27. Ibid., p. 24.
28. Taylor (ed.), *Aesthetics and Politics*, p. 61.
29. See David E. James, 'Cubism as Revolutionary Realism: John Berger and *G.*', *Minnesota Review*, 21 (Fall 1983), pp. 92–109.
30. Berger, *G.*, p. 133.

31. Berger, *A Painter*, p. 169.
32. Berger, 'Problems', p. 185.
33. Berger, *G.*, p. 137.
34. Ibid., p. 77.
35. Ibid., p. 72.
36. Ibid., pp. 137, 203.
37. Denis Mack Smith, *Italy: A Modern History* (Ann Arbor: Michigan University Press, 1959), p. 192.
38. Berger, *G.*, pp. 67, 75–6.
39. Ibid., pp. 7, 68, 77.
40. Ibid., p. 10.
41. F. T. Marinetti, 'The Founding and Manifesto of Futurism 1909', *Futurist Manifestoes,*. ed. Umbro Apollonio (London: Thames and Hudson, 1973), p. 22.
42. For a similar reading of the novel's conclusion, see Pamela McCallum, 'Postmodernist Aesthetics and the Historical Novel: John Berger's *G.*', *Minnesota Review*, 28 (Spring 1987), pp. 68–77.
43. Berger, *G.*, p. 305.
44. John Berger, *Pig Earth* (London, Pantheon, 1980), pp. 212–13.
45. John Berger, 'Ways of Witnessing', *Marxism Today* (December 1984), pp. 36–8, at p. 37.
46. John Berger and Nella Bielski, *A Question of Geography* (London: Faber and Faber, 1987), p. 48.
47. Lessing, *A Small*, pp. 5, 12.
48. Lorna Sage, *Doris Lessing* (London, Methuen, 1983), p. 45.
49. Lessing, *A Small*, p. 14.
50. Ibid., p. 79; Doris Lessing, 'Preface', *The Golden Notebook* (London: Granada, 1981), p. 14.
51. Lessing, *A Small*, pp. 82, 81.
52. Lessing, *Shikasta*, p. ix.
53. Lessing, *Golden*, p. 11.
54. Ibid., pp. 25, 251.
55. Ibid., pp. 15, 461–2, 265, 272.
56. Ibid., pp. 59, 262, 71.
57. Ibid., pp. 459, 457.
58. Ibid., pp. 600, 296.
59. Ibid., p. 418.
60. Sigmund Freud, *Civilisation and its Discontents*, trans. James Strachey (New York: W. W. Norton, 1961), pp. 60, 61; Karl Marx, *The Economic and Philosophic Manuscripts of 1844*, ed. Dirk J. Struik, trans. Martin Milligan (New York: International, 1964), p. 114.
61. Lessing, *Golden*, pp. 71, 237, 570–571, 573.
62. Ibid., pp. 353–4, 136.
63. Ibid., pp. 137, 235.
64. Elizabeth Wilson, 'Yesterday's Heroines: On Rereading Lessing and de Beauvoir', *Notebooks/Memoirs/Archives: Reading and Rereading Doris Lessing*, ed. Jenny Taylor (London: Routledge and Kegan Paul, 1982), pp. 57–75, at pp. 71, 72.
65. See, for example, Lessing, *Golden*, p. 443.
66. Ibid., pp. 223, 205, 211.
67. Ibid., pp. 447, 170, 327, 216.
68. Adrienne Rich, 'An interview with Adrienne Rich', *Critical Essays on Doris Lessing*, eds Claire Sprague and Virginia Tiger (Boston Mass: G. K. Hall, 1986), pp. 181–3, at pp. 181, 182.
69. Lessing, *Golden*, pp. 60, 252, 614.
70. Ibid., pp. 301, 462, 623, 609.

71. Ibid., pp. 80, 344.
72. Lessing, 'Profile', p. 20.
73. Doris Lessing, *The Memoirs of a Survivor* (Toronto: PaperJacks, 1976), pp. 71, 182.
74. Martin Green, 'The Doom of Empire: *Memoirs of a Survivor*', Sprague and Tiger, *Critical Essays*, pp. 31–7, at p. 34.
75. Ruth Whittacker, *Doris Lessing* (London: Macmillan, 1988), p. 16.
76. Berger, 'Ways of Witnessing', p. 37.

5

Dilemmas of the Contemporary Liberal

Liberalism is inseparable from individualism. Both were perceived to be under threat in the 1930s. Scarred by the horrors of the Great War and paralysed by their dread of fascism, many writers were pessimistic about the individual's capacity to survive, hence the numerous doomed figures who haunt the literature of the period: Eliot's Prufrock, Pound's Mauberley, Ford's Tietjens, Waugh's Tony Last, Woolf's Septimus Smith. E.M. Forster was to articulate this anxiety most clearly. He believed above all in 'personal relationships and the private life' but felt that the social order which had sustained his kind of existence was 'crumbling beneath him', leaving him the 'inheritor of a mode of life which is wanted no more'. Forster favoured social amelioration, but he could not reconcile himself to its consequences either for his personal life or for the world he inhabited. His solution was to turn his inability to come to terms with this 'collision of loyalties' into his subject matter. His essays and novels explored the dilemmas faced by individuals who are acutely aware that their privileged existence is in some sense unmerited and yet still believe that it puts them in touch with the things that make life most worth living: culture, the arts, personal relationships. Although Forster was deeply sensitive to social obligations, he staked his all on the individual: 'I have no mystic faith in the people. I have in the individual. He seems to me a divine achievement and I mistrust any view which belittles him'.[1]

Forster's soul-searching provides important clues to the work of John Fowles and Angus Wilson. Both writers see themselves as social democrats, although they are critical of the political traditions they support. Wilson, for example, observes of the families with which he lived in the 1940s that 'they became the centre of my attack upon the deficiencies of a liberal socialism to which I still give my own moral and cultural allegiance'.[2] He scrutinizes the weaknesses of his own humanist beliefs in novels such as *Hemlock and After* (1952) and *Anglo-Saxon Attitudes* (1956), taking Forster's liberalism as his point of departure. He focuses in particular on what he sees as liberalism's unwarranted confidence in the value of culture and the intrinsic worth of the individual, suggesting that Forsterian humanism frequently conceals gross self-deception and blindness to evil. Fowles's work, in turn, displays continuities with Forster's key preoccupations, and also, going still further back, with those of Matthew Arnold. His concern in novels such as *The French Lieutenant's Woman* (1969) and *Daniel Martin* (1978), not only with the social fate of the gifted individual but also with an aristocracy of the spirit, recalls both precursors. Thus although Fowles has described himself as a socialist, I shall suggest that his writing reveals him to be much closer to liberal thought and anxieties. What really interest him are the dilemmas faced by 'the intelligent trapped in the world of the stupid'. Fowles's persistent focus on the existential predicament of the gifted individual (Charles Smithson, Daniel Martin) has little to do with socialism but a good deal to do with an Arnoldian fear of mass society.

Fowles and Wilson have both stressed their allegiance to realism but have at the same time extended it in a variety of ways. Whereas Berger broke free from realist constraints by developing a form of literary Cubism in *G.*, and Lessing shattered the bonds of nineteenth-century realism through the fragmented structure of *The Golden Notebook*, Fowles and Wilson have sought to revivify traditional forms. Fowles grants experimental writers only grudging respect, regarding much of their writing as a form of contemporary 'rococo' and inveighing against its privileging of form over content.[3] The subsequent fetishization of experimentation results in a self-defeating formalism: 'We have used words in all the extreme ways. . . . We have reached the end of our field. Now we must come back'.[4] He is himself primarily 'interested in experiencing the world as it is' and in the forms of fiction that explore it most tellingly.[5] Thus although a novel like *The French Lieutenant's Woman* is metafictional and, in part, parodies Victorian literary conventions, it also signals its respect for nineteenth-century realism through its dense social texture, its detailed historical research, and its careful character studies.

Wilson's attitude to realism changed over time. In the early 1950s he was to champion it against modernism, particularly in its Bloomsbury variant. For Wilson, Virginia Woolf symbolized modernism's greatest weakness: its neglect of the social dimension. None of modernism's considerable aesthetic achievements could 'fully atone for the frivolity of ignoring man as a social being, for treating personal relationships and subjective sensations in a social void'.[6] But Wilson was quickly to change his mind. By 1961 he was claiming that a resurgent realism, trailing Leavisian moral values such as responsibility, health and maturity behind it, was exerting a tyranny stronger 'than the coterie dogmatisms of Bloomsbury'. His disaffection with realism stemmed from its advocates' tendency to portray the social realm as all-encompassing and to favour a documentary-like verisimilitude. The key to understanding Wilson's 'experimental turn' in novels such as *The Old Men at the Zoo* (1961) and *No Laughing Matter* (1967) lies in seeing that, although the social dimension of human life remained central to his work, he refused to believe that everything could be reduced to it or explained by it. Thus in 'The Dilemma of the Contemporary Novelist', he urged writers to reject 'the idea that fact is somehow a virtue' and argued that the novel is 'the most hopeful form of communication in the present age' because it discloses that the 'so-called real world . . . the world of fact, is not all that there is'.[7] His sensitivity to the theatrical and expressionist aspects of life is what led him away from a narrow realism to the multi-perspectival, linguistically exuberant, and parodic mode of *No Laughing Matter*.

Angus Wilson

Wilson's early novels, *Hemlock and After* and *Anglo-Saxon Attitudes*, explore his uneasiness with the liberalism he himself upholds. Both novels focus on central characters who are gradually made aware that their lives are based on self-deception. *Hemlock*'s Bernard Sands is a successful novelist who has carved a niche for himself in the cloistered world of English letters but prides himself on his refusal to compromise his 'anarchic humanism'.[8] Gerald Middleton, in contrast, perceives himself as a failure in both his professional and his private life; he has lacked the courage to break out of a loveless marriage, and his subsequent self-disgust has led him to squander his talents as a historian. Although Sands is at the outset self-satisfied, whereas Middleton is melancholy, both come to realize that they have reached middle-age without confronting the moral evasions that have characterized their adult lives. Sands, a self-confessed liberal sceptic, grasps that his humanist contempt for 'neo-authoritarianism' and 'dogmatic spiritual values' only conceals his own moral duplicity.[9] Middleton, in turn, recognizes that his inability to act at decisive moments has had lasting repercussions for the lives of his children and for his scholarly community.

Sands's initial certainty about the essential rightness of his values and actions symbolizes an over-confident pre-war brand of humanism that *Hemlock* takes to task. Forster had already in the 1930s worried about humanism's capacity to confront fascism, but his uneasiness on that score did not prevent him from continuing to affirm his belief in the individual as a repository of civilized values. This occasionally resulted in an ostrich-like refusal to think through the weaknesses of his position. In 'What I Believe', for example, Forster acknowledged 'that all society rests upon force' but argued that civilization is built in 'the intervals when force has not managed to come to the front'. But what was to be done when 'force' reared its malevolent head? Here is Forster's answer: 'I look the other way until fate strikes me. Whether this is due to courage or to cowardice in my own case I cannot be sure. But I know that if men had not looked the other way in the past, nothing of any value would survive'.[10] Bernard Sands has looked the other way all his life, so sure is he of his values, but as *Hemlock* unfolds he accepts the ambiguous nature of his own motives, the selfishness with which he has treated his family, and the presence of evil in a world he had hitherto believed to be benign. Moreover, his self-questioning is not just a private affair, having to do with his personal shortcomings as an individual, but is related to a wider post-war examination of humanism's failure to either explain or withstand the horrors of the Second World War. The Vardon Hall débâcle, which is a personal disaster for Bernard, is linked to 'one of those periodic worsenings of the world situation, which . . . crack the uneasy paste of hope and optimism of which so much hope is compounded' and which highlight 'the sense of individual impotence'. Bernard's growing apprehension of evil, in turn, is seen to have 'wider, historical applications'; it is 'perhaps from these little stagnant pools', he muses, 'that the mists and vapours arise . . . like Hitler'.[11]

Bernard's moral collapse is instigated by his recognition that the evil which gave rise to fascism exists in himself. Waiting for his former lover,

Terence, at Leicester Square, he witnesses a young homosexual's arrest by the police and is dismayed by his own response:

> He could only remember the intense, the violent excitement that he had felt when he saw the hopeless terror in the young man's face, the tension with which he had watched for the disintegration of a once confident human being. He had been ready to join the hounds in the kill then. It was only when he had turned to the detective that his sadistic excitement had faded, leaving him with normal disgust. But what had brought him to his senses, he asked himself, and, to his horror, the only answer he could find was that in the detective's attitude of somewhat officious but routine duty there was no response to his own hunter's thrill. Truly, he thought, he was not at one with those who exercised proper authority. A humanist, it would seem, was more at home with the wielders of the knout and the rubber truncheon.[12]

It is hard not to see the shade of Forster hovering over this climactic passage – Wilson's insistence on the corrupt and concealed motives of the naive liberal reads like a rebuttal of Forsterian sanguinity. Indeed, the passage involves a sleight of hand, which suggests that Wilson is keen to establish a direct link between Bernard's sadism and humanism's myopia. The last sentence takes us from the particular (Bernard's reaction) to the general (humanism as a whole), thereby implying that one individual's eager complicity with violence is symptomatic of all who espouse his political beliefs. But the text fails to establish this connection; it is merely asserted.

The Leicester Square incident shatters Bernard's previous self-confidence, leaving him to feel that his 'tattered humanism' is 'compounded through and through with alien motives and decisions'. His subsequent inability to act is contrasted to his wife's and Charles Murley's complacent willingness to exercise power as they see fit. Whereas Bernard's introspection paralyses him, Charles's and Ella's belief in 'the proper exercise of authority' enables them to act decisively but blinds them to the unseen, and often disastrous, consequences of their actions.[13] His position is weak because his grasp of humanism's blind-spots leads to quietism; theirs is flawed because their predisposition to intervene in human affairs leaves them ignorant of their own ambiguous motives. This dilemma cripples Bernard. He distrusts his own motives, refusing to accept their partial impurity, and the proper exercise of authority, refusing to accept its possibly harmful unintended effects.

Bernard's psychological paralysis effectively kills him; he discovers in his own heart the hemlock that poisons him. His death suggests that for Wilson there is no easy solution to the dilemmas faced by the post-war humanist. What follows hemlock is ambiguous: either Bernard's helplessness, a form of secular quietism that bows before 'the possible collapse of everything', thereby sharing Forster's belief in the efficacy of looking away; or Ella's and Charles's activism, a use of vested authority in which 'such a lot of wicked things get mixed up in the good one does'.[14] Bernard's death does not, then, allow Wilson neatly to complete the parallel with the life of Socrates but hints that his dilemmas remain unresolved.

Anglo-Saxon Attitudes raises similar concerns. Gerald, like Bernard, refuses to act because he fears the 'complicated webs of muddled human activity' and the 'sordid business' of life's entanglements.[15] So scared has he been of doing the wrong thing, of unintentionally hurting people, that he has retreated into a sybaritic life of art and sensual pleasure. But Gerald's inactivity has had disastrous consequences; it has allowed his wife to suffocate their children, deprived him of any right to intervene when he belatedly wants to help them, and permitted a scholarly fraud to distort his field for several decades. The latter is significant because it links Gerald's emphasis on personal relationships above all else to the inadequacies of a Forsterian liberalism. Gerald has suppressed his suspicions about the Melpham hoax out of loyalty to Lionel Stokesay, his benefactor. But Stokesay, 'one of the men of Munich', represents the naivety that led to appeasement.[16] Gerald's own unwillingness to confront the truth of the Melpham fraud and to act to set the record straight parallels his mentor's refusal to face the truth of fascism. Stokesay, Gerald reflects, had behaved as 'though he were running away from reality', but this indictment is no less pertinent to his own behaviour, since he has himself 'evaded the truth, past and present, for most of his life'. It is only when he confronts the self-deception and sentimentality with which he has viewed his life that he can begin, in Dollie's words, 'to grow up'.[17]

Wilson's own growing away from a naive and often self-serving humanism was to take him from the straightforward realism of these early novels to the parodic experimentalism and grand guignol of *No Laughing Matter*. The novel is a grand family saga that traces the fortunes of one family, the Matthews, focusing on the different paths in life taken by its various members. By giving almost all of his characters roles that take them to the heart of public life – actor, journalist, art collector, businesswoman, novelist – Wilson is able to explore their responses to some of the key events of the century's history. Divided into five books, the novel begins in Edwardian England and then moves through a succession of dates (1919, 1925–38, 1946, 1956, 1967) to the late 1960s. However, *No Laughing Matter* is not simply an updated version of the totalizing nineteenth-century burgher novel. Through its multi-perspective form, which entails several narrative viewpoints, elusive narrator, plays within the novel, and various pastiches of older literary styles, it both exposes the limitations of an earlier realism and pays tribute to its strengths.

Although the novel is replete with pastiches of different literary forms, its controlling mode is that of parody.[18] Fredric Jameson has suggested that in postmodernism pastiche has displaced parody. Postmodernism produces a dehistoricized sense of the present – the aesthetic corollary of which is depthlessness – with the result that once-productive parody has been superseded by motiveless pastiche. Postmodern society is 'bereft of all historicity'; pastiche represents such a dehistoricized culture's artistic mode *par excellence*. It is 'speech in a dead language' and is 'without any of parody's ulterior motives, amputated of the satiric impulse, devoid of laughter and of any conviction that alongside the abnormal tongue you have momentarily borrowed, some healthy linguistic normality still exists'.[19] On this view, *No Laughing Matter*, multiple-voiced, carnivalesque, and filled with mimicry, might easily be taken for another postmodernist text. But I shall suggest that it is driven by parody and that it self-consciously repudiates pastiche in order to maintain productive relations with the past. Wilson combats the waning of a historical consciousness by creating a panoramic canvas that refers outside itself to public events; he overcomes the depthlessness of much contemporary writing by employing a highly individual, baroque, and *written* (in Iris Murdoch's phrase) style that bears the indelible mark of a personal signature; finally, he makes dead pastiche serve living, motivated parody by building a critique of pastiche into his text. He employs parody in the spirit of Thomas Mann, who described his own style as 'a parody, not cynical but affectionate, of tradition'.[20] If his novel is postmodernist then it belongs not to a nihilist postmodernism that celebrates the dissolution of ethical and epistemological norms but to a referential postmodernism that problematizes representation while at the same time attempting to establish knowledge of reality.

No Laughing Matter both applauds the realist novel and subverts it. This Janus-faced stance manifests itself stylistically and structurally, but it is also dealt with thematically. At an anti-fascist rally in 1937 Herr Birnbaum, famous author of children's stories, is disappointed to hear that John Galsworthy will not be present. When Margaret Matthews, a successful writer herself, informs him that Galsworthy 'wasn't a very good novelist', Birnbaum concedes the point: 'No, I suppose not. But then the English novel is not an aesthetic novel, it is a social novel. *The Forsyte Saga* has great importance as the mirror of the British high bourgeoisie'.[21] Birnbaum's willingness to overlook the English novel's artistic defects and his faith in its capacity to reflect social life are not, however, shared by Angus Wilson. *No Laughing Matter* (provisionally entitled *Laughing Mirrors*) undermines Birnbaum's naive reflectionist aesthetic by both utilizing and parodying realist techniques.

Like Galsworthy's epic, *No Laughing Matter* is a family saga. And while there are similarities between the two works, it is the differences between them that point to Wilson's parodic revision of *The Forsyte Saga*. Parody, as Linda Hutcheon has argued, should not be regarded only as imitation for the purpose of ridicule. It may combine 'respectful homage' with an 'ironically thumbed nose'; it creates difference within similarity and thus allows artists to respond to the past by reworking it, recoding it in new forms.[22] *No Laughing Matter* both subverts an older novelistic tradition and acknowledges its strengths. Throughout the novel the narrow, insular world of *The Forsyte Saga* is associated with the resolutely middle-brow Pascoes, Sukey and Hugh, who refuse to face the social and historical transformations that confront them. Sukey disparages Margaret's ironic style of writing, complaining that unlike Galsworthy and Walpole she 'makes things more depressing than they really are'. When, during the Second World War, she and Hugh are unsure whether to shelter a Jewish refugee, she approves her husband's desire to escape into the safe milieu of his book: 'That's right, dear . . . You bury yourself in that awful old Soames. Why *should* you be worried with all this in the summer holidays?'. But the Pascoes' refusal to confront the encroachments of the wider world is ironized. Sukey's private pact with God – she offers her eldest two sons as a sacrifice so that the youngest, P.S., be spared – backfires cruelly. All survive the Second World War, but P.S. is killed during another international crisis – the division of Palestine between Israel and Jordan in 1948. And when Britain fails to reassert its status as a world power in the Suez débâcle of 1956, the response from those present to Sukey's hysterical reaction summarizes the inadequacy of her parochial worldview: '[T]he present crisis was no time for such ghosts, perhaps, in fact, it was just that sort of living in the past that had brought England to her present humiliations'.[23]

It is no accident that Wilson links large-scale historical disruptions of twentieth-century life with the collapse of Sukey's personal mythos. As Neil McEwan has pointed out, *No Laughing Matter* emphasizes both the importance of maintaining continuity with the past and the difficulty of doing so in a contemporary context.[24] Beginning in the Edwardian period, it depicts the dislocations between past and present caused by two world wars; focusing on the break-up of the Matthews family, it concludes with death and exile. The novel's subversion of the burgher epic discloses Wilson's belief that both the way of life it describes and its attendant narrative mode belong to a disappearing past. At the same time, *No Laughing Matter* reveals its awareness that the past conditions a gradually emergent present, whose cultural and artistic forms are at once continuous and discontinuous with it. Thus the text's formal innovations – parodies of various dramatic forms, characters' role-playing, and multiple points of view – question the accuracy with which the social novel of the past represented reality and attest the need to go beyond it. Herr Birnbaum's touching faith in its mirroring abilities is undermined, for Wilson, echoing Brecht, implies that if art reflects life it does so with distorting mirrors.

No Laughing Matter is a double-voiced text that explores literature and history. But it does not treat these as separate phenomena, viewing history as a set of events on which literature offers commentary. Rather, it emphasizes the complex ways in which a society's conception of history is shaped through the discourses that articulate and transmit it. Wilson does not suggest that fictional accounts and historical narratives are of the same ontological order or that they make the same kind of truth-claim. He acknowledges that there is a distinction between what Paul Ricoeur calls 'the *direct truth-claim* of history concerning past events, and the *indirect truth-claims* of fictional narrative'.[25] This distinction will, by the novel's end, prove to be crucial. But although Wilson refuses to conflate literature and history, he understands the multiple ways in which they intertwine. Literature is not only a discourse that can itself be historically located but also a discourse that locates history, because it contributes to a culture's self-understanding and because the writing of history is partially dependent on narrative models.[26]

The act that transmits knowledge of history is at one and the same time an interpretative act. It is fitting, then, as Jean Sudrann has argued, that *No Laughing Matter* begins less with a historical 'moment' than with a multi-layered account of the different ways it could be recorded and passed on.[27] The novel's opening words refer to the cinematic representation of the Exhibition which the Matthews family visits when the novel begins. Those who cannot be present catch 'quick jerky glimpses' of celluloid's reproduction of a world – the Wild West – that is itself an imaginative (and largely mythical) reconstruction of the past. But can the past, whether that of the frontier or that of Edwardian Kensington, be caught? The Matthews 'might so easily have been frozen and stored away in the files of the National Film Institute'. But although no mechanical means of reproduction were present, they would not in any case have equalled language's evocation of the scene:

And the loss in recall is probably not very great, since the jerky Colonel-Bogey-accompanied life of an old film news strip would ill serve to dissolve the limbs into that delicious, sunbathed, pleasure-sated rhythm which alone could bring back the exact feel of that far-off afternoon. In any case, what no recording machine yet invented could have preserved was the pioneer happiness, the primitive dream that for some minutes gave to that volatile, edged and edgy family a union of happy carefree intimacy that it had scarcely known before and was never to know again.[28]

Wilson's deliberately paratactic and individual style implicitly responds to Benjamin's claim that what 'withers in the age of mechanical reproduction is the aura of the work of art'.[29] This is less a claim that literature is superior to film than an attempt (*pace* Jameson) to recover this lost aura by flaunting its own particular gift: the power of the written word. At the same time the novel recognizes that realism has limitations and acknowledges that fiction must now compete with other modes of representation: television, cinema, photography.

That *No Laughing Matter* will explore the vexed question of representation, with particular emphasis on fiction, is made clear from the outset. If on the one hand it weighs the respective merits of the burgher novel and the art novel, then on the other hand it assesses the claims of realism and fantasy. The opening account of the Exhibition turns into a lengthy description of the different daydreams of each of the Matthews children. As the novel unfolds, these daydreams become fantasies that enable the young Matthews to cope with the intolerable pressures of living with their mercurial, irresponsible, at times vicious parents, Clara and Billy Pop. And while the text implies that fantasy functions as a valid form of self-defence, it also suggests that it may be debilitating, leading to an avoidance of reality. Sukey, for example, never breaks out of the distorting world of make-believe, but Marcus, who grows in stature as the novel progresses, is able to make the crucial transition from fantasy to reality. One of the text's central concerns is to show that although these two domains are linked in complex ways, a too-willing immersion in the latter may result in a crippling evasion of the former. And the issue of personal evasion for the purposes of psychic survival is in turn bound up with another question: does fiction itself, which creates imaginary worlds, face reality, or does it make reality bearable by recasting it in consoling but duplicitous artistic forms?

No Laughing Matter explores this question through its portrayal of Margaret Matthews and through its dramatic qualities, which encompass role-playing, mimicry and parody. Margaret's literary career is traced from its childhood beginnings to its adult successes. The novel reveals that her urge to write originates in a desire to escape the tensions of quotidian life and that her fictions enable her to displace threatening emotions. Already at the Exhibition Margaret imagines herself transmuting her experience of the day into literary form. But because she fears failure and disapproval she retreats behind the mask of an authorial persona, an internal alter ego. This early act of literary creation involves a double displacement. Experience is reinterpreted as fiction, and then responsibility for it is transferred: 'There, now it was someone else, and Aunt Mouse and all other mice could jeer as much as they wished, it would not touch her'. This form of self-protection, in which Margaret both rewrites experience and distances herself from her own revision of it, is the main impulse behind her creativity. When she is woken by a tempestuous parental quarrel she dispels her 'childhood terror' by once again fictionalizing her life: 'Slowly, practisedly she relaxed by means of the familiar stringing together of words'. Yet although unresolved conflicts become the well-spring of Margaret's creativity, her inability to confront them in life may well have poisoned her talent at source, for she seems unable to go beyond a harshly ironic mode of writing. The pleasure she takes in employing irony is tinged with self-criticism: 'And yet, and yet, by ironically placing so carefully it somehow failed to capture the contradictory whole'. Praised at first for her mordant social satires (as was Wilson), she distances herself from her early work, noting that 'she had spent more than a quarter of a century since then trying to adapt the tongue to poetry, to attune the ear to deeper music than mere mimicry'.[30]

Margaret's concern that ironic realism cannot do justice to the complex nature of reality is a small cog in the massive machinery of the novel, which is geared to investigating how human beings shape reality into stories in order to make sense of it. Through story-telling, *No Laughing Matter*'s characters endow their lives with form, structure and meaning. Wilson does not judge their personal narratives, but he does distinguish between those narratives that overtly distort experience and those that recast it into new forms in order the better to comprehend it. A good illustration of this distinction is provided by the different accounts of Sukey's wedding. In the first place, Wilson offers no purportedly neutral description of events against which his characters' versions could be compared. The wedding is initially presented through Margaret's fictionalized interpretation of it, which seems authentic and persuasive because it depends on an ironic reversal that results in self-criticism and censure of the Matthews' snobbery. But Margaret's account of the wedding's events is later contested by both Sukey and Marcus.[31] Their contestations of her story raise alternative validity-claims, challenging its veracity on the grounds of empirical truth. The pertinence of such a challenge is not negligible for Wilson, as my discussion of the last third of the novel will make clear. But he also suggests, contra Herr Birnbaum, that art cannot stand in a straightforward mimetic relation to the world. Sukey's dismissal of her sister's work leads Hugh to reflect solemnly that 'if one knew a lot of these writers, even chaps like Galsworthy or Hugh Walpole, one would be surprised how they'd twisted facts'. Jack's more sophisticated response is that Marcus's objections are misplaced because cultural artefacts must be judged according to internal criteria: 'A work of art is a work of art'.[32] But Wilson is defending neither the deliberate distortion of reality nor a thoroughgoing aestheticism. His point, rather, is that in the absence of an Archimedean perspective from which individuals' competing accounts of reality could be judged, a reflectionist aesthetic must be qualified. On his view, narratives do not stand outside experience, mirroring it, but are thoroughly incorporated in it, shaping, configuring, and interpreting it both as it takes place and later, when it is rethought. In *No Laughing Matter* language is shown to signify and resignify reality rather than to reflect it.

The five parodies within the novel serve various functions: they expose the novel's own fictional nature, revealing it to be a cultural artefact that is itself participating in a literary reconstruction of history; they show how earlier literary forms have differed in their interpretations of the past and question their claims to veracity; they juxtapose these various forms within the text's wider framework and thus problematize both the concept of representation in general and this particular novel's attempt at it. But it is not just the plays within the novel that emphasize the theatricality of human behaviour; the Matthews' persistent role-playing, most notably in The Game, is equally significant. Like the story-telling that recodes bad experiences into fiction so that they can be borne, The Game transforms suffering into a parodic simulacrum of it so that it can be displaced. Quentin's lengthy defence of its procedures stands as a *mise-en-abîme* for Wilson's own parodic tactics in this novel:

> Was the man or woman able to be another also the most suited to defend that other's interest? Yes, for simulation, whatever its motive, demands identification. But was he or she sufficiently detached to be able to offer a defence intelligible to others as defending counsel should, without the confusions and blurs of subjective statement? Yes, for simulation and mimicry also demand observation: in them compassion is tinged by mockery or mockery by compassion, and identification is distanced by the demands of technique. But could this simple mixture of opposites which mimicry requires, of affection with distaste, of respect with contempt, of love with hatred – be justly defined as a sort of reasoned apology? Yes, if passed through the tempering fire of Mr. Justice Scales (Quentin). The rules established, the Game could now proceed.

The Game functions both as a metaphor for *No Laughing Matter* as a whole and as a way of exploring its characters' personalities. Quentin's observation that mimicry requires a degree of empathy, that mockery and compassion may be complementary rather than contradictory, perfectly describes the novel's parodic mode. Wilson's parodic mimicry offers a 'critical revision' of old literary forms and thereby discloses both his distance from them and his recognition that, like palimpsests, they lie just beneath current fictive modes.[33]

The Game allows the Matthews children to articulate their grievances, but does it enable them to confront the past or does it encourage them to evade it? The answer to this question is important, for it bears as much on Wilson's narrative mode as on the nature of the characters he portrays. *No Laughing Matter*, in fact, seriously undermines The Game, implying that in adulthood it becomes an obstacle to maturity because instead of acknowledging the past it displaces it. The Game, story-telling, the invention of private imaginary worlds, and role-playing all encourage the same denial of personal and public history in which Bernard Sands and Gerald Middleton engaged. Granny Matthews, for all her limitations, knows that the past must be confronted: 'I suppose, really, growing up is when you can first see that life's all one thing, that however silly you have been in the past it's all part of you, you can't refuse it. . . . [S]uddenly one day I saw that it was all part of my life, I couldn't turn my back on any of it. I think that's when I grew up'. Billy Pop paraphrases this as 'having a sense of the past'. Having a sense of the past does not mean nostalgically looking through old photograph albums (Margaret) or old dressing-up boxes (Marcus). Indeed, the nostalgic view of history is given short shrift in this text. Sukey's wartime broadcasts, which depict 'the good old days', are 'muck', as Billy Pop pithily remarks. And

Marcus's tongue-in-cheek use of a mythical English past (which reads now as a prophetic comment on the way the heritage industry packages history) is shown to be motivated by commercial astuteness: 'Everyone said the English and Americans would want a French name, but I risked Plantagenet and it worked. All those old queens in wimples made such wonderful advertisements'.[34] Recycling images from a glorious history that is as fabricated as the Edwardian daydream with which the novel begins, Marcus self-consciously evokes a noble past solely in order to promote sales. In contrast to the notion of history as commercial kitsch, *No Laughing Matter* suggests that having a sense of the past entails not distorting it by way of personal or national fantasies, facing its continuing influence, and acknowledging that the different ways in which it has been interpreted condition current perceptions of reality.

The paradox that, by being playful, literature may examine reality seriously lies at the heart of *No Laughing Matter*. The text displays an ambivalent attitude both to its own stylistic reliance on comedy and parody and to its characters' use of caricature and burlesque. For although mimicry, role-playing, and fantasy are aspects of reality, they may also be evasions of it. Wilson's awareness of this means that he must find a way not only to control his text's carnivalesque exuberance and multiple perspectives but also to establish a critical distance from its characters' escapes into private fantasy and public pantomime. From Book Three onwards Wilson gradually eliminates pastiche and humour, thereby clarifying his sense of their limitations as narrative strategies and modes of behaviour. Books Three and Four, which deal with the years 1937–56, show how defenceless play-acting and fantasy are against the depredations of history.

The public events of 1937 and 1938 have shattering consequences for most of the Matthews. Sukey is chastized by the Jewish refugee Frau Liebermann, who forces her to question both her own and Britain's isolationism; Quentin grasps the extent of Soviet purges and abandons communism; Marcus, whose lover is Jewish, is appalled by his experience of fascism and acknowledges the limitations of his aestheticism; Rupert and Margaret join the anti-fascist cause. Gladys's unwitting dispossession of an impoverished refugee couple is, in turn, linked to the Munich Pact by way of the novel's theatrical metaphor. At her trial Margaret hopes that humorous tomfoolery will save the day, for Gladys will 'surely seek to buy [the judge] off with a somersault or a false nose'. But the time for comedy is long past, and Gladys is given a 4-year sentence. Outside the courthouse not one of the Matthews can 'bear the prolongation of any family play'. This personal drama, which symbolizes the dispossession of the Jews on a local level, is paralleled by the public charade presided over by Chamberlain, which will result in a global holocaust. And Munich comes 'to most of the Matthews brothers and sisters as a horrible, long-awaited, too predictable curtain to an exhausting play'.[35] In 1942 Clara and Billy Pop are killed in a Baedeker raid, the description of which closes Book Three and offers the novel's final dramatic pastiche. The Game, in turn, is last played in 1946 after the Matthews' house – a symbol of cultural rootedness – has been sold, and the Matthews family – a symbol of national continuity – has been dispersed by internal conflicts, self-imposed exile and death.

Books Three, Four and Five show that some of the Matthews remain trapped in childhood while others have made the transition to adulthood. But they also clarify the novel's use of parody and defend the seriousness of its enterprise. Quentin's justification of The Game's satiric mode (empathy *and* critique, respect *and* contempt) represents part of this defence. But Wilson signals both his grasp of comedy's shortcomings and his commitment to art's truth-telling obligations in two key scenes: Marcus's response to the unmotivated pastiches of a pseudo-painter; Herr Birnbaum's heartfelt speech at the anti-fascist rally in 1937.

When Marcus and Jack, both art collectors, are shown a series of paintings by a fellow homosexual, Jack feels constrained to admire them; Marcus, however, makes no attempt to conceal his feelings. When the painter explains that his imitations of older styles are ironic pastiches, Marcus brushes him off:

> 'To begin with, all this stuff is entirely derivative – faces from Munch, buildings from Chirico and what you call irony of Rouault is just bad, imitation Rouault. Personally if you were another Munch or Chirico I shouldn't care a fuck because I'm not interested in a lot of modish illustrations to dream books. But your trouble is that you can't paint. You're simply not competent to do what in any case, I think, would be a waste of a real painter's time. It's as bad as that.'[36]

Apart from the man's lack of skill, his canvases are bad because their ostensibly ironic treatment of earlier art is *only* derivative. For Marcus, this kind of unmotivated pastiche is to be rejected because it is parasitic, rather than productive. This scene can illuminatingly be contrasted with Douglas Crimp's discussion of the difference between the modernist Manet and the postmodernist Rauschenberg. Whereas Manet's *Olympia* uses Titian's *Venus* as a model, Rauschenberg silk-screens reproductions of paintings by Velazquez and Rubens onto his own works. In Rauschenberg's work, according to Crimp, 'the fiction of the creating subject gives way to frank confiscation, quotation, excerption, accumulation and repetition of already existing images'.[37] Pastiche, in Jameson's terms – a bracketing and then effacing of 'the past as "referent"' that eventually 'leav[es] us with nothing but texts'.[38] How far Wilson is from this view of art is made clear not only by Marcus's implicit clarification of his own parodic mode but also by his subsequent apologia for art and Birnbaum's defence of literature.

The scene just discussed has a wider resonance. Jack finds Marcus's uncompromising stance unacceptable, but Marcus refuses to repent: 'I've got one thing I know about – painting. . . . It's the only thing I've got and I'm not going to tell lies about it for any purpose whatsoever'. Marcus is essentially an aesthete, and his defence of art rests primarily on its plastic qualities, but his faith in art's truth-telling capacity is the counterpart to Herr Birnbaum's social realist belief in literature's referential function and his defence of art on epistemological grounds. At the anti-fascist rally attended by Rupert, Margaret and Quentin, it is Herr Birnbaum, initially the butt of the text's joke against the English novel, who really understands what is at stake. His grasp of fascism's debasement of language and his plea for resistance to its perversion of literature are central to a work itself obsessed with the sense-making properties of art:

I have lived all my life for the language of my country, the German language. . . . But to find the right language, the right words in our great tongue, has been a hard life time's task. And now with the coming of our Fuhrer, I have known two hells. The one is smaller. This hell alone is for me and for the other German artists who must leave Germany or remain silent. We must speak as I am now doing in a half tongue, in a language that is not our own. . . . The other hell is deep and very black. To know that the language I have tried to use to give the children life of the mind is being used today, perverted, strangled, to bring to the children of my country a real and permanent death – the death of their spirit.[39]

Marcus's and Birnbaum's defences of art's importance force the reader once more to confront *No Laughing Matter*'s own use of language. The novel rejects the dead language of pastiche in favour of a vital parodic mode that, in Thomas Mann's words, adds to what is appropriated because its borrowings 'acquire a symbolic life of their own'.[40] But in so far as Wilson builds a critique of empty pastiche and a defence of motivated parody into his text, he also qualifies his own use of the latter by drastically cutting down on comedy and mimicry. The significance of this should not be overlooked, for *No Laughing Matter* asks the reader to discriminate among different uses of language. The crucial point is that although Wilson acknowledges that the heteroglossic richness produced by different individuals' competing accounts of reality cannot be contained by a totalizing perspective, he does not conclude that the unattainability of a decisive overview must culminate in a relativization of ethical values. Thus when Marcus first grasps the horror of fascism he accepts that the 'easy moral rules' by which he has lived cannot apply when '"nice" people' reveal 'the obscenities of their minds and wills'.[41] The fight against fascism is central to this text because it reveals Wilson's belief that the world can neither be encompassed by language nor reduced to it. *No Laughing Matter* ultimately shows that reality cannot be treated as simply the product of mutually incommensurable language games among which it is impossible to adjudicate.

In his account of postmodernism Jameson argues that within its force-field 'distance in general (including "critical distance" in particular) has very precisely been abolished'.[42] He thus denies that it is possible to achieve the kind of critical perspective I have argued Wilson achieves, one that is both implicated in the postmodern, and highly sceptical of it. So is *No Laughing Matter* a postmodernist novel? Given the contested nature of postmodernism, this must remain a moot point. If, as Hutcheon argues, postmodernism attempts 'a re-evaluation of and a dialogue with the past in the light of the present', which 'does not deny the *existence* of the past' but questions 'whether we can ever *know* that past other than through its textualized remains', then it can be regarded as a postmodernist text.[43] But I am more concerned to argue that the postmodern constellation has not entirely eliminated literature that, however epistemologically self-aware and aesthetically up-to-date, is still strongly referential and deeply committed to resisting the kind of dehistoricization mourned by Jameson.[44] *No Laughing Matter* rejects the dead language of pastiche, refuses the blandishments of a distorting nostalgia, and resists the waning of historicity. It acknowledges the difficulty both of maintaining contact with the past and of representing it, but it establishes precisely the critical distance that Jameson deems unattainable by utilizing a Mannian

parodic mode, which at once refers to the past and foregrounds its own
constitutive role in interpreting that past. The novel also skirts the
reflectionist impasse that bedevils realism and is the target of postmodern
critiques by shifting to a productive view of mimesis. Ricoeur's view of
mimesis as 'not simply reduplication but [as] creative reconstruction by
means of the mediation of fiction' perfectly describes *No Laughing Matter*'s
experimental realism, which is resolutely referential but recognizes that
discourses configure reality. This is a writing characterized by what Ricoeur
calls 'iconic augmentation'; it is productive as well as reproductive.[45]
Utilizing a multi-layered parodic mode, the novel points outwards to a
society beyond itself and gestures inwards to its own contribution, as a
culturally embedded and intertextually conceived form, to society's ongoing
struggle for historical self-understanding.

John Fowles

John Fowles has averred a commitment to both socialism and feminism on
several occasions.[46] *Daniel Martin*, a post-war 'Condition of England' novel
that grapples with various political, cultural and artistic issues, echoes these
sentiments. Dan dismisses the Tory grandee Fenwick as 'no more than an
egotist' who believes 'that the fortunate must at all costs be allowed to retain
their good fortune'; and the resurgent relationship between Jane and Dan, in
part a redemption of lost time in personal terms, has a public dimension, for
Jane's Lukács- and Gramsci-inspired socialist convictions encourage Dan to
re-examine his politics, leading him by novel's end to become 'a fully paid-
up member of the Labour Party'.[47] Although the Preface to *The Aristos* and
the conclusion to *Daniel Martin* represent Fowles's clearest expressions of
commitment to democratic socialism, novels such as *The French Lieutenant's
Woman*, which urges emancipation from oppressive social structures, and *A
Maggot* (1985), which sympathizes with a whole tradition of religious Dissent,
are also utopian texts firmly opposed to reaction.

Why is it, then, that *The Aristos*, for example, was apparently so misunder-
stood? And why, when reading Fowles, does one so often feel uneasy,
suspecting that somehow the avowed socialist and feminist stance does not
fit with the fictional worlds being projected? Fowles's writing, I suggest,
discloses a tension between political beliefs that seek to reorganize society
and biological/archetypal convictions that hold this to be impossible. A clue
to this opposition is provided in *Daniel Martin* when, in the middle of a
theoretical discussion, the eponymous protagonist reflects that 'it was less
Gramsci than his exegetist that interested me – *as always*, far less the political
than the biological view of life'.[48] By focusing on the role of history, the
representation of gender, and the conflict between an existentially conceived
free will and a scientifically conceived determinism in his novels, I shall
argue that Fowles's politics ultimately reveal a greater affinity with an
Arnoldian paternalism than with democratic socialism.

Two of Fowles's novels, *The French Lieutenant's Woman* and *A Maggot*, are
'historical' novels, at least in the sense that they are set in the past, in
nineteenth-century and eighteenth-century England respectively; a third,

Daniel Martin, is explicitly concerned with contemporary history. But neither of the first two novels is primarily concerned to reconstruct the period in which it is set. *The French Lieutenant's Woman* attends more closely to the detail of Victorian social life than does *A Maggot* to the minutiae of Georgian England, but the interest of both novels lies elsewhere. The author is quite clear about this. He writes of the former work, in 'Notes on an Unfinished Novel', that the existential dilemma faced by Charles Smithson was of central importance and that he deliberately and anachronistically gave his protagonist moral preoccupations and personal anxieties that he could not logically have entertained. It was the existential conflict between a form of *mauvaise foi*, in this context the implicit acceptance of determinism through the choice of a conventional hide-bound life, and its opposite, a socially marginal life that is authentic, because freely chosen, which interested the writer. It is not 'a historical novel, a genre in which [he] ha[s] very little interest'.[49] *A Maggot* is equally removed from the question of historical verisimilitude. In his Preface to the book, Fowles stresses its provenance in the realms of the imagination, averring that he 'would not have this seen as a historical novel'. He points out in his Epilogue that he has consulted no historical documents, thereby reiterating this view: 'I repeat, this is a maggot, not an attempt, either in fact or in language, to reproduce known history'.[50]

In Fowles's work the separation between history and fiction is clear-cut. The history serves as a backdrop to more contemporary concerns; indeed, it might be argued that he has set some novels in the past precisely because the psychological distance between the present and the past helps to focus the issues that preoccupy him, putting them in sharper relief. His work erects a *cordon sanitaire* between history and literature. History, he contends in *A Maggot*, 'is essentially a science, and immensely different in its aims and methods from those of fiction'.[51]

Fowles's fictional objectives, then, are clearly demarcated from his reliance on a historical discourse that he considers is scientific and therefore at odds with the workings of the imagination. One corollary of this view is that history comes to function as a kind of background to a given novel's events, it being those events that are of the first importance. A second consequence of this view can be apprehended in the confident, assertive tone employed by Fowles's narrators – in texts such as *The French Lieutenant's Woman* and *A Maggot* – whenever they make historical pronouncements. The narrator of the former adopts a consistently authoritative stance when parcelling out non-diegetic historical information, which, rather than being challenged or undermined, is corroborated by other textual features: the literary and historical epigraphs to each chapter, which, in an echo of Victorian fiction, serve to authenticate the narrative they enclose; the footnotes, which, although they ironize the narrator's intrusiveness and pedantry, are also genuinely informative; the frequent references to the years within which the action takes place, 1867–9, which allow discussion of topical issues such as the impact of science (Buffon, Lyell, Darwin) on religious thought, the perceived consequences of the Second Reform Act (Arnold), and Mill's efforts to extend 'universal' suffrage to include women (his defeated Commons motion of 1867, and his publication of *The Subjection of Women* in 1869); and, finally, the documentary tone adopted in several passages.[52] *A Maggot*, whose narrator is far less in evidence, relies on a similarly authoritative historical discourse that is as little problematized as it is in *The French Lieutenant's Woman*.

This is at first sight disconcerting, but in fact it is unsurprising when one realizes that these novels seek less to reconstruct the past than to evoke imagined worlds in which *contemporary* dilemmas can be foregrounded and explored. In *A Maggot*, for example, Fowles writes of a character: 'Like all mystics (and many novelists, not least the present one) he is baffled, a child, before the real now; far happier out of it, in a narrative past or a prophetic future, locked inside that weird tense grammar does not allow, the imaginary present'.[53] This desire for an escape from the present, a flight from what in *A Maggot* is called 'the real now' and in *The French Lieutenant's Woman* 'the real reality', hints at a fear of entrapment in a historically determined present that precludes the possibility of individual freedom of choice, self-expression, and purposive action.[54] Charles Smithson, for example, that 'ammonite caught in the vast movements of history', perceives himself to be 'a man struggling to overcome history'.[55] Daniel Martin notes that 'what have appeared to be [his] own freely taken decisions provide very little evidence of more wisdom than the blind dictates of destiny'.[56] Ayscough and Jones, in *A Maggot*, are 'like most of us, still today, equal victims in the debtors' prison of History, and equally unable to leave it'.[57]

Most of Fowles's novels are characterized by an urgent sense of the need to elude a history that threatens to constrain the individual. Thus, despite the fact that two of his novels are set in the past, they are in some respects curiously dehistoricized. Not only does Fowles deliberately map contemporary concerns onto the past, but also he seeks trans-historical constants that belie the cultural specificity of the periods in which his novels are set. Such constants are most clearly discernible in his conception of gender and his sympathy for the existentialist predicament.

The representation of gender in *The French Lieutenant's Woman* turns on two fairly obvious sets of contrast: Sarah/Charles and Sarah/Ernestina. It is the enigmatic social outcast in each case who functions as the moral touchstone against which the other characters must be judged. In this sense, Sarah Woodruff stands at the heart of the text, justifying its title; but in another, equally significant, sense she is of secondary importance, for Charles Smithson is in many respects the novel's central protagonist, and Sarah merely the means by which he attains an incipient sense of self.[58] On this reading, Charles's predicament comes to the fore while Sarah's recedes into the background, the novel thus inverting the order of priorities that its title suggests. A second aspect of the representation of Charles and Sarah concerns the assumptions made about them and the imagery used to portray them, both of which ultimately serve to uphold gender stereotypes. *The French Lieutenant's Woman* thus exhibits a tension between an apparent desire for female emancipation – a prevalent theme in the novel – and a regressive view of the form such emancipation might take.

The description of the first encounter between Charles and Sarah contains in embryonic form the key contrasts between them that will subsequently be developed in greater detail:

> She turned to look at him – or as it seemed to Charles, through him. . . . It was certainly not a beautiful face, by any period's standard or taste. But it was an

unforgettable face, and a tragic face. Its sorrow welled out of it as purely, naturally and unstoppably as water out of a woodland spring. There was no artifice there, no hypocrisy, no hysteria, no mask; and above all, no sign of madness. The madness was in the empty sea, the empty horizon, the lack of reason for such sorrow; as if the spring was natural in itself, but unnatural in welling from a desert.

Again and again, afterwards, Charles thought of that look as a lance; and to think so is of course not merely to describe an object but the effect it has. He felt himself in that brief instant an unjust enemy; both pierced and deservedly diminished.

The various hints thrown out here will be developed as the book unfolds: the emphasis on Sarah's acuity, her ability to see through cant and subterfuge; the contrast between artifice and naturalness, and the suggestion that the environment is at fault ('desert'), not the individual trapped in it; the proleptic dismissal of the fears concerning Sarah that will haunt Charles at various moments in the text – madness, hysteria, dissimulation; the conflict between Charles and Sarah; and his initial recognition of her superiority over him. All this is subsequently amplified in detail. The contrast between artifice and naturalness turns neatly into an opposition between Ernestina, Charles's conventional bride-to-be, and Sarah, the harbinger of a socially unacceptable authenticity. Ernestina represents the role-playing self; Sarah, the unmasked self. As Charles gradually realizes, it is because he and Ernestina are both playing parts that they are 'enveloped in a double pretense'. Whereas his fiancée seems all too willing to embrace the social roles imposed on her, Sarah embodies 'an intelligence beyond convention'. Thus marriage to Ernestina is 'a fixed voyage to a known place', which threatens to stifle the 'vast potential' he has perceived in his future and that is symbolized by Sarah.[59]

If the Sarah/Ernestina contrast shows the latter in a harsh light, then the Sarah/Charles contrast is no less unforgiving toward the text's male protagonist, for his limitations are mercilessly exposed.[60] Charles's behaviour frequently lacks candour; having 'more than one vocabulary', he is 'almost three different men', and, the narrator pointedly remarks, 'there will be others of him before we are finished'. Charles is in fact far more of a chameleon than Ernestina, hence the stress placed on his recognition of this fact and on his decision to reject the mode of life that precipitates this behaviour: 'He gave the crown of her head a long look, then stood. He caught sight of himself in a mirror; and the man in the mirror, Charles in another world, seemed the true self. The one in the room was what she said, an imposter; had always been, in his relations with Ernestina, an imposter, an observed other'.[61]

In existentialist terms Charles and Ernestina are both guilty of bad faith. But what of Sarah Woodruff, the disruptive figure who is the novel's moral *point d'appui*? It is here that the text's internal contradictions are most discernible, for Sarah is in some respects portrayed as an unconventional character and in other respects as the classic, stereotypical heroine. Thus she is direct and forthright, refusing the mask of demureness cultivated by Ernestina; she is active rather than passive, with a stare 'like a rifle' or 'a lance', and 'an independence of spirit'; she is associated with traditional manifestations of masculinity, having 'the air of a girl coachman' or 'a female soldier'; she is perceptive, able to see people 'as they were and not as they tried to seem'; above all, she is consistently authentic – indifferent to fashion, dismissive of social propriety and contemptuous of a hypocritical moral rectitude. At the same time, however, Fowles endows her with characteristics that could hardly be more conventionally feminine. She is 'a figure from myth', a 'siren', a 'Calypso', a 'Sphinx', and a 'Virgin Mary'; she is associated throughout with nature and animality, showing a 'wild shyness' and being described as a 'wild animal . . . trembling, dumb'; she is 'sensual', with 'darker qualities'; finally, although her physical appearance does not conform to Victorian fashion, her face is 'well modeled, and completely feminine'.[62]

Sarah Woodruff is thus a curious hybrid of apparently incompatible 'male' and 'female' attributes. But she is no Woolfian androgyne, no escapee from the straitjacket of gender stereotypes. She is always nature to Charles's nurture. For all his shortcomings, Charles is urbane, intelligent, educated, and scientifically inclined; Sarah, in contrast, is unself-conscious, intuitive, and emotionally sensitive. Her 'essence', according to the bewitched narrator, is a 'fused rare power' of 'understanding and emotion'. Sarah's perceptiveness is systematically associated with instinct. Thus her intelligence is 'not in the least analytical or problem-solving'; nor is it self-aware, for although she can see through people, she does so '[w]ithout being able to say how'. This portrayal of Sarah as fundamentally intuitive goes hand in hand with the way she is compared to mythic figures, as these confirm her status as archetypal woman. First introduced as 'a figure from myth', she never shakes off the ahistorical connotations that accrue to this image. Sarah's options are limited not only by the Victorian context but also by her innate female 'essence'; fusing the language of archetypes with that of science, the narrator falls back on a 'biology is destiny' position, claiming that 'she appeared inescapably doomed to the one fate nature had so clearly spent many millions of years in evolving her to avoid: spinsterhood'.[63]

The representation of Sarah as natural and intuitive is conventional, and it is consistent with another stereotype employed by Fowles – woman as enigma. Sarah is rendered mysterious in several ways: by the images, such as sphinx, used to describe her; by her lack of self-consciousness; and by the mode of narration, which provides interior views of Charles's character but almost always describes Sarah from the outside.[64] The effect of this narrative strategy is to displace Sarah, ostensibly the novel's subject, from the text's centre and to marginalize her within the novel's modern idiom just as effectively as Mrs Poulteney has done within its Victorian context. She is silenced, rendered voiceless. To be sure, she speaks in *propria persona*, challenging Charles on various occasions, but because she is presented as a character unable to articulate her sense of self, and because the reader is denied any detailed insight into the workings of her mind, she is far less the subject of her own utterances than the object of others' words about her. Furthermore, as the novel progresses, Charles's existential predicament assumes centre-stage (the reader being made privy to his internal anxieties and external movements), whereas Sarah drops completely out of sight. This shifts the attention decisively onto the male protagonist, turning the novel

into a kind of *Bildungsroman* in which Charles's moral growth is of pre-
eminent importance and the relatively unchanging Sarah is merely the
means by which he achieves it. A similar pattern is exhibited in *Daniel
Martin*. Jane is also presented externally; is associated, for all her intelligence,
with 'feeling' rather than 'thinking'; and is portrayed as the means by which
Dan can change.[65]

The objectification of Sarah is, I think, unwitting, but it is apparent at key
textual moments. If her look at Charles is lance-like in that it pierces his
pretences, then his look – with which the narrator is complicit – is that of the
male voyeur:

> The girl lay in the complete abandonment of deep sleep, on her back. Her coat had
> fallen open over her indigo dress, unrelieved in its calico severity except by a small
> white collar at the throat. The sleeper's face was turned away from him, her right
> arm thrown back, bent in a childlike way. A scattered handful of anemones lay on
> the grass around it. There was something intensely tender and yet sexual in the
> way she lay; it awakened a dim echo in Charles of a moment from his time in Paris.
> Another girl, whose name now he could not even remember, perhaps had never
> known, seen sleeping so, one dawn, in a bedroom overlooking the Seine.

This carefully staged scene, so reminiscent of the composition of a nude painting,
makes Sarah the object of Charles's unreturned gaze and suggests she is
interchangeable with other women. The voyeuristic note is sounded again
later in the text when Sarah describes her (fictive) seduction by Varguennes,
leaving Charles to imagine himself as 'at one and the same time Varguennes
enjoying her and the man who sprang forward and struck him down'.[66]

The text positions Sarah in such scenes as object rather than subject. This
shift from observer to observed, which diminishes her significance and limits
her scope for self-expression, is confirmed in both of the novel's two endings.
In the first of these, Charles's last, baffled words to a Sarah who has been
unable to explain herself are met with the following response: 'The head
against his breast shakes with a mute vehemence'. In the second ending, she
is equally inarticulate; arresting Charles by calling out his name, it is 'as
though she were trying to tell him something she could not say in words'.
The narrator, once again, is complicit with this view of Sarah as an enigma as
much to herself as to the uncomprehending Charles and the benighted
reader. His final 'look' back at her fails to enlighten him, for she remains
firmly outside his purview: 'There are tears in her eyes? She is too far away
for me to tell'.[67]

The French Lieutenant's Woman is thus internally contradictory. Fowles
gives with one hand and takes away with the other. Sarah Woodruff is at
once endowed with non-gendered attributes, commended as the worthiest
character in the book, and placed as its central subject, *and* portrayed as an
archetypal figure from the world of dream and myth, turned into the means
by which a male protagonist can develop (she finishes up as muse and
amanuensis), and transformed from speaking subject to unvoiced object. As
Bruce Woodcock has persuasively argued, the novel offers a powerful
critique of masculinity but perceives femininity as simultaneously socially
constructed and archetypal; this unresolved contradiction leads to 'an
idealisation of the feminine and the female which itself remains unquestioned'.[68]

Fowles's idealization of what in *The Aristos* he calls 'the female principle' is discernible in almost all of his writing, and he seeks to substantiate it by drawing on archetypes and then justifying them on biological grounds.[69] In 'Notes on an Unfinished Novel', for example, relying on the kind of binary opposition that is prevalent in his work, he writes: 'I see man as a kind of artifice, and woman as a kind of reality. The one is cold idea, the other is warm fact. Daedalus faces Venus, and Venus must win'. The distinctions invoked here are well-worn: male/female; artifice/reality; Daedalus/Venus; coldness/warmth. In *The Aristos* these distinctions are couched in biological terms, and it is women who are most closely tied to biology. They 'know more about human nature, more about mystery'; when they 'resist emancipation' it is as a result of biological drives, and they 'know what they are about'.[70] Fowles's 'feminism' in no way questions or challenges the terms in which gender has traditionally been conceived. He seeks instead to praise – using ahistorical and biological arguments – that which has previously been demeaned ('the female principle'), thereby reinscribing the very logic that has in the past contributed to women's oppression.

Fowles's valorization in 1969 of a 'superior' female nature can interestingly be contrasted with the position being argued by Harriet Taylor and John Stuart Mill at the time in which *The French Lieutenant's Woman* is set. Taylor, for example, refuses to countenance alleged innate differences between the genders and rejects all attempts to assign a 'proper sphere' to women on the basis of their 'nature': 'We deny the right of any portion of the species to decide for another portion . . . what is and what is not their "proper sphere". The proper sphere for all human beings is the largest and highest which they are able to attain to'.[71] Mill, following in Taylor's tracks, devotes much of *The Subjection of Women* to arguments against views that attribute a particular kind of nature to women, emphasizing the social construction of gender.[72] He counters two claims frequently made by opponents of women's suffrage in the Victorian period: firstly, that women's biological makeup determines their psychological nature, endowing them with character traits such as passivity, intuition, and emotional sensitivity; secondly, that women are morally and spiritually superior to men and must be prevented from participating in public affairs lest they become corrupted. Whereas Mill rebuts both these arguments, Fowles implicitly endorses them. His 'feminism' relies on a belief in innate female superiority over men but treats women as the instruments of male development. It turns out to be remarkably close to the anti-suffrage 'defence' of women, which proclaimed their greater virtue at the price of their unsuitability for public life. Taylor had already exposed the hierarchy of power that underpins all versions of this kind of view in her 'Enfranchisement of Women', pointing out 'that persons usually mean by virtues the qualities which are useful or convenient to themselves'.[73]

Taylor's and Mill's writings show that Fowles's views about gender were already being strenuously argued against in the very period in which his novel is set. They also suggest that his lack of real interest in that period results in a monolithic and Whiggish account of it that is often misleading, contrasting as it does the restrictions of the past with the relative freedoms of the present. Fowles's reliance on biologically sanctioned archetypes leads to an unhistorical conception of male and female characteristics that is as irrelevant today as it is inaccurate when applied *tout court* to the Victorians.

Furthermore, his notion of an eternal male/female conflict dovetails neatly with his commitment to an existentialist worldview, because, despite Sartre's well-known claim that existence precedes essence, his emphasis on a human universality of condition is compatible with Fowles's belief in the universal opposition between Daedalus and Venus. Indeed, existentialism has been criticized for its bias towards a 'human condition' that is insufficiently historicized, and Fowles's lack of interest in the history of the period suggests a lack of attention to 'the real reality' from which *The French Lieutenant's Woman* claims *Homo sapiens* is by definition in flight.[74]

Fowles asserts in his Preface to *The Aristos* that his primary goal was 'to preserve the freedom of the individual', and in *The French Lieutenant's Woman* he enshrines 'freedom' and 'autonomy' as the modern novelist's sacred imperatives. But Fowles is haunted by the fear that few people are capable of the kind of awareness required by existentialism and that most will conform to social expectations rather than choose alternative lifestyles. There is thus a conflict between those whom he variously calls the Few, the *aristoi*, or the Elect, and the Many or the *hoi polloi*. It is here that the incompatibility between Fowles's nominal espousal of socialism and his deep-rooted commitment to a version of existentialism tinged with bits of Heraclitus, Arnold, and Forster can be seen most decisively. Consider the following passage, in which he clarifies his conception of the conflict between the Many and the Few:

> I meant simply that unless we face up to this unnecessarily brutal conflict (based largely on an unnecessary envy on the one hand and an unnecessary contempt on the other) between the biological Few and the biological Many; unless we admit that we are not, and never will be, born equal, though we are all born with equal human rights; unless the Many can be educated out of their false assumption that biological superiority is a state of existence instead of what it really is, a state of responsibility – then we shall never arrive at a more just and happier world.[75]

A passage such as this illustrates a similar kind of principle at work to the one I identified in Fowles's representation of gender. The ostensible recognition of equal rights and desire for a fairer social order is undermined by a series of problematic premises: that the frustration felt by oppressed groups is the product of 'unnecessary envy' and 'false assumptions' rather than a valid claim for the redress of social injustice; that there is little difficulty about identifying who are the Few and who the Many; that people can be assigned to these groups on biological grounds; and that the Few have a paternalistic duty to re-educate those unfortunates who belong to the other group. The opposition that Fowles sets up here between the Few and the Many – like that between the male and female principles – transcends history. It is explicable in terms of both biology and a quasi-Platonic concept of Ideal Form, for the spirit of the Elect survives the supersession of its historically contingent manifestations.[76] Fowles's conception of the elect, then, like his view of women, is predicated on a curious blend of idealism, idealization, myth and biology.

Fowles's language when he discusses the Few and the Many betrays the fact that his sympathy lies more with the predicament of the Few than with that of the Many, and it is for this reason that Fowles seems to me to be politically close to figures like Arnold and Forster. There are several similarities between these writers and Fowles: a belief in the need for a social élite that, in a nineteenth-century locution of Arnold's, can preserve and transmit 'the best that has been thought and said in the world'; a commitment to the idea of culture and a concomitant certainty that these writers know what true culture is; a fear that society is threatened by decline, precipitated in Arnold's case by a nation unprepared for full democracy, and caused in Fowles's case by massification; and an emphasis on individual self-transformation rather than on political change.[77] Fowles, for example, writes: 'every culture, however undemocratic, or however egalitarian, needs a kind of self-questioning, ethical élite, and one that is bound by certain rules of conduct, some of which may be very unethical, and so account for the eventual death of the form, though their hidden purpose is good: to brace or act as structure for the better effects of their function in history'.[78] Forster, in turn, writes: 'I believe in . . . an aristocracy of the sensitive, the considerate and the plucky. Its members are to be found in all nations and classes, and all through the ages. . . . They represent the true human tradition, the one permanent victory of our queer race over cruelty and chaos'. Later, prefiguring Fowles, he calls them 'the elect, the chosen, the Best People'.[79] Arnold, of course, argued for the indispensability of such 'aliens' in *Culture and Anarchy*, and in 'The Function of Criticism at the Present Time' suggested that 'it is only by this small circle resolutely doing its own work that adequate ideas will ever get current at all'.[80]

Arnold's confident assumption that this small circle has access to 'adequate' ideas and is able to ascertain how things 'are' relies on an implicit denial of the contested – ideological – nature of ideas. Fowles's similar conception of culture is more high-handed than Arnold's. In *Daniel Martin*, for example, he mounts a full-scale offensive against mass culture (Hollywood and British cinema, the communications industry), which is portrayed as uniformly atrocious; resisting this barbarity is 'genuine culture', which is never defined.[81] Whereas Arnold suggests that culture should 'not try to teach down to the level of inferior classes', Fowles has few such qualms.[82] Ninety-nine per cent of humanity, he avers, are 'not particularly moral . . . not particularly artistic, and . . . not particularly intelligent'.[83] It is hardly surprising, then, that in *Daniel Martin* the central protagonist tries to 'inject some culture' into his daughter, and that in *The Aristos* Fowles maintains that what 'the many need above all else is education; they need to be led, not to be leaders'.[84]

Arnold's mistrust of political reform (machinery) and his fear that a nation unprepared for democracy will descend into anarchy leads him to focus on internal self-transformation rather than external political change. Fowles's existentialist conception of the individual, which in *The French Lieutenant's Woman* he explicitly links to Arnold's Victorian notion of the 'best self', results in a similar focus. This brings me back to my initial claim that Fowles's avowed commitment to socialism is undermined by his lack of interest in history, his biological and archetypal conception of gender, and his existentialist emphasis on the individual. Fowles is, in fact, far more concerned with the individual than with the polity, and the individual that interests him is a member of, or an aspirant to, the elect. His primary concern is not so much to change society as to protect those who have at least a degree of freedom, autonomy and power from those who do not. He is at one in this with the anarchy-fearing Arnold whose best self, in Raymond Williams's words, did not rise when confronted with the sight of the smashed Hyde Park railings.[85] As Arnold wrote, the 'system of checks and every Englishman doing as he likes' was 'seen to have been convenient enough so long as there were only the Barbarians and the Philistines to do what they liked, but to be getting inconvenient, and productive of anarchy, now that the Populace wants to do what it likes too'.[86]

Fowles's worries are similar. He sympathizes with the plight of the less fortunate in a society to which he is genuinely hostile, but he is more concerned to protect the privileges of the Few from the claims of the Many. This concern to protect the Few is in the end ratified by an appeal to a form of socio-biology. Thus, in *The Aristos*, Heraclitus's view that humanity is divided into the *aristoi* and the *hoi polloi* is said to be '*biologically* irrefutable'; in his interview with James Campbell, Fowles reiterates his belief in '[b]iological elitism'; and in *Daniel Martin* Fenwick's claim that equality between people is 'a genetic impossibility' is endorsed by Dan.[87] In short, Fowles's progressive desire for political amelioration is persistently undermined by a regressive causality that explains socio-economic inequalities by way of genetic and evolutionary theory. The result of this recourse to socio-biology is a non-socialist displacement of blame away from the economic and political organization of society onto those who are its victims, for in an evolutionary sense they can be said to occupy the position they are meant to occupy. Elsewhere, however, Fowles seems to acknowledge that the conflict between the privileged individual and the disadvantaged group reflects the liberal's classic dilemma between self-centred personal liberty and other-centred social obligation. In the following passage he is speaking of Daniel Martin, but he could as easily have been referring to himself: 'His dilemma was the most familiar of all twentieth-century dilemmas, of course: that of the man, the animal, required to pay in terms of personal freedom for the contempt he felt at the abuse of social freedom – and unable to do it'.[88]

Notes

1. E. M. Forster, *Two Cheers For Democracy* (London: Penguin, 1972), pp. 65, 64, 83, 113, 68, 66.
2. Angus Wilson, *The Wild Garden* (London: Secker and Warburg, 1963), p. 47.
3. John Fowles, *The Aristos* (London: Triad/Granada, 1981), pp. 189–90.
4. Ibid., p. 192.
5. John Fowles, 'An Interview with John Fowles', *Contemporary Literature*, 17. 4 (Autumn 1976), pp. 455–69, at p. 459.
6. Angus Wilson, *Diversity and Depth in Fiction: Selected Critical Writings of Angus Wilson*, ed. Kerry McSweeney (London: Secker and Warburg, 1983), p. 131.
7. Wilson, *Diversity*, p. 241.
8. Angus Wilson, *Hemlock and After* (Harmondsworth: Penguin, 1956), p. 11.
9. Ibid., p. 14.
10. Forster, *Two Cheers*, pp. 78, 79.
11. Wilson, *Hemlock*, pp. 146–7, 108.

12. Ibid., p. 109.
13. Ibid., p. 126.
14. Ibid., pp. 205, 235.
15. Angus Wilson, *Anglo-Saxon Attitudes* (Harmondsworth: Penguin, 1978), pp. 290, 215.
16. Ibid., p. 21.
17. Ibid., pp. 102, 16, 330.
18. For a useful critical discussion that emphasizes pastiche, see Malcolm Bradbury, 'The Fiction of Pastiche: The Comic Mode of Angus Wilson', *Critical Essays on Angus Wilson*, ed. Jay L. Halio (Boston: Hall, 1985), pp. 139–55.
19. Fredric Jameson, *Postmodernism, or The Cultural Logic of Late Capitalism* (London: Verso, 1991), pp. 18, 17.
20. Thomas Mann, *The Letters of Thomas Mann, 1895–1955*, trans. Richard and Clara Winston (London: Penguin, 1975), p. 444–5.
21. Angus Wilson, *No Laughing Matter* (London: Secker, 1967), p. 370.
22. Linda Hutcheon, *A Theory of Parody: The Teachings of Twentieth-Century Art Forms* (London: Methuen, 1985), p. 33.
23. Wilson, *Laughing*, pp. 186, 298, 437.
24. Neil McEwan, *The Survival of the Novel: British Fiction in the Later Twentieth Century* (Totowa N. J.: Barnes, 1981).
25. Paul Ricoeur, *A Ricoeur Reader: Reflection and Imagination*, ed. Mario J. Valdes (Hemel Hempstead: Harvester, 1991), p. 105.
26. See Hayden White, 'The Historical Text as Literary Artifact', *The Writing of History: Literary Form and Historical Understanding*, eds R. H. Canary and H. Kozicki (Madison: Wisconsin University Press, 1978), pp. 41–62.
27. Jean Sudrann, 'The Lion and the Unicorn: Angus Wilson's Triumphant Tragedy', Halio, *Critical Essays*, pp. 130–9.
28. Wilson, *Laughing*, pp. 11, 11–12.
29. Walter Benjamin, 'The Work of Art in the Age of Mechanical Reproduction', *Illuminations*, ed. Hannah Ahrendt, trans. Harry Zohn (New York: Schocken, 1978), pp. 217–53, at p. 221.
30. Wilson, *Laughing*, pp. 18, 52, 78, 411.
31. Ibid., pp. 186, 200.
32. Ibid., pp. 186, 199.
33. Hutcheon, *Theory*, p. 15.
34. Wilson, *Laughing*, pp. 106, 395, 396, 461–2.
35. Ibid., pp. 392, 393.
36. Ibid., p. 385.
37. Douglas Crimp, 'On the Museum's Ruins', *The Anti-Aesthetic: Essays on Postmodern Culture*, ed. Hal Foster (Port Townsend, WA: Bay, 1983), pp. 43–56, at p. 53.
38. Jameson, *Postmodernism*, p. 18.
39. Wilson, *Laughing*, pp. 385, 379–80.
40. Mann, *Letters*, p. 362.
41. Wilson, *Laughing*, p. 291.
42. Jameson, *Postmodernism*, p. 48.
43. Linda Hutcheon, *A Poetics of Postmodernism: History, Theory, Fiction* (London: Routledge, 1988), pp. 19–20.
44. For good use of Benjamin's concept of the 'constellation' *vis-à-vis* postmodernism, see Richard Bernstein, *The New Constellation: The Ethical/Political Horizons of Modernity/Postmodernity* (Oxford, Blackwell, 1991).
45. Ricoeur, *Reflection*, p. 134.
46. Fowles, *Aristos*, p. 158.
47. John Fowles, *Daniel Martin* (St Albans: Triad/Panther, 1978), pp. 339, 664.

48. Ibid., p. 419, emphasis added.
49. John Fowles, 'Notes on an Unfinished Novel', Bradbury, *The Novel*, pp. 147–65, at p. 147.
50. John Fowles, *A Maggot* (London: Picador, 1991), pp. 6, 455.
51. Ibid., p. 455.
52. See John Fowles, *The French Lieutenant's Woman* (Boston: Little, Brown, 1969), pp. 88, 206–7.
53. Fowles, *Maggot*, p. 389.
54. Ibid., p. 389; Fowles, *French*, p. 107.
55. Fowles, *French*, pp. 344, 306.
56. Fowles, *Daniel*, p. 169.
57. Fowles, *Maggot*, p. 237.
58. I am indebted for this point to Bruce Woodcock, *Male Mythologies: John Fowles and Masculinity* (Brighton, Harvester, 1984). The tenor of my discussion of gender owes a good deal to this first-rate book.
59. Fowles, *French*, pp. 16–17, 138, 151, 139.
60. Ibid., pp. 24, 50, 417.
61. Ibid., pp. 155, 393–4.
62. Ibid., pp. 16, 128, 177, 61, 11, 152, 451, 148, 127, 128, 129.
63. Ibid., pp. 67, 61, 11, 63.
64. Ibid., pp. 104, 290.
65. Fowles, *Daniel*, pp. 646–7, 603, 611.
66. Fowles, *French*, pp. 79, 186.
67. Ibid., pp. 472, 477, 479.
68. Woodcock, *Male*, p. 12.
69. Fowles, *Aristos*, p. 157.
70. Ibid., pp. 157, 158, 90.
71. Harriet Taylor, 'Enfranchisement of Women', *Collected Works of John Stuart Mill*, Vol. 21, *Essays on Equality, Law, and Education*, ed. John M. Robson (Toronto: Toronto University Press, 1984), pp. 393–416, at p. 400.
72. John Stuart Mill, *The Subjection of Women*, ed. Mary Warnock (London: J. M. Dent, 1986), p. 273.
73. Taylor, 'Enfranchisement', p. 406.
74. Fowles, *French*, p. 107. For a critique of Sartre along these lines, see Iris Murdoch, *Sartre: Romantic Rationalist* (London: Chatto and Windus, 1987).
75. Fowles, *Aristos*, pp. 7, 10.
76. Fowles, *French*, pp. 305–6.
77. Matthew Arnold, *Culture and Anarchy*, ed. J Dover Wilson (Cambridge: Cambridge University Press, 1988), p. 6.
78. Fowles, *French*, p. 306.
79. Forster, *Two Cheers*, p. 81.
80. Matthew Arnold, 'The Function of Criticism at the Present Time', *Selected Prose of Matthew Arnold*, ed. P. J. Keating (Cambridge: Cambridge University Press, 1978), pp. 146–7.
81. Fowles, *Daniel*, p. 99.
82. Arnold, *Culture*, p. 70.
83. Fowles, 'Interview', p. 468.
84. Fowles, *Daniel*, p. 104; Fowles, *Aristos*, p. 111.
85. Raymond Williams, *Culture and Society, 1780–1950* (Hammondsworth: Penguin, 1963).
86. Arnold, *Culture*, p. 121.
87. Fowles, *Aristos*, p. 9; Fowles, 'Interview', p. 468; Fowles, *Daniel*, p. 337, 412.
88. Fowles, *Daniel*, pp. 278–9.

6

Feminist Critical Fictions

History has in recent years emerged as a contested terrain within feminist social critique. Unsurprisingly, debates have focused as much on theory and methodology as on specific areas of empirical research. Of particular note has been the emphasis placed by post-structuralist historians on the discursive formations through which objects of enquiry are constructed. Foucauldian historians such as Joan Wallach Scott, for example, stress not only that questions around issues of gender have hitherto played a minor role in the study of history, but also that these questions cannot simply be tacked onto existing historiographical models. For Scott, the attempt by early second-wave feminists to focus attention on the lives of women, which had previously been marginal to the discipline, was compromised because they failed to theorize the reasons for which such marginalization took place. Their additions to the domain of history, however valuable they were, remained mired in a positivist conception of it that resulted in an impasse. Writers like Scott insist that the discipline of history and the academic apparatus that sustains it need to be reconceptualized if issues such as gender, subjectivity and sexuality are to become objects of study. Scott thus promotes a practice that focuses on the way that history constructs its subject matter and produces particular knowledge regimes. Her goal is to study 'the variable and contradictory meanings attributed to sexual difference, to the political processes by which those meanings are developed and contested, to the instability and malleability of the categories "women" and "men", and to the ways those categories are articulated in terms of one another, although not consistently or in the same way every time'. By writing a form of metahistory, she aims to shatter the presuppositions according to which history has suppressed the problematic of gender.[1]

This approach to history is indebted to Foucault's concept of genealogy: 'a form of history which can account for the constitution of knowledges, discourses, domains of objects etc., without having to make reference to a subject which is either transcendental in relation to the field of events or runs in its empty sameness throughout the course of history'.[2] The anti-essentialism of Foucault's position recommends it to feminists who consider that terms such as sex, gender, nature, man, and woman do not denote categories that are givens but disclose discursive formations that require explanation. Feminists who concentrate on the deployment of such categories invariably stress their historicity and their polyvalence, refusing to reduce heterogeneity to sameness. Luce Irigaray points out that she is not interested in elaborating a theory of 'woman', for example, since 'in a woman('s) language, the concept as such would have no place'.[3] Gayatri Chakravorty Spivak argues that 'since there is no discursive continuity among women, the prime task is situational anti-sexism, and the recognition of the heterogeneity of the field, instead of positing some kind of woman's subject, women's figure, that kind of stuff'.[4] The notion of a universal patriarchy, whose oppressive functions are everywhere the same, is similarly rejected. For Judith Butler, 'genealogy investigates the political stakes in designating as an *origin* and *cause* those identity categories that are in fact the *effects* of institutions, practices, discourses with multiple and diffuse points of origin'.[5]

The displacement of a monolithic category such as 'women', now seen as a heuristic construct, suggests not that feminism loses its point but that it becomes more differentiated, since it is acknowledged that 'women' are traversed by a wide range of intersecting determinants such as age, class, ethnic and family background, region, religion, and politics.[6] Such differentiation calls the concept of *écriture féminine* into question, for this notion depends on a view of women as a relatively homogeneous category. Rita Felski thus attacks theories of *écriture féminine* on the grounds that the connection they posit between feminism and fluid, polysemic, diffuse, open-ended forms of 'experimental' writing is arbitrary. For Felski, the 'phallo-centric' language that such writing ostensibly disrupts itself needs to be theorized in a nuanced way; instead of being hypostatized as a seamless and abstract entity, it needs to be seen in terms of the multiple discourses through which social reality is articulated and contested. Felski considers that 'there exists no necessary relationship between feminism and experimental form, and that a text can thus be defined as feminist only insofar as its content or the context of its reception promote such a reading'.[7] Terry Lovell makes much the same point: 'Feminism does not carry imperatives as to form. Feminist intervention is possible and necessary at all levels of cultural production, and in most genres'.[8]

What is the significance of this for the work of Angela Carter and Sara Maitland? I want to suggest that Carter and Maitland both eschew the notion of a 'woman's language' in favour of a form of feminist fictional critique that takes socially produced discourses as its target. For them, to invert a sentence of Felski's, the text's 'subversive significance' lies 'in its critical distance from the real', and not 'in its ruptures of semantic and syntactic order'.[9] Like the post-structuralist feminist historians with which I began this chapter, they focus on the social construction of categories such as gender, sexuality and identity. Carter considers writing as a woman to be 'part of the slow process of decolonialising our language and our basic habits of thought'.[10] Her preferred strategy is to contest those habits of thought by rewriting the stories and myths that have been central to Western conceptions of gender. She describes herself as being 'in the demythologising business', explaining that she focuses on culturally dominant accounts in order to make them implode upon themselves: 'I am all for putting new wine into old bottles, especially if the pressure of the new makes the old bottles explode'.[11] Maitland, whose work resembles Carter's, also challenges the discourses that have construed gender in ways that oppress women. But she explicitly rejects the concept of a woman's language, replacing it with the notion of a woman's discourse. Writing from a socialist-feminist standpoint, she considers that literary works should be 'vehicles of social revolution'.[12] But whereas Carter is resolutely secular, Maitland sets up a dialogue between feminism and theology by focusing on biblical texts, particularly those that sanction and promote institutional androcentrism. Her fictional mode thus owes as much to the work of theologians such as Phyllis Trible, whose *Texts of Terror* re-examines the appalling treatment of women in certain biblical narratives, as it does to the work of Carter, whose reworking of myths, fairy tales, and genres made a good deal of Maitland's own writing possible.[13]

Although Carter and Maitland both engage in critical rewriting, there are key differences between their approaches to the question of gender. One way of thinking about these differences is suggested by Elizabeth Grosz's distinction between two ways of conceptualizing the body: as an 'inscriptive' entity, which is construed as 'a *social*, public body' that 'is marked, scarred, transformed, and written upon or constructed by the various regimes of institutional, discursive, and nondiscursive power as a particular kind of body'; or as a 'lived body', which is seen to start with a 'body schema' that it internalizes, ultimately enabling the subject to acquire 'an underlying sense of unity beneath the disparate, heterogeneous sensations it experiences'. Whereas the first of these models 'conceives the body as a surface on which social law, morality, and values are inscribed, the second refers largely to the lived experience of the body'.[14] Although such distinctions are always simplistic, I would suggest that Carter's and Maitland's representations of identity loosely correspond to Grosz's schema. Carter's deconstruction of cultural codes depends upon her depiction of characters as intertextual ciphers, who are quite literally put together out of bits and pieces of other writings. Maitland's novels are basically realist in tenor, and although they contain mythic elements, they focus in detail on the lived experiences of her central protagonists. Whereas Desiderio, Eve/lyn, and Fevvers are over-determined and deliberately 'flat' metafictional constructs, Liz, Anna and Karen are presented as 'round' human characters whose struggles are meant to arouse the reader's empathy.[15]

These differences in style affect not only these writers' representations of gender but also the form that their subversions take. Carter's work, I suggest, displays a persistent tension between carnival and the everyday, between magical fantasy and rational critique. Her novels draw attention to the limitations of a parodic and carnivalesque narrative mode by stressing that linguistic excess must be coupled with hard-headed political analysis. In contrast to those critics who read *The Infernal Desire Machines of Dr Hoffman* (1972) in Freudian or Lacanian terms, I see it as engaged in a dialogue with Plato's *Republic,* and argue that many of the concerns it raises spill over into *The Passion of New Eve* (1977), *Nights at the Circus* (1984) and *Wise Children* (1991). Maitland's novels, particularly *Virgin Territory* (1985), engage in a strategy of reclamation. They recover women's experiences, focusing on modes of knowing that have been lost or deformed. *Virgin Territory* explores one woman's attempt to free herself from the subjugated position to which her internalized religious values have consigned her. Her emancipation comes when she rejects the authority of the Church Fathers who refuse to grant her autonomy and, in a strategy that recalls Irigaray's work, starts to think through her various mothers, thereby creating an oppositional matriarchal genealogy.

Angela Carter

The strategy of rewriting has become all too familiar in recent years, but Angela Carter is significant because of the awareness with which she walks the tightrope between carnivalesque fantasy and rational critique. For all her Rabelaisian humour and linguistic exuberance – perhaps the most immediately noticeable features of her writing – she is conscious of their limitations. Thus she builds into her novels a searching examination of her own *modus operandi*, which acknowledges the boundaries to her literary subversions and asks hard questions about the political efficacy of her narrative strategies. This is especially the case with *The Infernal Desire Machines of Doctor Hoffman*, *The Passion of New Eve*, and *Nights at the Circus*, which mark a shift in Carter's writing toward a more theoretically explicit form of critical fiction. In *Hoffman*, Carter responds obliquely to Plato's challenge to the poets to offer a defence of their art; the novel explores what is lost by strict adherence either to ascetic rationalism or to bachanalian eroticism. *New Eve* and *Nights*, in turn, confront in different ways the problem of gender; the former describes an apocalyptic moment that destroys fixed conceptions of male and female identity, whereas the latter rewrites history as utopia, envisaging the closing of the last century as the opening of a brave new feminist world.

Each of these novels has a distinctive tone and set of concerns, but they share a hostility to binary thinking and reveal structural similarities. All three texts break down dichotomies such as male/female, order/chaos, reason/passion, and exploit the ambiguous space that opens up between them. In *Hoffman*, Albertina explains that her father 'worked in that shadowy land between the thinkable and the thing thought of', precisely the terrain where Carter should be located.[16] Liminal states, thresholds, margins – all these surface again and again in Carter's work because they undermine intellectual certainties, thereby providing her with a point of entry for her own cultural critique. But liminality also serves a structural function in these texts, for each is organized around protagonists who undergo rites of passage which are inseparable from the experience of marginality. All three novels offer picaresque variants of quest narratives; uproot their protagonists from stable environments, placing them on hazardous roads where they face various ordeals; and situate them in inhospitable regions – jungle (*Hoffman*), desert (*New Eve*), Siberian wastes (*Nights*) – where their experiences erase their former identities. These structural parallels are reminiscent of Victor Turner's description of rites of passage in *The Ritual Process*. Turner identifies three stages to such rites – separation, experience of the limen, aggregation. He argues that liminality, which is 'betwixt and between the positions assigned and arrayed by law, custom, convention, and ceremonial', dissolves social boundaries. The neophyte in liminality, who is a critic of 'closed or structured societies', must undergo 'ordeals and humiliations, often of a grossly physiological character' in order to become 'a *tabula rasa*, a blank slate'. Liminality, reliant on myths, symbols, rituals and art, facilitates 'periodical reclassifications of reality and man's relationship to society, nature, and culture'.[17]

The parallels between the trajectory of Carter's narratives and Turner's account of social transitions in pre-literate cultures are clear, as are the novelist's reasons for exploiting this anthropological material – it allows her to contest hegemonic ideologies within her own culture. But such a strategy is strewn with pitfalls. To begin with, it encourages a writing that veers close to a form of contemporary myth or allegory; because it may imply that cultures very different from Carter's own are isomorphic with it, such writing risks reinscribing at a different level the very essentialism it elsewhere rejects. Another potential difficulty arises out of the focus on liminality itself, for liminality is by definition transitional and should lead somewhere. In Turner's model, for example, separation and marginality are followed by aggregation, a reincorporation into the social group. Given Carter's oppositional stance, this form of closure, which threatens prematurely to resolve social contradictions on an imaginative plane, is problematic for her; by the same token, to remain in the world of the limen or the carnivalesque world-turned-upside-down is to invert power structures within a given realm of discourse but to offer no way of changing those structures and moving beyond them. Part of my task in this chapter is to show how Carter's work circumvents these difficulties.

Carter's hostility to myth is well-known. In *The Sadeian Woman* (1979) it is defined as 'consolatory nonsense', attacked for trafficking in 'false universals', and accused of relying on archetypes which conceal 'that relationships between the sexes are determined by history and by the historical fact of the economic dependence of women upon men'.[18] She considers herself, as already noted, to be 'in the demythologising business'.[19] But much of her own work, however hostile to myth, partakes of its attributes: a fabulistic and timeless quality (*Hoffman*); a rejection of one kind of mythical language only to substitute it by another (*New Eve*); an emblematic conception of character (*New Eve* and *Nights*); and an allegorical approach to narrative (*Nights*). Is there then a contradiction between *what* Carter's novels say about myth and the *way* they say it? Does Carter's use of fantasy, fairy tale, and magic realism trap her in the despised mythic role of an 'occult priestess' who is 'allowed to speak but only of things that male society does not take seriously', who 'can hint at dreams . . . can even personify the imagination; but . . . only because [she] is not rational enough to cope with reality'?[20] The problem is hardly negligible, for as Terry Lovell points out, non-realist writing frequently 'connotes "not to be taken seriously". It licenses escape, fantasy, pleasure'.[21]

I want to argue that Carter maintains her balance on the tightrope between fantasy and rationalism by at once employing a fabulistic mode and drawing attention to its limits. Each of the novels I discuss uses liminality or carnival to challenge specific targets, either disrupting them from within, as do Hoffman and Mother, or ridiculing their pretensions through the laughter and eroticism of the grotesque body, as does Fevvers. But at the same time, each exposes the limits to the critique it offers by showing that fantasy must be attended by analysis and by providing deliberately aporetic endings that refuse closure. Carter's chosen style enacts what her novels explore: the impossibility of choosing between reason and desire, or between abstract disengagement and sensuous involvement, without serious loss. Carter's novels acknowledge the benefits conferred by the intellect but, by refusing the closure represented by Turner's aggregation, they invite their readers to share in the Keatsian 'wild surmise' with which she closed *The Magic Toyshop*.

The Infernal Desire Machines of Dr Hoffman works on many levels, but I want to focus primarily on its response to Plato's negative view of the poets in the *Republic*. That Carter has the *Republic* in mind is clear: the novel describes a city-state run on rational principles by a kind of Philosopher-King, the ascetic Minister; the city is under threat from Hoffman, who is 'waging a massive campaign against human reason itself' and desires 'a regime of total liberation'; the besieged city tries 'to keep what [is] outside, out, and what [is] inside, in';[22] and the subsequent conflict between Hoffman and the Minister, representatives of unfettered desire and disengaged thought respectively, replays the Platonic conflict between the appetitive and the rational parts of the soul.[23] The figure of Desiderio, caught between two equally intransigent opponents, eventually moves beyond the dichotomous choice they propose, embracing a position that is closer to the Plato of the *Phaedrus* than of the *Republic*.

In the *Republic* Plato appears to oscillate between two conceptions of literature: on the one hand, it is so trivial as to be hardly worth discussing; on the other hand, it is supremely important (because it can corrupt) and must be subservient to the dictates of a philosophically conceived morality.[24] Plato seems to veer from the view that literature is outside the moral realm altogether to the view that it directly competes with philosophy's truth-claims and is therefore its most dangerous rival. In *The Laws*, for example, the Athenian responds as follows to the poets' request that they be allowed entry into the state:

> [W]e are poets like yourselves, composing in the same genre, and your competitors as artists and actors in the finest drama, which true law alone has the natural power to 'produce' to perfection. . . . So don't run away with the idea that we shall ever blithely allow you to set up stage in the market-place and bring on your actors whose fine voices will carry further than ours. Don't think we'll let you declaim to women and children and the general public, and talk about the same practices as we do but treat them differently – indeed, more often than not, so as virtually to contradict us.[25]

The battle-lines could not be drawn more clearly. The poet competes with the philosopher, threatening to drown out his voice and to sway the innocent from the path of virtue and law. Most disturbing of all, however, the poet – like the rhapsode in the *Ion*, the rhetor in the *Gorgias*, and the sophist in the *Sophist* – lacks real knowledge; his appeal is to the lowest segment of the soul, to the irrational desires. Philosophy and law promise to subjugate these unruly appetites and to teach them their place in a carefully elaborated hierarchy of values; poetry and the arts risk giving them a primacy in human affairs that they do not deserve and cannot sustain without leading the state into chaos.

In *Hoffman*, this conflict finds its counterpart in the battle between the austere Minister and the diabolical Doctor. They stand diametrically opposed to one another: on one side reason, philosophy, law, unity, structure, restraint; on the other side desire, imagination, anarchy, anti-structure, freedom. The Minister is 'not a man but a theorem, clear, hard, unified and harmonious'. He is an analogue of the city, representing 'the grand totality of [its] resistance'. His guiding light is reason and his 'only weapon in the fight is inflexible rationalism'. His ascetic conception of the 'perfectly symmetrical' state is almost a parody of the Platonic republic: 'It has the architechtonic structure of music, a symmetry imposed upon it in order to resolve a play of tensions which would disrupt order but without which order is lifeless. In this serene and abstract harmony, everything moves with the solemnity of the absolutely predictable'.[26] Hoffman, in contrast, is described as 'a poet' whose aim is 'to render the invisible visible'. He proliferates 'images along the obscure and controversial borderline between the thinkable and the unthinkable' in order to release the liberatory power of desire.[27] The difference between the two figures is philosophical. Whereas the Minister aspires to an epistemological certitude that can be mathematically grounded, Hoffman seeks to dissolve all rational procedures in the heady wines fermented by the imagination. When the Minister renounces the Doctor he does so in Platonic language, describing him as 'a forger' who 'has passed off upon us an entire currency of counterfeit phenomena'.[28] It is for this reason that he orders all mirrors to be smashed. The poet, a shape-shifting, mercurial figure, is a threat to the legally constituted state because the multiple 'lawless images' he disseminates through mirrors contest its account of reality: 'Since mirrors offer alternatives, the mirrors had all turned into fissures or crannies in the hitherto hard-edged world of here and now and through these fissures came slithering sideways all manner of amorphous spooks'.[29]

The Minister and Hoffman are locked into a rigid dualism – reason and philosophy versus desire and imagination. It is Desiderio who is able to go beyond this dichotomy. Desiderio is little more than a cipher culled from numerous literary sources; he is a disappointed Platonist who shares the Minister's admiration for perfect stasis but believes it to be unattainable; he is a *fin-de-siècle* Decadent straight out of Huysmans' *A Rebours* (his name also recalls Théophile Gautier's *Fortunio* (1837)); he is a disillusioned lover, a 'man without much passion' who yet desires passion, like Ford Madox Ford's hapless Dowell; and, like Eve/lyn in *New Eve* and Walser in *Nights*, he is Turner's neophyte, an outcast, who goes on the road only to undergo numerous ordeals.[30] Initially a passive observer of Hoffman's guerrilla warfare, Desiderio is dragooned into service against him because he is an unimpressionable, blank figure. But as a result of the experiences that he undergoes he is enabled to see through the debilitating dichotomy of lawlessness and moralism.

Of particular significance here are his love for Hoffman's daughter Albertina (modelled in turn on Proust's Albertine) and his meeting with the Count and his servant Lafleur, thinly disguised versions of the Marquis de Sade and his valet Latour. Albertina signifies passion; she awakens the somnolent Desiderio, inflaming him with desire. Just as her father's hetero-geneous iconography offers alternatives to the uniformity upheld by the city, she introduces Desiderio to undreamt-of aspects of his own identity. He and she are like two 'disseminating mirrors' that 'reflect each other' and multiply images 'without end'. These multiplying images, products of a reciprocal gaze, invite the reconstruction of the self, which is portrayed as a shifting, variable entity: 'In the looking glass of her eyes, I saw reflected my entire being whirl apart and reassemble itself innumerable times'. But whereas Albertina hints at the benign effects of Hoffman's worldview, the Count discloses its malignant consequences. In his case the complete liberation of desire leads to an all-devouring egotism in search of ever more refined ways of satisfying his appetites. A grotesque narcissist, he denies the existence of the other because 'his lusts always blind[ ] him completely to anything but his own sensations'. Although Desiderio is shaken out of his torpor by his passion for Albertina, he rejects the Count's extreme expression of a Hoffmanesque libertinism. In a typically Sadeian bordello, the various manifestations 'of every imaginable warped desire' are to him 'nothing but malicious satires upon eroticism' and provoke only 'laughter and revulsion'.[31] Carter's words in *The Sadeian Woman* are apposite here: 'Sexuality, in this estranged form, becomes a denial of a basis of mutuality, of the acknowledgement of equal rights to exist in the world, from which any durable form of human intercourse can spring'.[32]

The contrast between the Count and Albertina is central to the novel, for the relationship between the latter and Desiderio suggests that Eros may be energizing without being destructive. It helps to break down the assumption that the Minister and Hoffman offer a straightforward choice between morality and licentiousness. Desiderio himself at times conceives of the choice in such stark terms, lamenting at one point that he has 'the casting vote between a barren yet harmonious calm and a fertile yet cacophonous tempest'. Yet although he ultimately sides with the forces of order, he is aware of what has thus been lost, and this sense of loss, which permeates the novel, becomes as much its subject as all that has gone before. Desiderio grasps that Hoffman and the Minister are *doppelgänger* who refuse to acknowledge the existence of what they repress, each manifesting the very qualities he despises in the other. In his battle with Hoffman the Minister becomes a 'witch-doctor', whereas his opponent is 'triple-refined Mind in person'.[33] Desiderio must choose, but he desires neither option because both are, at a deeper level, flip-sides of the same coin: totalitarianism.

Desiderio eventually sides with the Minister, destroying both Hoffman and Albertina. But the text refuses to sanction this choice. It opts for an aporetic form of closure that undermines his decision. First, the novel thwarts reader expectations that its protagonist's actions represent a 'resolution' of the text's dilemma: 'Those are the dreary ends of the plot. Shall I tie them up or shall I leave them unravelled?'.[34] Secondly, the novel portrays the old Desiderio as an enervated figure who scorns the 'gentle contentment' enjoyed by the city as a result of his decision and who mourns the consequent death of desire. He thinks less of the benefits conferred by an ordered society than of the price it exacts.[35] The young, acting Desiderio stands to the old, narrating Desiderio rather as the Plato of the *Republic* stands to the Plato of the *Phaedrus*. Whereas in the *Republic* Plato is deeply suspicious of poetry, in the *Phaedrus* he seems to acknowledge that it can express truths inaccessible to dialectic and that this means the latter's claims to knowledge must be reappraised.[36] Furthermore, his earlier view, in the *Ion*, for example, that poets are in the grip of an irrational possession that should be derided, is modified to one that accords such inspiration a high degree of respect. In the *Phaedrus* Socrates sees the frenzy that creates poetry as springing from a divine source.[37] Like Plato, the elderly Desiderio's conception of the respective claims made by reason and desire, soul and body, philosophy and poetry, is more discriminating. By acting 'for the common good' he has contributed to a social stasis that has killed those passions that 'could shine more brightly than a thousand suns'. He is the 'earth and water' that extinguishes Albertina's 'air and fire', but, unlike the Minister, he refuses to suppress his knowledge that '[r]eason cannot produce the poetry disorder does'. At night, Albertina disturbs his dreams, for Hoffman's amorphous spooks have vouchsafed him a glimpse 'of an alternate world in which all the objects are emanations of a single desire'.[38]

The elegiac tone that haunts *Hoffman*'s closing pages resists a dualistic conception of reality that can only pit philosophy and poetry against one another. *The Passion of New Eve* and *Nights at the Circus* attack another binary opposition, that of male/female, in order to propose a more complex view of human identity. Both texts criticize traditional accounts of gender analytically but couch their critiques in a form of fantasy. *New Eve* is explicit about its aims:

> Our external symbols must always express the life within us with absolute precision; how could they do otherwise, since that life has generated them? Therefore we must not blame our poor symbols if they take forms that seem trivial to us, or absurd, for the symbols themselves have no control over their own fleshly manifestations, however paltry they may be; the nature of our life alone has determined their forms.
>
> A critique of these symbols is a critique of our lives.
> Tristessa. Enigma. Illusion. Woman? Ah![39]

The novel confronts the cultural iconography of our time, suggesting that its representations of gender are deceptions, shadow dances behind which lie complex structures of power. It not only destroys dominant myths of feminine and masculine but also disdains the attempt to replace them at one stroke by a technological version of divine fiat. In *New Eve*, myths are first replaced by other myths, but ultimately all myths are displaced by history – after the apocalypse, Year One and a move out of myth into time. *Nights*, in contrast, is an exuberantly utopian text, brimming with humour and optimism. A fantastic allegory, it reverses the dire predictions of early twentieth-century writers such as Max Nordau and Oswald Spengler, imagining the new century as the threshold to a communitarian society. Whereas *New Eve* shifts from myth to history, *Nights* remains in the realm of the imaginary – it is a narrative that 'does not belong' to 'authentic history'.[40] It employs the language of carnival to overturn existing social hierarchies, adapting Bakhtin's grotesque realism to its own purposes. If *New Eve* insists on Blake's coexistence of contrarieties, evoking it through images of the hermaphrodite and the uroboros, then *Nights* offers a world-turned-upside-down, turning authority over to pigs, chimps, clowns, and fabulous bird-women who are neither fact nor fiction.

New Eve rewrites the biblical account of creation, focusing less on the details of Genesis than on its consequences. The novel's central protagonist, another of Carter's overdetermined ciphers, is at once a male egotist who must be reborn, a modern counterpart to the Bible's Eve, and a secular surrogate for Christ who undergoes kenosis in the desert and subsequently experiences a technological version of the Passion. He is also a parody of masculinity, just as Leilah is a parody of stereotypical male fantasies about women. Like Desiderio, Evelyn is an anti-hero on a quest. Initially an arch-misogynist, he is a casually brutal voyeur who provides a classic example of the objectifying stare. A favourite occupation is watching Leilah watching herself in a mirror as she dons a grotesquely eroticized garb of femininity; she is the willing accomplice of her own fetishization, 'a perfect woman' because 'like the moon, she only gave reflected light'. In a text obsessed with the social construction of images (nursery tales, myths, religion, Hollywood, the mass media) and with their often pernicious effects, Evelyn's metamorphosis into new Eve entails less a biological transformation than a cultural one, for the experiences he undergoes, which lead him to disavow his earlier view of women as objects of desire and instruments of pleasure, are the result of misogynist violations of his person. Thus the subject, Evelyn, is punished by being turned into 'the object of all the unfocused desires that had ever existed in [his] own head'; is shown what happens when 'life parodie[s] myth, or be[comes] it'; and is purified by becoming 'a tabula erasa [sic.], a blank sheet, an unhatched egg'.[41]

It is not the surgical intervention by which Mother creates Eve out of Evelyn that transforms him but his experiences as a 'woman', most notably at the hands of the patriarchal Nietzschean, Zero, an exaggerated version of Evelyn's young self, and in his relation to Tristessa. Evelyn writes of Zero's sexual violence that it 'forced me to know myself as a former violator at the moment of my own violation'.[42] Tristessa, in turn, is the ultimate parody of male fantasies about women; a flawless cinematic illusion, s/he represents their literal embodiment as s/he is in fact a man masquerading as a woman. Tristessa is 'the sensuous fabrication of the mythology of the flea-pits' who has 'no ontological status, only an iconographic one'. Both Eve/lyn and Tristessa are thus hermaphrodites of sorts; at once male and female, they become non-gendered beings. The ambiguous gender identities of these two characters, one a 'man' cross-dressing as a 'woman', the other a 'man' trapped in a 'woman's' body by virtue of surgical intervention, suggests not only that sexual identities are amorphous but also that they are culturally inscribed. These are Grosz's bodies, '*machinic* organism[s] in which "components" can be altered, adjusted, removed, or replaced'.[43] The mock wedding between Tristessa and Eve/lyn is thus one in which they simultaneously take up 'masculine' and 'feminine' subject positions, since both are 'the bride, both the groom'. The wedding is witnessed by a gallery of haphazardly assembled waxwork stars whose sexual identities are equally confused, for 'Ramon Navarro's head was perched on Jean Harlow's torso and had one arm from John Barrymore Junior, the other from Marilyn Monroe and legs from yet other donors'. And when Tristessa and Eve/lyn make love, they people 'this immemorial loneliness with all we had been, or might be, or had dreamed of being, or had thought we were – every modulation of the selves we now projected upon each other's flesh, selves – aspects of being, ideas – that seemed, during our embraces, to be the very essence of our selves'. Despite its lyricism, the text almost breaks down under the difficulty of evoking the labile nature of sexual identity, admitting finally that it has no answers to the questions it has posed:

> Masculine and feminine are correlatives which involve one another. I am sure of that – the quality and its negation are locked in necessity. But what the nature of masculine and the nature of feminine might be, whether they involve male and female, if they have anything to do with Tristessa's so long neglected apparatus or my own factory fresh incision and engine-turned breasts, that I do not know. Though I have been both man and woman, still I do not know the answer to these questions. Still they bewilder me.

The rigid demarcations between masculine and feminine sanctioned by various mythologies are in this text dissolved as decisively as Tristessa's glass mausoleum, 'that hall of mirrors' in which Evelyn has lived his 'whole life' is smashed.[44] *New Eve* thus dramatizes Judith Butler's claim that if 'one is not born, but rather *becomes* a woman, it follows that *woman* itself is a term in process, a becoming, a constructing that cannot rightfully be said to originate or to end'.[45]

It is clear, however, that *New Eve* rejects the false universals posited by myth in favour of a contingent historicity. In 'The Language of Sisterhood' Carter claims that, 'since myth is more malleable than history', women rewrite it 'in order to accommodate [them]selves in the past'.[46] *New Eve* goes one step further; it suggests that myth needs to be abandoned altogether. Mother's attempt to control myth ultimately fails because history overtakes it. History proves 'too slippery for her to hold' and renders myth 'obsolete'. The language of myth is both redundant and pernicious. Perhaps symbols of 'Divine Virgins, Sacred Harlots and Virgin Mothers' once served a purpose, but now 'the gods are all dead' and women, formerly consigned to Blake's realm of ahistorical space, are urged to break through to his domain of historical time.[47]

The critique offered by *New Eve* leaves a problem: what to offer in place of that which has been rejected? *Nights at the Circus* responds to this question by participating in the creation of a new iconography. It offers a magical allegory of an alternative social world, which is represented by the circus and presided over by the Rabelaisian Fevvers, who is 'warts and all the female paradigm'.[48] The carnivalesque world of the circus demystifies and debunks the hierarchical social order to which it is marginal; like Sleary's circus in *Hard Times*, it offers a different set of values. Through numerous inversions, it emphasizes process over stasis, humour over seriousness, the body over the mind, and everywhere pits the unofficial against the official. Indeed, its controlling mode is that of inversion, evident in the portrayals of the bodily, gargantuan and vulgar Fevvers; the analytical and improbably learned Lizzie; the cowardly and emotionally weak Samson; the eminently malleable New Man, Walser; the aptly named Sybil, Colonel Kearney's porcine decision-maker; and the deceptively knowing chimps who eventually take over the circus.

In accordance with grotesque realism's comedic tactics, *Nights* is superbly parodic. Carter punctures male portentousness in an instant, as in the scene which sees Walser deliver Hamlet's 'What a piece of work is a man' soliloquy to an audience of studious apes, a performance accompanied by the Strong Man reaching orgasm 'in a torrent of brutish shrieks'. This kind of mockery is extended to a burlesque of literary models. Consider the following passage:

> 'And once the old world has turned on its axle so that the new dawn can dawn, then, ah, then! all the women will have wings, the same as I. This young woman in my arms, whom we found tied hand and foot with the grisly bonds of ritual, will suffer no more of it; she will tear off her mind forg'd manacles, will rise up and fly away. The dolls' house doors will open, the brothels will spill forth their prisoners, the cages, gilded or otherwise, all over the world, in every land, will let forth their inmates singing together the dawn chorus of the new, the transformed – '
>
> 'It's going to be more complicated than that.' interpolated Lizzie. 'This old witch sees storms ahead, my girl. When I look to the future, I see through a glass, darkly. You improve your analysis, girl, and then we'll discuss it.'
>
> But her daughter swept on, regardless, as if intoxicated with vision.

A tissue of quotations, this passage uses Bakhtin's punning *grammatica jocosa* both to invest other writers' words with new meanings and to mock their pretensions to seriousness. The most obvious model here is Joyce; Fevvers is another Icarus, and in the previous paragraph, underlining the links with Joyce, she has alluded to Lizzie's years of 'exile and cunning'. The passage above parodies the priggish Stephen's scholastic account of his aesthetic theories in *Portrait*, Lizzie playing the ironizing role of Cranly, reminding Fevvers that her Icarian euphoria will result in disaster if she does not temper it with rational critique. Like Stephen, Fevvers perceives herself as having a 'prophetic role', but her weapons are those of mockery and laughter rather than of silence and cunning. Fittingly, then, *Nights* ends on this note, with Fevvers' joyous guffaws spreading across the globe in 'a spontaneous response to the giant comedy that endlessly unfolded beneath it, until everything that lived and breathed, everywhere, was laughing'.[49]

Carter's use of carnival – introduced as early as *The Magic Toyshop* – might seem a risky strategy. Critics of carnival have argued that it is often conceived in an essentializing way, as innately oppositional and subversive; that it relies on a nostalgic notion of 'real community'; that it often reinforces existing power structures because it is a licensed form of release from social restraint; and that its transformations take place within certain kinds of discourse but are unable to challenge the hierarchy of discourses, which comfortably contains their apparent subversiveness.[50] I have suggested that throughout her œuvre Carter walks a tightrope between carnivalesque fantasy and rational analysis, that her preferred mode *is* fabulistic but never exclusively so. I want to underline this point by showing that in the texts here examined – and in *Wise Children* (1991), her last novel – Carter reveals that she shares these critics' reservations and exploits her narrative mode's limitations.

That Carter is at times sentimental about the marginal groups she describes is hard to deny. The sentimentality is evident in the portrayal of the circus in *Nights* and in the nostalgia for the traditions of vaudeville that have been superseded by the mass media in *Wise Children*. In both texts, however, as well as in *Hoffman* and *New Eve*, Carter sets clear boundaries to the liberatory possibilities her texts release. She is, in fact, something of an inverted Platonist, for she is primarily committed to the literary imagination but supplements it with analysis and critique. If Plato recognizes that dialectic needs to be supported by poetry, then Carter recognizes that literature requires help from critique. For all their inventiveness, vitality and humour, each of the works discussed above invites the reader to question its own procedures. *Hoffman* undermines the decision reached by Desiderio, refuses closure, and emphasizes the futility of a simple dichotomy between the free play of desire and the rigid control of reason; the text demands that both be seen in a more discriminating way. *New Eve* is similarly open-ended. It employs a kind of contemporary mythology to expose the workings of older myths, but then supplants both forms by suggesting that the uses to which myth can be put are strictly limited; its archetypal essentialism is to be challenged by a contingent historicism. *Nights*, finally, adopts a carnivalesque mode that undermines gender hierarchies but also deflates its own messianism, using Lizzie as the *eiron* forever reprimanding Fevvers' *alazon*.

In *Wise Children*, the subversive world of carnival and the transformative power of the grotesque body, symbolized by that ever-expanding Falstaffian, Perry, is more firmly problematized. In the scene where the 100-year-old Perry and the 75-year-old Nora threaten to 'fuck the house down', to destroy the entire social order lorded over by the centenarian patriarch Melchior, the novel pulls back: 'But such was not to be. There are limits to the power of laughter and though I may hint at them from time to time, I do not propose to step over them'. These limits have already been signalled in the text, when Nora comments that as a young woman she had not 'lived in history' but had sought only 'the moment' because '[t]omorrow never comes', and when she admits that she 'never listened to the news in those days'. Carter later reels in this lightly thrown out line when she has Nora reflect on the significance of her love-making with Perry:

> While we were doing it, everything seemed possible, I must say. But that is the illusion of the act. Now I remember how everything seemed possible when I was doing it, but as soon as I stopped, not, as if fucking itself were the origin of illusion.
> 'Life's a carnival,' he said. He was an illusionist remember.
> 'The carnival's got to stop, some time, Perry,' I said: 'You listen to the news, that'll take the smile off your face.'
> 'News? What news?'

Perry, 'not so much a man, more of a travelling carnival', is 'incorrigible'. Nora, however, recognizes that everyday reality, in the form of 'tomorrow' or 'the news', will always succeed that of the world-turned-upside-down.[51]

Angela Carter's narrative mode is, to borrow once more from Victor Turner, 'betwixt and between' fantasy and analysis, allegory and rationalism. Her texts are deliberately aporetic, not only because they refuse decisive forms of closure but also because they refuse to opt finally for one of these two discourses, thereby repressing the other. Carter's form neither implies that carnival and fantasy can suffice nor suggests that rationalism and critique be eschewed; rather, it urges a view of the novel as a composite form in which both kinds of discourse supplement one another, allowing the writer a fuller apprehension of reality. This very oscillation between two modes of cognition is a central aspect of Carter's search for truth. Peter Stallybrass and Allon White are surely correct to argue that carnival has become 'a common trope *within*' a 'particular site of discourse' and that only 'a challenge to the hierarchy of *sites* of discourse . . . carries the promise of politically transformative power'.[52] Carter's work makes a similar point through its double-voiced style. *Hoffman, New Eve, Nights* and *Wise Children* repeatedly warn their readers that, however inspiring submersion in the magical, fantastic, and carnivalesque may be, the play of 'holiday time', which permits mockery, will be followed by the reality of 'everyday', which demands praxis.

Sara Maitland

Sara Maitland's work is influenced as much by socialist-feminism as by revisionist theology. Her essay 'Futures in Feminist Fiction' (1989) explains a good deal about her fictional strategies. The essay, which intervenes in debates about *écriture féminine* and genre, explains why the much-vaunted 'Feminist Novel' seems never to have been written. For Maitland, any attempted answer to this question must consider 'what happens culturally and politically at large, as this will both inform the Women's Liberation Movement and inform the fictional genres within which we both read and write'. Her own view is that the direction national politics took in the 1980s has led to such a far-reaching loss of faith in socialism that those on the Left have fallen victim not so much to disillusionment as to disvisionment: 'We have to face the real possibility that through social circumstance we may now be in the process not of being *disillusioned*, but of being *disvisioned*: an act of violence, not therapy'. Whereas the former may be positive, in that it can provide therapeutic liberation from false ideals, the latter is damaging, since it dispossesses people of valid political aspirations. The distinction is significant for Maitland because she wants feminist writing to be driven by empowering visions: 'The futures of feminist fictions depend on whether there is any real content, any envisioning or transforming content, in the act of making public the products of the imagination'. In Maitland's view, feminist writing in the 1980s has not fulfilled the emancipatory imperative, but 'the failure of feminist fictions' should not be attributed to the Women's Movement alone but should be analysed in the broader context of this general social disvisionment.[53] Whereas women's writing in the 1970s (the period in which second-wave feminism took off in Britain and America) was suffused with optimism and was characterized by 'the belief that there is such a thing as a feminist fiction in the structural, formal, generic sense', in the recessionary 1980s it was either subsumed by other genres or splintered into various sub-genres.[54] Although much valuable work has been done, the hopes and aspirations of the 1970s have not come to fruition.

'Futures in Feminist Fiction' reveals a nostalgia for the 1970s and for an identifiable and culturally dominant feminist literary mode. As mentioned earlier, one of the immediate problems inherent in any attempt to elaborate an *écriture féminine* or 'the feminist novel' is that it tends to subsume difference into identity. Although Maitland argues that feminist writers have somehow failed to conjure up a decisive literary mode of their own, thereby invoking the idea of *écriture féminine*, her subsequent emphasis on genre and discourse suggests a way of circumventing such homogenization. In the latter part of her essay she eschews the concept of a woman's *language*, choosing to speak instead of a woman's *discourse* and to relate it to genre. Her choice of these two terms is deliberate; she uses them 'in absolute preference to the concept of a language of our own'. Carter, as we have seen, is deeply hostile to all mythic accounts of women, and Maitland is equally suspicious of their predilection for politically regressive constructions of gender. The concept of a woman's language is compromised by the kind of biological essentialism that Carter and Maitland both repudiate.[55] The concept of discourse, however, resists any such essentialism since it focuses on language's social dimension and stresses that language is inseparable from its use; that of genre, in turn, shifts emphasis onto the way that different literary forms can reinterpret and critically revise other modes of writing. Maitland's approach to feminist critical fiction through discourse and genre thus hints at a thoroughly historicized writing practice that makes calculated interventions within specific social and literary contexts. It also encourages a view of writing as an ongoing process (of dialogue and contestation, for example), which refuses the premature closure of unresolved conflicts. What Maitland calls 'being-in-engagement', leads to a kind of writing that does not succumb to the defeatism so easily produced by disvisionment but that (echoing Adrienne Rich) can 'make visionaries of us all . . . can re-vision us'.[56]

Maitland's texts combine realism with elements of fantasy and the supernatural in order to investigate the ways in which myths are culturally manifested and to disclose and confront their representations of gender. In *Arky Types* the character 'Sara' remarks that her rejection of most narrative modes leaves little '[e]xcept reclaiming the myths', explaining later that she does not want to recount well-known stories but to use them.[57] Reclamation and use entail Hutcheon's 'critical revision', of course, since the purpose behind such rewriting is to break free from earlier conceptions of gender as well as to transform them for strategic purposes in the present.[58] Crucial to this project is Maitland's articulation of the differences among women. But Maitland does not regard her exploration of women's heterogeneity as inimical to a search either for continuities between women's lives or for a sense of community that thrives as much on differences as on affinities. 'Requiem', a short story in *Weddings and Funerals*, discloses these concerns. It treats the particle/wave duality of light as a metaphor for the impossibility of doing justice to difference. 'Requiem' takes this duality as the point of departure for a dialogue between Sara, an authorial persona, and two early Christian martyrs, Perpetua and Felicity, with whom she wrestles because they 'resist' her twentieth-century preconceptions about them and her desire to 'use them for [her] own morally uplifting purposes'. Sara's insistence that the two martyrs' lives and fates are part of history and should be more widely known is met by Perpetua's demand that her story be retranslated. What is at stake here is not the translation from Latin into English vernacular but the hermeneutic problem of fusing the horizons between a contemporary feminist and a third-century martyr: 'The dialogue wavers, wavers and breaks up. It is nearly impossible. It is impossible to sustain. Our voices die away, battered by the differences of vision, of understanding, of time and space, the different knowings, the different timings and spacings'. The story refuses to be baulked by these insurmountable differences. It affirms community, without seeking to deny them: 'We are different. The gap may not be closed. She is dead. I am alive. We are sisters'. The story rejects the idea that 'woman' is a trans-historical category whose character traits remain more or less fixed. It acknowledges that the historical and cultural gap remains unbridged, but at the same time it affirms a solidarity with women of the past by virtue of certain shared experiences. In the words of Rowbotham, which close the story, this is an attempt to weave the 'threads and strands of long-lost experience into the present' and to rediscover 'the dimensions of female existence lost in the tangled half-memories of myth and dream'.[59]

Maitland's attitude to archetypes is not uniform. Whereas her works always deconstruct their ideological functions and effects, they also reinterpret them in order to suggest that they can be invested with new meanings. This is particularly the case with certain myths and biblical narratives. In *Daughter of Jerusalem*, for example, the main story taking place in the present is counterpointed by a series of biblical vignettes. No authorial gloss on these stories is provided; they simply conclude each chapter. Yet the interaction between the main narrative and these scriptural intertexts is productive. The novel's juxtaposition of two disparate narrative modes (modern fiction and ancient parable) and two traditions of thought (secular and religious) asks the reader to re-examine both. In keeping with Maitland's historicist approach to writing, the novel does not establish easy parallels between the past and the present. It focuses on the ways in which the bible has been interpreted so that it could be used against women, reinterpreting it in order to disrupt this strategy. The story of Deborah and Jael, which is a celebration of female power, works at the diegetic level by highlighting Liz's fury with Ian for beating her and warning of her capacity for vengeance, but at the same time establishes a wider historical and intertextual resonance:

> Back in the tent she does not hesitate: the weight of the hammer is with her now, the pointed stick is no longer alien but a part of her person. With her first stroke she breaks the skin, penetrates the bone, the point is finding its own pathway into the depths of the man. He groans once, unable to resist the strength of her stroke, she has heard that groan before. She goes berserk; long after it is necessary, bang, bang, bang, rhythmical, powerful she bangs, in and in; the blood and the flesh flow out over the sheepskin coverlet, over the pillow, she is delighted with her power, her strength. Bang, bang, bang. Her moment in history, her song, her story, her revenge.

The association of sex with violence in this passage not only recalls Bram Stoker's *Dracula*, reversing that text's bloody killing (and symbolic rape) of the female vampire, but also raises the issue of male violence against women. The reversal enacted in this passage, where Jael initially 'fondles the tent peg . . . stroking the pointed end, caressingly' but then turns it against Sisera in an ecstasy of murder, functions at once as a symbolic act of retribution on behalf of those women who have suffered male violence and as a personal message to her own husband, for when he 'sees what she has done he will be very, very frightened, of her, of her'.[60]

Maitland's polemical challenge to patristic interpretations of biblical texts is two-pronged: she re-examines the struggles and achievements of scriptural women with a contemporary eye; she attests the connection between knowledge and what Habermas terms 'human interests', thereby nailing her feminist colours to a hermeneutically conceived theological mast.[61] Her rereadings of biblical narratives turns them into empowering feminist parables, which reclaim parts of the tradition from a patriarchal dispensation.

A similar fusion of disparate modes characterizes *Virgin Territory*, which explores the internal spiritual struggle of a Catholic nun who finds herself unable to square her religious beliefs with her incipient feminist consciousness. The novel combines realism with supernaturalism; it is narrated from an omniscient and psychologically motivated point of view but weaves mythic, magical and spiritual elements into its narrative. *Virgin Territory* focuses on Anna's breakdown, which is precipitated by the rape of a fellow nun; given a year's sabbatical from her convent, she enters upon a journey of self-discovery during which she wrestles with her vocation, challenges patriarchal authority within the Church, and acknowledges her dormant sexuality.

Anna's internal conflict is dramatized through the opposition between the patristic account of male/female roles, which portrays them as biologically determined and scripturally sanctioned, and her own sense of identity, which leads her to reject the discourses that have hitherto defined her. Those discourses have ensured that, as a woman, she occupies a subordinate and largely submissive role within the Church. Anna's struggle represents a reworking of the ancient conflict between the body and the soul, which is enacted in the text by the different voices that torment her: on the one hand, the inchoate murmurings of the autistic child, Caro; on the other hand, the stern imperatives of the Church Fathers. For the Fathers, it is precisely women's bodily nature that renders them untrustworthy. They articulate a conception of womanhood that ensures its subordinate status, since they conceive the male as the paradigm model for humanity and the female as a defective 'other', as what Aquinas, following Aristotle, was to call a 'misbegotten male'; this belief, in turn, leads directly to the view that only men have been authorized to interpret the Church's canonical texts.[62] The Fathers' attacks on Anna's fallen condition are articulated in sexual terms: 'Your mind is not pure. Blessed are the pure in heart for they shall see God. You are filthy. You are muck. You are bad'.[63] Exaggerated though this invective sounds, it merely expresses in modern idiom what was frequently asserted by the early Church Fathers. Tertullian, for example, claimed that since 'the ignominy . . . of the first sin and the odium of bringing ruin upon mankind' belonged to woman, she should remember that God's judgement upon her 'endures even today' and with it 'endures [her] position of criminal at the bar of justice'.[64] The Fathers in *Virgin Territory* equate womanhood with sin in precisely this way: 'You are disgusting. You are a woman. You are bloody and bad'. And Anna has internalized this self-alienating conception of herself, as Karen, the woman she comes to love, is aware: 'she was attuned to . . . Anna's distance from her own body. As though inside the habit there was nothing there'.[65]

Anna starts to break free from the Church's negation of her sexual identity as a result of her love for Karen, the lesbian feminist who questions her vocation, and her work with Caro, the autistic child for whom she is a part-time physiotherapist. Karen challenges Anna on an intellectual (conscious) level, forcing her to acknowledge those areas of her experience that the Church has suppressed; Caro speaks to her on a more visceral (unconscious) level, inviting her to re-examine her entry into a patriarchal social order.[66] During Anna's dark night of the soul, it is Caro who is pitted against the Fathers. Whereas they seek to impose their patriarchal values on Anna by alternately threatening, wheedling and cajoling, Caro, who calls to Anna from the safety of her internal haven, urges her to protect her inner core from violation. The brain-damaged child has an overdetermined function in the novel; she can be seen to represent either the unconscious or the body (caro), which is opposed to Anna's (anima) emphasis on the spirit. Whichever interpretation one opts for, it is clear that Anna's sense of identity has been deformed by the Fathers' phallocentrism, which not only defines 'woman' negatively in relation to a male 'norm' but also arrogates to itself the symbolic power of generation.

Luce Irigaray has argued that androcentric culture is based not on patricide, as Freud argued, but on matricide, on the systematic denial of mothers as the 'foundation of the social order'.[67] Within this economy women are not only refused an autonomous corporeality but also socially constructed in such a way that they become the guardians of male corporeality, functioning as patriarchy's unconscious.[68] Elizabeth Grosz describes Irigaray's inversion of Freud as follows: 'Freud's concept provides a dazzling metaphor of women's simultaneously repressed/oppressed social position and the permanent possibilities of resistance – the threat the unconscious poses to civilisation in its symptomatic "return"'.[69] If Caro is conceived in these terms then she can be read as the unconscious that returns in order to refuse the role to which patriachy has assigned Anna. Consider the following passage, which introduces the autistic child:

> They had to put her on a table and work her limbs, trying to convert them from tail to legs, trying to make their movements conform to the movements of human beings. They were trying to pattern her, Anna felt, as she had been patterned into a good nun. Caro fought back. And Anna began to believe that she could hear the deep voice that was the centre of the child, that uttered and mumbled and growled. Not like the Fathers, a clarion from above, but something different altogether, a black quiet muttering that Anna had to listen to attentively to catch the individual words.

Caro functions as Anna's unconscious, gradually teaching her not only to see how she herself has been enculturated but also to develop modes of being and speaking that bypass the language of the Fathers. The helpless Caro is being given physical therapy that it is hoped will enable her to overcome her 'handicap'. But Caro refuses to surrender to the treatment. She asserts her otherness, resisting all attempts to translate it into sameness: 'I crept in and grew and flourished in the dark damp hole. It is wild. I do not want to come out'.[70] Caro's struggle becomes Anna's; her visible rejection of physical therapy leads Anna to confront the hidden coercion of which she herself has been a victim. Like Caro, she has been shaped to conform to an ideal of the human form that is imposed on her.

The conflict between the claims made on Anna by the Fathers and by Caro, as well as the autocratic manner in which the former 'name' reality whereas the latter implicitly questions it, is central to the text's own exploration of the relationship between language and power. The Fathers' voices disclose Anna's internalization of their values; their way of interpreting the world, their language, is imprinted on her mind. Through the process of socialization Anna has inculcated their spiritual worldview at the core of her being: 'Sr. Anna was Pallas Athene, the virgin created by the Fathers. A creation of the Fathers and virgin only because they like it that way. She was at the beck and call of the Fathers who ranted in her head, in her dreams and in her private spaces'.[71] The Fathers' power derives from their ability to colonize Anna's mind and to bring about her self-alienation. Unlike Eve/lyn, Desiderio, or Fevvers, Anna represents the 'lived body'; she has *internalized* a conception of the self that, although the product of an externally imposed theory of gender identity, has inscribed itself in her very innards, hence the Fathers' ability to speak to her from her most 'private spaces'.

The twin issues of identity and language are central to feminist critique. This is a point at which secular and religious traditions meet, for feminist theologians systematically focus on what Rosemary Radford Ruether calls 'the process of the critical naming of women's experience of androcentric culture'.[72] The issue of naming is crucial to *Virgin Territory*. Its importance is signalled when the text alludes to the opening of John's gospel: 'There was a great power in naming, calling things by name was the act of creation; the eternal Word naming the darkness and chaining it to light and form'. The allusion is significant because it signals a challenge not to language *per se* but to a specific discourse that has historically functioned in a certain way. The generative power metaphorically described by the gospeller has been appropriated by patriarchy, which, in Irigaray's words, 'superimposes upon the archaic world of the flesh a universe of language [langue] and symbols which cannot take root in it except as in the form of that which makes a hole in the bellies of women and in the site of their identity'.[73] But if the Fathers represent one mode of authoritative naming then Karen, who aids Anna in so many ways, represents another. In a bold move, Maitland suggests that beneath their mutually antagonistic conceptions of the world Karen and the Fathers reveal a will to power that is disturbingly similar; both trade in certainties and seek to impose those certainties on others: 'Anna knew now how she had never been able to answer Karen, never been free to contradict her; she had been powerless before Karen's naming of the universe; she had played Eve to Karen's Adam – it was not good in her but it was no better in Karen. Karen allowed space only for certainty, she took no account of tentativeness'. Learning from Caro, whose torment reflects her own, Anna searches for a 'discourse of her own', for a language of self-understanding that is marked by the absence of reductive certainties. By the novel's end she has rejected all three of the possible subject-positions offered to her by Caro, Karen, and the Fathers: retreat into that impossible space, the pre-oedipal unconscious; embracement of the 'truth' of the body in the form of lesbian sexuality; continuation as a virgin-nun, controlled by the Church.[74]

Two procedures are required if Anna is to free herself from the discourses that have entrapped her: firstly, she must escape others' naming of reality and name it for herself; secondly, she needs to see the numerous links between her experiences and those of other women. Although Caro's obduracy provides Anna with the strength to combat the Fathers, she cannot overcome them once and for all, as they are so integral a part of her identity. To be sure, Caro is a potent symbol of resistance: 'The power of the Fathers was everywhere manifest. There seemed, except in the muttered rumblings of Caro, little or no defence against it'. Yet the infant's interruptions are of limited efficacy, since the Fathers' control of religious discourse is the locus of their authority over women, as Anna recognizes: 'she ought not to have spoken, because words were the possession of the Fathers, and in using them she was dragged back into their power'. In order to escape the cognitive dissonance produced in her by alien linguistic codes, Anna retreats into an internal space:

> Inside her there is something silent. Silent, almost sullen. Stubborn, pig-headed. There comes a point, she discovers, where words become impossible, even dangerous; a point when all the words are taken over and belong to other people and you are left with none of your own. At that point you know that only sullenness will pay. . . . Caro knew and showed her that they can punish you, yell at you, cajole and tempt you, and even if they want to they can kill you. But in the end they cannot make you consent. They cannot make you obey. There comes a time when you just have to hunker down in a grim sullenness, not answer back, not try to explain, not respond.

This retreat into silence is potentially disastrous. As Mary Jacobus writes in a different context: 'Women face the choice: entry into culture on condition of submission to phallocentricity; refusal, and a reinscribing of the feminine as marginal madness or nonsense'.[75] But Anna's silence, her refusal of entry into culture, is only a first step. It is followed by renaming and then by the reconstruction of a suppressed matriarchal lineage that offers the possibility of new ways of knowing. In accordance with Maitland's position in 'Futures in Feminist Fiction', Anna does not step outside language but disrupts and reworks it from within. In a statement that doubles as a description of Maitland's own *modus operandi*, Anna outlines the nature of her challenge to the Fathers as follows: 'I shall use your power too, because I've served in your courts and know your ways; the ways of words, and bright skeins of discourse and cleverness. I shall unknot your threads and reweave them my own way'.[76]

If naming constitutes one half of Anna's self-healing then the attempt to re-establish contact with the lost mother makes up the other:

> To Anna it was gloriously simple, not easy but simple. She must go back to the womb and be born again in the power of the spirit. She must go back to the beginning to the place that Caro has invited her, not trying to graft the form-lessness on but stripping naked to meet it. She must go back to the dark damp belly. She will go back to the Amazon valley where she has once been with Kate. She will go to the headwaters and float down the great river until she comes to the land of the mothers and she will stay there and learn to be a grown-up woman.[77]

It is here that *Virgin Territory* seems to me to be closest to Irigaray. Consider this, from 'The Bodily Encounter with the Mother':

> There is a genealogy of women within our family: on our mothers' side we have mothers, grandmothers and great-grandmothers, and daughters. Given our exile in the family of the father-husband, we tend to forget this genealogy of women,

and we are often persuaded to deny it. Let us try to situate ourselves within this female genealogy so as to conquer and keep our identity. Nor let us forget that we already have a history, that certain women have, even if it was culturally difficult, left their mark on history and that all too often we do not know them.[78]

When this view of genealogical thinking is set next to Foucault's view of it as 'local, discontinuous, disqualified, illegitimate knowledges', we can see how resonant Maitland's imagery becomes. It suggests the potency of suppressed knowledges, the importance of transforming mother–daughter relations in order to break out of the oedipal scenario, and the need for developing modes of being and knowing that slip through the interstices of androcentric culture. Maitland is surely also thinking of Woolf's well-known claim that 'we think back through our mothers if we are women. It is useless to go to the great men writers for help'.[79] On the spiritual side, the matriarchal imagery leads to a non-gendered concept of the divinity, which most probably draws on Julian of Norwich.[80] When Anna picks up a copy of Meinrad Craighead's *The Sign of the Tree* she is so overwhelmed by its description of God as mother that 'her darkness' is all of a sudden 'ablaze with light'.[81]

The matriarchal imagery that increasingly comes to the fore towards the novel's end has as its counterpart the invocation of mythical figures such as Artemis, Koré, Pallas Athene, Persephone, and Medea. By identifying with these literary role models, Anna reclaims territory that, far from being virgin, has been strategically colonized. Given Maitland's suspicion of myth, how are we to interpret the text's recourse to it? I would suggest that *Virgin Territory* displays an ambivalent attitude to myth. The novel's epigraph, which is a quotation from Sheila Rowbotham, suggests one view: 'For feminists the existence of universal and ahistoric psychic patterns clearly has to be contested because these inevitably confirm and legitimate male power'.[82] This critical perspective is later articulated by Karen, who, like Carter, thinks that myths and archetypes seek to pass themselves off as 'immutable transhistorical psychic truths' but are really 'indulgent consolations' in the service of patriarchal power:

> 'All those symbols of strong women, all those mythological virgins and Amazons and matriarchs, they're not about us, they're about men and their lousy little fears, and their lusts and their power. Quite possibly virginity had a radical function and radical manifestations too if you want to insist; but negative, negative, defined against male supremacy. . . . Look at the archetypes; what have you got? You get the wife and mother, and the sex symbol and the friend-and-companion, and you get the virgin, all in this nice tidy balanced square, polarised, orderly, acceptable. But who's standing in the middle of the square? Who's holding it together, keeping it in focus? Men, that's who, they're doing the defining.'

Karen's undermining of myth points to the way it can promote hegemonic interests by making what is contingent appear to be universal. But another approach to myth, which is in keeping with the novel's re-visioning strategy, is to reclaim it by inverting it, to turn it back upon itself in the form of critique. The novel challenges myth's proclivity to universalize by disclosing how it upholds certain hierarchies of power, but at the same time utilizes myth's potency by reclaiming it for feminism. This is what Diana Fuss might call a strategic deployment of essentialist categories for interventionist purposes.[83] In doing so, *Virgin Territory* suggests that neither myth nor scripture is fixed and immutable, set in tablets of stone, but that both are pre-eminently historical in character and are therefore subject to revision, contestation, and change.

Notes

1. Joan Wallach Scott, *Gender and the Politics of History* (New York: Columbia University Press, 1988), pp. 10, 10–11.
2. Michel Foucault, 'Truth and Power', *Power/Knowledge: Selected Interviews and Other Writings, 1972–1977*, ed. Colin Gordon (Brighton: Harvester, 1980), pp. 109–33, at p. 117.
3. Luce Irigaray, *This Sex Which is Not One*, trans. Catherine Porter and Carolyn Burke (Ithaca: Cornell University Press, 1985), p. 123.
4. Gayatri Chakravorty Spivak, *The Post-Colonial Critic: Interviews, Strategies, Dialogues*, ed. Sarah Harasym (New York: Routledge, 1990), pp. 57–8.
5. Judith Butler, *Gender Trouble: Feminism and the Subversion of Identity* (London: Routledge, 1990), pp. x–xi.
6. See, for this anxiety, Robert Scholes, 'Reading Like a Man', *Men in Feminism*, eds Alice Jardine and Paul Smith (New York and London: Methuen, 1987), pp. 204–18. For a response to Scholes, see Diana Fuss, *Essentially Speaking: Feminism, Nature and Difference* (London: Routledge, 1989).
7. Rita Felski, *Beyond Feminist Aesthetics: Feminist Literature and Social Change* (London: Hutchinson Radius, 1989), pp. 31–2.
8. Terry Lovell, 'Writing Like a Woman: A Question of Politics', *The Politics of Theory*, ed. Francis Barker et al. (Colchester: Essex University Press, 1983), pp. 15–26, at p. 24.
9. Felski, *Beyond*, p. 33.
10. Angela Carter, 'The Language of Sisterhood', *The State of the Language*, ed. Leonard Michaels and Christopher Ricks (Berkeley and Los Angeles: California University Press, 1980), pp. 226–35, at p. 226.
11. Angela Carter, 'Notes from the Front-Line', *On Gender and Writing*, ed. Michelene Wandor (London: Methuen, 1988), pp. 69–77, at pp. 69, 75.
12. Sara Maitland, 'Futures in Feminist Fiction', *From My Guy to Sci-Fi: Genre and Women's Writing in the Postmodern World*, ed. Helen Carr (London: Pandora, 1989), p. 195.
13. Phyllis Trible, *Texts of Terror: Literary and Feminist Readings of Biblical Narratives* (Philadelphia, PA: Fortress Press, 1984).
14. Elizabeth Grosz, 'Feminism and the Crisis of Reason', *Feminist Epistemologies*, eds Linda Alcoff and Elizabeth Potter (London: Routledge, 1993), pp. 187–215, at pp. 196, 196–7, 200, 196.
15. The terms are Forster's. See E.M. Forster, *Aspects of the Novel* (Harmondsworth: Penguin, 1980), Ch. 4.
16. Angela Carter, *The Infernal Desire Machines of Doctor Hoffman* (London: Penguin, 1972), p. 194.
17. Victor Turner, *The Ritual Process: Structure and Anti-Structure* (London, Routledge and Kegan Paul, 1969), pp. 95, 111, 103, 128–9.
18. Angela Carter, *The Sadeian Woman: An Exercise in Cultural History* (London: Virago, 1990), pp. 5, 6, 6–7.
19. Carter, 'Notes', p. 71.
20. Carter, *Sadeian*, p. 5.
21. Lovell, 'Writing', p. 25.

22. Carter, *Hoffman*, pp. 11, 38, 12.
23. In the *Republic*, Socrates claims that 'an excessive desire for liberty at the expense of everything else is what undermines democracy and leads to the demand for tyranny'. See Plato, *The Republic*, trans. Desmond Lee (London: Penguin, 1974), at 562e.
24. Ibid., 595–603, 607a. See also Plato, *The Laws*, trans. Trevor J. Saunders (London: Penguin, 1982), at 817d.
25. Plato, *Laws*, at 817b.
26. Carter, *Hoffman*, pp. 13, 28–9, 206, 35. Carter's target here may also be Karl Popper, who identified Plato as the father of totalitarianism. See Karl Popper, *The Open Society and Its Enemies*, Vol. 1, *The Spell of Plato* (London: Routledge and Kegan Paul, 1957).
27. Carter, *Hoffman*, pp. 24, 22, 206. In Platonic terms Hoffman appeals to the lowest part of the soul – the passions. See Plato, *Republic*, at 605b.
28. Carter, *Hoffman*, p. 37. Plato, of course, famously charges the poets with misrepresentation of the truth, at *Republic* 377–83.
29. Carter, *Hoffman*, p. 12.
30. Ibid., p. 97. The similarities between Desiderio and Dowell are brought out towards the end of the novel. Compare Carter, *Hoffman*, p. 207 with Ford Madox Ford, *The Good Soldier* (Harmondsworth: Penguin, 1981), p. 227.
31. Carter, *Hoffman*, pp. 202, 168, 135.
32. Carter, *Sadeian*, p. 141.
33. Carter, *Hoffman*, pp. 207, 24, 209.
34. Ibid., p. 219.
35. Ibid., p. 207.
36. For this reading of the *Phaedrus*, see Martha Craven Nussbaum, ' "This Story Isn't True": Poetry, Goodness, and Understanding in Plato's *Phaedrus*', *Plato on Beauty, Wisdom, and the Arts*, ed. Julius Moravcsik and Philip Temko (Totowa, N.J.: Rowman and Littlefield, 1982), pp. 79–125.
37. Plato, *Phaedrus*, trans. C.J. Rowe (Warminster: Aris and Phillips, 1988), at 245a.
38. Carter, *Hoffman*, pp. 207, 213, 221, 206, 14.
39. Angela Carter, *The Passion of New Eve* (London: Virago, 1977), p. 6.
40. Angela Carter, *Nights at the Circus* (London: Picador, 1985), p. 97.
41. Carter, *New Eve*, pp. 34, 75, 77, 83.
42. Ibid., p. 102.
43. Grosz, 'Feminism', p. 199.
44. Carter, *New Eve*, pp. 129, 135, 134, 149–50, 191.
45. Butler, *Gender Trouble*, p. 33.
46. Carter, 'Language', p. 228.
47. Carter, *New Eve*, pp. 172–73, 175. The references to Blake's *The Vision of the Last Judgement* are at pp. 53, 77.
48. Carter, *Nights*, p. 286.
49. Ibid., pp. 111, 285–6, 285, 286, 295.
50. See Peter Stallybrass and Allon White, *The Politics and Poetics of Transgression* (London: Methuen, 1986).
51. Angela Carter, *Wise Children* (London: QPD, 1991), pp. 220, 125, 155, 222, 169.
52. Stallybrass and White, *Politics*, pp. 202, 201.
53. Maitland, 'Futures', pp. 193–203, at pp. 199, 194, 195, 196.
54. See Michelene Wandor (ed.), *The Body Politic: Writings from the Women's Liberation Movement in Britain, 1969–1972* (London: Stage 1, 1972); Maitland, 'Futures', p. 196.
55. For a critique of *écriture féminine* along these lines, see Felski, *Beyond*, pp. 5–7, 30–44.
56. Ibid., pp. 199, 202. Maitland is here surely drawing on Adrienne Rich, 'When We Dead Awaken: Writing as Re-Vision', *On Lies, Secrets, and Silence: Selected Prose*

1966–1978 (London: Virago, 1980).

57. Sara Maitland and Michelene Wandor, *Arky Types* (London: Methuen, 1987), p. 196.
58. Linda Hutcheon, *A Theory of Parody: The Teachings of Twentieth Century Art Forms* (London: Methuen, 1985), p. 15.
59. Aileen La Tourette and Sara Maitland, *Weddings and Funerals* (London: Brilliance Books, 1984), pp. 136, 139–40, 140, 141.
60. Sara Maitland, *Daughter of Jerusalem* (London: Blond and Briggs, 1978), p. 161.
61. Jürgen Habermas, *Knowledge and Human Interests*, trans. Jeremy J. Shapiro (Boston: Beacon, 1971).
62. Thomas Aquinas, *The 'Summa Theologica'*, Part 1, *Treatise on Man*, trans. Fathers of the English Dominican Province (London: Burns Oates and Washburne, 1922), Question 92, Article 1, pp. 274–7.
63. Sara Maitland, *Virgin Territory* (London: Pan, 1985), p. 113.
64. Tertullian, 'Women's Dress', *Fathers of the Church: A Selection from the Writings of the Latin Fathers*, trans. F. A. Wright (London: George Routledge and Sons, 1928), p. 52.
65. Maitland, *Virgin*, pp. 216, 114.
66. For a Lacanian reading of the novel, see Caroline Guerin, 'Iris Murdoch – A Revisionist Theology? A Comparative Study of Iris Murdoch's *Nuns and Soldiers* and Sara Maitland's *Virgin Territory'*, *Journal of Literature and Theology*, 6. 2 (June 1992), p. 160.
67. Luce Irigaray, 'The Bodily Encounter with the Mother', *The Irigaray Reader*, ed. Margaret Whitford (Oxford: Blackwell, 1992), pp. 34–46.
68. Luce Irigaray, 'Women-mothers, the Silent Substratum of the Social Order', ibid., pp. 47–52. See also Elizabeth Grosz, *Sexual Subversions: Three French Feminists* (St Leonards, NSW: Allen and Unwin, 1989), p. 107.
69. Grosz, *Sexual Subversions*, p. 107.
70. Maitland, *Virgin*, pp. 64–5, 196.
71. Ibid., p. 32.
72. Rosemary Radford Ruether, 'Feminist Interpretation: A Method of Correlation', *Feminist Interpretation of the Bible*, ed. Letty M. Russell (Oxford: Basil Blackwell, 1985), p. 117. See also Elisabeth Schussler Fiorenza, *Bread Not Stone: The Challenge of Feminist Biblical Interpretation* (Boston: Beacon, 1984); Daphne Hampson, *Theology and Feminism* (Oxford: Basil Blackwell, 1990).
73. Irigaray, 'The Bodily Encounter', p. 41.
74. Maitland, *Virgin*, pp. 110, 213, 226, 235, 232.
75. Mary Jacobus, *Women Writing and Writing about Women* (London: Croom Helm, 1979), p. 12.
76. Maitland, *Virgin*, pp. 73, 190, 236, 215.
77. Ibid., p. 231.
78. Irigaray, 'The Bodily', p. 44.
79. Virginia Woolf, *A Room of One's Own* (London: Granada, 1980), p. 114.
80. Julian of Norwich, *Revelations of Divine Love*, trans. Clifton Walters (London: Penguin, 1966), especially chapters 57–61. See also Luce Irigaray, *L'Éthique de la Différence Sexuelle* (Paris: Les Éditions de Minuit, 1984).
81. Maitland, *Virgin*, p. 230.
82. Ibid., p. 7.
83. Fuss, *Essentially*, p. 20.

7

Postmodernism and the Problem of History

Writing in the aftermath of the Second World War, Karl Löwith could find neither pattern nor purpose to history. The dream of a rational and teleological *Universalgeschichte*, predicated on a quasi-theological notion of salvation, had been smashed, leaving him to conclude that 'neither a providential design nor a natural law of progressive development is discernible in the tragic human comedy of all times'.[1] Ruled by contingency, human history seemed to be a catalogue of failures. The loss of meaning he identified finds a more complete articulation in recent pronouncements that history has come to an end. Primarily associated with postmodernism, these views in fact extend further, for they include New Right theorists such as Arnold Gehlen and Francis Fukuyama as well as disillusioned Leftists who argue that we have entered the era of *posthistoire*. In this respect, a Marxist like Jameson is not so far from neoconservatives, with whom he has little else in common. Jameson mourns the loss of temporality within postmodernity, arguing that it gives rise to 'depthlessness', loss of affect, and a view of the past as 'little more than a set of dusty spectacles'.[2] Theorists of *posthistoire* also invert the metanarrative of progress, turning it into one of decline: history in the Hegelian or Marxist sense has come to an end and offers no hope of rationalization or revolution; it undermines faith in the collective subject and in human agency; it teaches that any vision of totality is chimerical and must be replaced by plurality. Contemporary culture thus presides over the death of meaning, disclosing that although life goes on and history continues, History is finished since life no longer has any purpose. Hence Lutz Niethammer's claim that the 'problematic of posthistory is not the end of the world but the end of meaning'.[3]

The idea that History has come to an end is inseparable from recent debates over the nature of history as a scholarly discipline. The challenge to Ranke's ideal of reconstructing the past *wie es eigentlich gewesen ist* and to the positivists' scientistic elaboration of a covering law model has come from a variety of sources – feminist, Marxist, narrativist, post-structuralist, post-colonial, New Historicist. These different theoretical perspectives all question history's claims to know the past, basing their work on the assumption 'that History has been undone'. This undoing is characterized by scepticism about the claims historians used to make: that the past exists in a pre-established form which simply requires human beings to discover it; that the historian can speak from a universal (objective) standpoint; that what constitutes the subject of history does not change with time and is agreed upon by most practitioners; that the historian can offer a totalizing, synoptic account of the past, which is complete in all necessary particulars.[4] This kind of questioning has meant that the nature, methodology, and theoretical underpinning of history has had to be rethought. Various historians have advanced alternative theses. Firstly, that because the historian cannot be free from bias all attempts to totalize the past will be defeated by some kind of exclusion; historians should acknowledge that they cannot be fully disinterested and should endeavour to be openly self-reflexive in their work.[5] Secondly, that the authority attributed to historical sources needs to be questioned; sources predominantly take the form of written documents, and, since these must be interpreted just like all other written works, history is better seen as the study of the textuality through which conflicting accounts of the past are mediated than as the study of the past as it really was.[6] Thirdly, a corollary of the second point, that the old distinction between text and context is untenable; theorists claim that it relies on primary sources to posit an authentic historical reality (context) in relation to which secondary sources (all other texts) are interpreted, but to proceed in this way, they argue, is to ignore the extent to which context is itself a textual construct.[7] Fourthly, that traditional emphasis on continuities, developments, and progress generates misleadingly unified accounts of history, which should be replaced by genealogical and archaeo-logical approaches that are alert to conflicts, discontinuities, and aporias.[8]

It is easy to see the link between this kind of theoretical questioning and claims that History's death-rattle can be heard. Both empty history of meaning. The former leads to scepticism about the possibility of historical knowledge, and it is only one step from such scepticism to the position that History reveals no pattern, meaning, or purpose. All is ceaseless, but pointless, change. But perhaps 'radical' theorists go too far in their undermining of history, and apologists for *posthistoire* go too far in their (otherwise sensible) repudiation of the salvationism inherent in nineteenth-century philosophy of history. Any number of contemporary historians attest the value of the linguistic turn the discipline has recently taken.[9] But as Martin Jay points out in his assessment of the Habermas – Gadamer debate, it all depends on what sort of linguistic turn one is talking about.[10] As is well known, Habermas attacked Gadamerian hermeneutics because it afforded no vantage point from which to challenge tradition, and therefore undermined the kind of social critique that was central to critical theory. Many historians recognize the predominantly textual nature of what constitutes the historical record, but see this as the necessary ground of research into history, not as an insuperable obstacle to knowledge of the past. Dominick La Capra, for instance, criticizes Hayden White for giving the impression that the historian is 'a free shaping agent with respect to an inert, neutral documentary record'. Historians confront a complex documentary record that requires careful interpretation since it 'is itself always textually processed' before they approach it, but, La Capra insists, this record clearly constrains their shaping of it into a historical account.[11] Paul Ricoeur refers to the documentary 'trace' by means of which the historian reconstructs the past. For Ricoeur, accounts of the past are not isomorphic with it; historians are 'well aware that . . . reconstruction is a different construction than the course of events reported', but they are 'moved by the vow to do justice to the past'. Historiography should thus be seen as an analogical discipline, since this distinction retains reference to a real, lived past but introduces the mediating role of the historian's own discourse'.[12]

Postmodern accounts of history have had a clear impact on a good deal of recent fiction. This is hardly surprising, for if history is held to be a mode of enquiry whose procedures resemble those of fiction, there is likely to be interest in the narrative possibilities that interaction between the two genres might produce. If history has splintered into disparate discourses, none of which is necessarily more reliable than any other, making it little more than a form of story-telling tricked out in scientifically respectable language, then fiction's propensity to fabulate receives a new lease of life. History, it turns out, is not only itself a form of fabulation but is also reliant on the very narrative strategies that historians previously claimed belonged to the imaginative world of literature, but not to the more scholarly one of history. The novels that Linda Hutcheon calls 'historiographic metafictions' thus play with the boundaries between 'real' and 'invented' in order to expose the constructed nature of historical discourse by disclosing its reliance on the narrative modes associated with literature.[13] The nostalgia for the historically 'real' that characterizes the work of both Jameson and theorists of *posthistoire* frequently haunts these fictions. The anxiety that history cannot truly be known gives rise to a kind of cultural pessimism. In Graham Swift's *Waterland* (1983), Tom Crick spends his life searching for the 'Grand Narrative' of history but is forced to conclude that it 'is a yarn'.[14] In *Flaubert's Parrot* (1984), Geoffrey Braithwaite's search for the real Gustave Flaubert ends in defeat, leaving him to muse that the past is like a piglet 'smeared with grease' and to wonder whether history 'is merely another literary genre: the past is autobiographical fiction pretending to be a parliamentary report'.[15] These statements seem to suggest a fairly extreme scepticism; they meld all too well with postmodern claims that history, conceived as a text, cannot be known because the interpreter has no access to an unmediated, pre-discursive historical 'real'. But writers such as La Capra, Ricoeur, and Quentin Skinner remind us that the textualization of history takes a variety of forms. We therefore need to look closely at novels such as *Waterland*, *Flaubert's Parrot*, *The History of the World in 10½ Chapters* (1989), and *Midnight's Children* (1981) in order to see what stance they take *vis-à-vis* the problem of history. I want to suggest in the following chapter that these novels, particularly those by Barnes and Rushdie, offer a far more critical reading of certain postmodern claims about the unrepresentability of the historically 'real' than might initially be thought to be the case.

Graham Swift

It is simple for postmoderns to lampoon nineteenth-century historians. Consider the following remarks made by Robert Mackenzie in *The Nineteenth*

Century – A History (1880): 'Human history is a record of progress – a record of accumulating knowledge and increasing wisdom, of continual advancement from a lower to a higher platform of intelligence and well-being'.[16] How different from this Whig conception of history are the views of Tom Crick, the disillusioned historian in Graham Swift's *Waterland*, written 100 years later: 'History: a lucky dip of meanings. Events elude meaning, but we look for meanings. Another definition of Man: the animal who craves meaning – but knows – '.[17] The difference can all too easily be seen as that between a positivist historiographer and a postmodernist sceptic; Mackenzie's faith in the metanarrative of progress has been displaced by Crick's agnostic willingness to accept a variety of mutually jostling *petits récits*. But maybe this explanation, convenient though it is, is too tidy. Perhaps it merely turns the linear Whig emphasis on progress into an equally linear postmodernist stress on decline; historians once misguidedly thought humanity was becoming increasingly rational, but they now know better. Historians of the past can thus be treated as the whipping-boys of the more sophisticated present. How, then, should the following passage be read?

> [E]ven with regard to those occurrences which do stand recorded, which, at their origin have seemed worthy of record, and the summary of which constitutes what we now call History, is not our understanding of them altogether incomplete; is it even possible to represent them as they were? . . . It is, in no case, the real historical Transaction, but only some more or less plausible scheme and theory of the Transaction, or the harmonised result of many such schemes, each varying from the other and all varying from truth, that we can ever hope to behold.[18]

Apart from the idiom and the unusual capitalizations, this sounds like grist for the postmodernist mill. The writer is Thomas Carlyle, however, and the date is 1830. Carlyle's awareness of the difficulties inherent in historical enquiry, his suspicion of grand explanatory narratives, his distrust of the linearity enforced on historians, his acceptance of the huge gaps in the historical record, and his emphasis on the lives of ordinary people, predate currently fashionable concerns by well over 100 years, although Carlyle refused to embrace scepticism.[19]

Is it obvious, then, that Tom Crick's jaded pronouncements about his discipline render him a postmodernist? What kind of historian is Crick? The only historian to whom he makes reference in the course of his narrative is, in fact, Thomas Carlyle, whose *The French Revolution* he has read more than once, and Carlyle's conception of history turns out to be remarkably close to his own. Carlyle makes several points in 'On History'. He argues that historians have a partial perspective and should aim 'only at some picture of the things acted, which picture itself will at best be a poor approximation'. History is a 'complex Manuscript, covered over with formless inextricably-entangled unknown characters'; it is 'a *Palimpsest*' from which 'some letters, some words, may be deciphered', but it 'can be fully interpreted by no man'. The historian, moreover, can neither explain the grand events of the past nor identify them. The 'cardinal points on which grand world-revolutions have hinged' might easily pass unnoticed, for 'no hammer in the Horologe of Time peals through the universe when there is a change from Era to Era'. The very writing of history entails falsification, as it imposes a neat linearity (hence a sense of teleology) on events that took place simultaneously: 'It is not in acted, as it is in written History: actual events are nowise so simply related to each other as parent and offspring are; every single event is the offspring not of one, but of all other events, prior or contemporaneous, and will in its turn combine with all others to give birth to new: it is an ever-living, ever-working Chaos of Being, wherein shape after shape bodies itself forth from innumerable elements'. Carlyle's conviction that historians can neither explain the significant occurrences of the past nor do justice to its sheer density leads him to shift emphasis away from grand events and onto social history: 'Laws themselves, political Constitutions, are not our Life, but only the house wherein our Life is led: nay, they are but the bare walls of the house: all whose essential furniture, the inventions and traditions, and daily habits that regulate and support our existence, are the work not of Dracos and Hampdens, but of Phoenician mariners, of Italian masons and Saxon metallurgists, of philosophers, alchymists, prophets, and all the long-forgotten train of artists and artisans'. The writer who dwells 'with disproportionate fondness in Senate-Houses, in Battle-fields, nay, even in Kings' Ante-chambers', ignoring the lives of ordinary people, will in future 'pass for a more or less instructive Gazetteer, but will no longer be called a Historian'.[20]

Tom Crick's conception of history resembles Carlyle's in several respects. He trusted as an adolescent that history would provide him with the answers he craved, but as an adult he has lost this faith:

> I began to demand of history an Explanation. Only to uncover in this dedicated search more mysteries, more fantasticalities, more wonders and grounds for astonishment than I started with, only to conclude forty years later . . . that history is a yarn. And can I deny that what I wanted all along was not some golden nugget that history would at last yield up, but History itself, the Grand Narrative, the filler of vacuums, the dispeller of fears of the dark?[21]

Crick realizes, to his chagrin, that the synthesizing, totalizing account he desires is an impossible dream. He faces instead the numerous *petits récits* beloved of Lyotard, but, unlike the latter, cannot be sanguine at the prospect. He is not just perplexed at history's inability to explain the past; he is tormented by it. Like Carlyle, however, he concludes from this that history cannot focus purely on spectacle and grand event; his own story attempts to do justice not only to the detail of social life but also to the solidity and simultaneity of events that Carlyle thought linear narrative concealed. Crick's tale functions on a variety of levels. It disrupts linear chronology by juxtaposing four different periods (the 1790s, the nineteenth century, the 1940s, the present day); it achieves density by recounting several intersecting stories (the history of the Atkinson and Crick families from the eighteenth to the twentieth centuries, Crick's own experiences during the 1940s, and his contemporary predicament); and it displaces grand events such as the French Revolution, the First World War, and the Second World War from a position of centrality, treating them rather as the backdrop to the daily lives of his protagonists. Crick's emphasis on what Carlyle called the 'sedulous endeavours' of those who inhabit 'the dark untenanted places of the Past'[22] is unmistakable:

> And that is how, children, my ancestors came to live by the River Leem. That is how when the cauldron of revolution was simmering in Paris, so that you, one

day, should have a subject for your lessons, they were busy, as usual, with their scouring, pumping and embanking. That is how, when foundations were being rocked in France, a land was being formed which would one day yield fifteen tons of potatoes or nineteen sacks of wheat an acre and on which your history teacher-to-be would one day have his home.

Crick shifts attention away from the spectacle of history, away from the view that its most significant features are wars, political intrigues, and revolutions, displacing it with the representation of daily life and the role played by geography in forming it. This shift in emphasis is articulated early in the text when he first introduces the metaphor (which foregrounds natural history) that will later prove to be central to his conception of history: 'So forget, indeed, your revolutions, your turning-points, your grand metamorphoses of history. Consider, instead, the slow and arduous process, the interminable and ambiguous process – the process of human siltation – of land reclamation'.[23]

Crick is no Carlyle clone, however. Although many of his views resemble Carlyle's, he disagrees with the latter over the nature of society, lacks his confidence that doubt can be dispelled by action, and discerns no divine message in the text of the world. In 'Characteristics' (1831) Carlyle distinguishes between the Artificial, which is 'conscious, mechanical', and the Natural, which is 'unconscious, dynamical'. There is a dualism between negative and positive poles, for 'the Perfect, the Great is a mystery to itself, knows not itself; whatsoever does know itself is already little, and more or less imperfect'. Consciousness contaminates unconsciousness and produces a dissociation of sensibility not dissimilar to that later articulated by T. S. Eliot. Society 'was what we can call *whole*', for '[t]hought and the voice of thought were also a unison'.[24] Crick correctly identifies the myth of a lost golden age and 'the idea of a return . . . a restoration' as a key influence on the sansculottes' fervour: 'did they really have in mind a Society of the Future? Not a bit of it. Their model was an idealised ancient Rome. Laurel wreaths and all. Their prototype the murder of Caesar. Our heroes of the new age – good classicists all – yearned, too, to go back – '.[25] He pours scorn on 'this insidious longing to go backwards', describing the nostalgia for a 'time before history claimed us, before things went wrong' as a 'bastard but pampered child'.[26] His own cyclical view of the past (about which more below) leads him to satirize all notions of a past arcadia or a future utopia and to offer instead a bleak conception of history as a form of retrenchment.

A second major difference between Carlyle and Crick concerns the former's faith (most clearly expressed by Teufelsdröckh's Everlasting Yea in *Sartor Resartus*) that the 'disease of metaphysics', which breeds scepticism, can be overborne by purposeful activity: 'A region of Doubt . . . hovers forever in the background; in Action alone can we have certainty. Nay, properly Doubt is the indispensable inexhaustible material whereon Action works, which Action has to fashion into Certainty and Reality'.[27] Crick, in contrast, is powerless to act. Indeed, his attempts to master his fate have catastrophic consequences, for they result in his wife's infertility, his brother's suicide, and his own enforced early retirement. Unable to comprehend his past life, help his distraught wife, or resist his marginalization within the school where he teaches, he is doomed to passive reflection. Like Saleem Sinai's in *Midnight's Children*, his is 'as peripheral a role as that of any redundant oldster: the traditional function, perhaps, of reminiscer, of teller-of-tales'.[28]

Crick oscillates between two broad conceptions of history, although he diverges from both at certain moments in his narrative. One of the novel's two epigraphs announces this split stance, defining history either as an enquiry and investigation into the past or as a tale and a story. The first characterization posits history as a discipline with a referential foundation; the second portrays it as an art with an imaginative basis. Crick tacks between these two views of history throughout his narrative, apparently unable to adjudicate between them. Nor does he appear to conceive them in dialectical terms; they are opposites, rather, locked into the ebb and flow of a systole–diastole pattern whose course is set.

The significance of these two conceptions can be clarified by comparing different characters' responses to the reality of their lives. For Crick, to live in the Fens is to face the 'great, flat monotony of reality; the wide, empty space of reality'. The 'nothing-landscape' of the Fens provokes one of two responses: the desire to master one's destiny through action or the wish to escape the senselessness of life through imagination: 'How did the Cricks outwit reality? By telling stories. Down to the last generation, they were not only phlegmatic but superstitious and credulous creatures. Suckers for stories. While the Atkinsons made history, the Cricks spun yarns'.[29] Tom Crick is himself a product of both Atkinsons and Cricks; the conflict between agency and spectatordom, action and narration, wars within him. Other characters adopt one stance or the other, and the division between them tends to follow genetic lines. The Atkinsons, as Crick's long account of their family history attests, are energetic and enterprising businessmen who subdue the geography of the Fens by turning its particular features to their advantage. The Cricks, in turn, are cautious and reticent folk who cope with the landscape of the Fens by seeking refuge in fairy-tales.

Tom Crick's view of history is inextricable from the twin impulses of reality-avoidance and reality-confrontation. Helen Atkinson, for example, 'believes in stories' because 'they're a way of bearing what won't go away, a way of making sense of madness'. She is able to survive her experience of incest with her crazed father because she turns it into a narrative: 'You can't erase it. But make it into a story. Just a story. Yes, everything's crazy. What's real? All a story. Only a story . . .'. Henry Crick, in contrast, is unable to perform the same operation on his memories of the trenches in the First World War because their horror defeats all attempts to make sense of them: 'He thinks: there is only reality, there are no stories left. About his war experiences he says: "I remember nothing"'. Story-telling thus operates in an equivocal, ambiguous way in *Waterland*. On the one hand it functions as the means by which characters can endow their lives with meaning, but on the other hand it encourages them to displace the painful aspects of reality into the realm of make-believe. This ambivalence is equally present in Crick's approach to history, for whereas at times he describes it as 'a yarn' and as a form of myth, at others he considers its substance to be 'for ever determined and unchangeable' and acknowledges that he must ask 'where the stories end and reality begins'. The tension between these two views is evident in a passage such as the following:

> Ah yes, he's hooked by now, it's got serious, this historical method, this explanation-hunting. It's a way of getting at the truth – or, as you would have it, Price, a way of coming up with just another story, a way of dodging reality . . . .
>
>   But it's no longer story-time in the land of the Leem. Reality's already imposed itself in the form of a sodden corpse. And it's going to get more pressing, more palpable still . . .[30]

The tension between the referential basis of a past to which the historian 'owes a debt' and the apparent inaccessibility of that past to the interpreting historian, which leads the sceptic to assert that history is merely a form of fabulation, could not be clearer.[31] It is a tension Crick is unable to resolve. He admits that his 'becoming a history teacher can be directly ascribed to the stories which [his] mother told [him] as a child, when . . . [he] was afraid of the dark', and he later reiterates this rationale for his vocation: 'It helps to drive out fear. I don't care what you call it – explaining, evading the facts, making up meanings, taking a larger view, putting things into perspective, dodging the here and now, education, history, fairy-tales – it helps to eliminate fear'. This account of history as the means by which existential anxieties may be assuaged (displaced?) coexists uneasily with another, rather more sober, view of it:

> [H]istory is that impossible thing: the attempt to give an account, with incomplete knowledge, of actions themselves undertaken with incomplete knowledge. So that it teaches us no short-cuts to Salvation, no recipe for a New World, only the dogged and patient art of making do. I taught you that by for ever attempting to explain we may come, not to an Explanation, but to a knowledge of the limits of our power to explain. Yes, yes, the past gets in the way; it trips us up, bogs us down; it complicates, makes difficult. But to ignore this is folly, because, above all, what history teaches us is to avoid illusion and make-believe, to lay aside dreams, moonshine, cure-alls, wonder-workings, pie-in-the-sky – to be realistic.[32]

On this view, history offers not consoling myths that hold a frightening reality at bay but disturbing truths that look it squarely in the face.

Crick's ethos is in some ways that of a post-Enlightenment thinker. This is suggested by his modest conception of history as a form of reclamation, his rejection of the Whig belief in progress, and his fear of an impending apocalypse. Not for him the optimism of a Condorcet, who could write his celebrated 'Esquisse d'un tableau historique des progrès de l'esprit humain' (1793) while awaiting the guillotine. But his conception of history is in certain respects more akin to that of an ancient Greek like Polybius than to philosophers like Hegel or Marx. Two aspects of his views suggest this: his belief in historical cyclicality, and his claim that there is a perpetual conflict between innate human nature and the artifice of society.

Crick makes it clear throughout his narrative that he disbelieves in the idea of progress. He replaces this notion with his metaphor of history as the painstaking reclamation of land: 'There's this thing called progress. But it doesn't progress. It doesn't go anywhere. Because as progress progresses the world can slip away. It's progress if you can stop the world slipping away. My humble model for progress is the reclamation of land. Which is repeatedly, never-endingly retrieving what is lost'.[33] The noble dream of Kant's *Universalgeschichte*, through which humanity was to become ever more rational, has been left far behind. So has the 'ruse of reason' by way of which Hegel could claim that history, for all its disasters, had a meaning and purpose unknown to its actors. Crick's scaled-down model for history has jettisoned the Enlightenment's transcendental aspirations and replaced belief in progress with an ethic of retrenchment. The metaphor of reclamation also challenges the significance usually attributed to cataclysmic occurrences such as the French Revolution. It undermines the metanarrative of history because it shifts focus away from grand events, suggesting that these are not easily identifiable, and denies that the meaning of the events that historians do analyze can be understood. Crick's emphasis on reclamation thus marks a decisive shift from an epistemological orientation towards the past to a pragmatic one.

Pragmatism is a reasonable option if you believe that history is cyclical. Crick certainly does. His entire narrative is geared towards exemplifying this view, which he frequently asserts: 'We believe we are going forward, towards the oasis of Utopia. But how do we know . . . that we are not moving in a great circle?'. He provides his own answer to this rhetorical question on several occasions, averring each time that history is indeed recursive and glossing his account of the French Revolution's various phases thus: 'How it repeats itself, how it goes back on itself, no matter how we try to straighten it out. How it twists, turns. How it goes in circles and brings us back to the same place'. Cyclical theories of history tend to be conservative and pessimistic because they see change as ephemeral and hold out little hope that it could ever result in progress. Strictly cyclical conceptions of history are undialectical, and this is why it is important to differentiate them from the theories of philosophers such as Vico and Hegel who emphasize that the movement of history is not that of a circle but that of a spiral. Crick's view is clearly of the former, undialectical variety, since he not only describes history in circular terms but also claims that it 'brings us back to the same place'.[34] This view is close to that of Polybius, for example, who writes in his *Histories*: 'Such is the cycle of political revolution, the course appointed by nature in which constitutions change, disappear, and finally return to the point from which they started'.[35]

Crick's bleak view of his discipline is apparent in his metaphor of reclamation, his loss of faith in providence, and his contention that history follows a cyclical pattern. His resolutely non-teleological stance means that he inverts both Carlyle's claim that there has been a dissociation of sensibility (a linear story of decline) and Kant's claim that history leads to the development of humanity's potential (a linear story of progress). Civilization, Crick avers, is an 'artifice' that is 'easily knocked down' but is no less 'precious' for that. It is a construct, an invention, a more or less consciously developed set of social protocols and institutions about which there is nothing natural whatsoever: 'Children, there's this thing called civilisation. It's built of hopes and dreams. It's only an idea. It's not real. It's artificial. No one ever said it was real. It's not natural, no one ever said it was natural. It's built by the learning process; by trial and error. It breaks easily. No one ever said it couldn't fall to bits. And no one ever said it would last for ever'. Crick's impatience with the myth of innate goodness of natural man functions as the counterpart to his suspicion of Kant's dream of human perfectibility. Instead of progress there is the 'dogged and vigilant business' of reclaiming what has been fought for and is always being lost.[36]

Crick, then, inverts Kant's model of history as the means by which humanity progresses. But he is close to Kant in one respect. The latter argues in 'An Idea for a Universal History from a Cosmopolitan Point of View' that the impulse that provokes people to abandon their initial contented state, hence to embark on the path of progress, is 'propelled by vainglory, lust for power, and avarice'. This 'evil' impulse finds its origin in nature: 'Man wishes concord; but Nature knows better what is good for the race; she wills discord. He wishes to live comfortably and pleasantly; Nature wills that he should be plunged from sloth and passive contentment into labor and trouble, in order that he may find means of extricating himself from them'. These negative drives stand at the origin of history, but they are gradually stripped away as history unfolds and humanity becomes increasingly rational.[37] Crick does not believe in progress but, like Kant, considers that human beings' appetites and drives provide the motor of history: 'Supposing it's revolutions which divert and impede the course of our inborn curiosity. Supposing it's curiosity . . . which is our natural and fundamental state of mind. Supposing it's our insatiable and feverish desire to know about things . . . which is the true and rightful subverter and defeats even our impulse for historical progression'. Whereas Kant posits the transformation of this kind of discontent ('Curiosity will never be content', Crick remarks) into wisdom, Crick sees it as so fundamental to human nature that it is unalterable.[38] It is for this reason that revolutions must fail and that history can only move in circles:

> Children, there's something which revolutionaries and prophets of new worlds and even humble champions of Progress . . . can't abide. Natural history, human nature. . . . Because just supposing – but don't let the cat out of the bag – this natural stuff is always getting the better of the artificial stuff. Just supposing – but don't whisper it too much abroad – this unfathomable stuff we're made from, this stuff that we're always coming back to . . . is more anarchic, more subversive than any Tennis-Court Oath ever was. That's why these revolutions always have a whiff of the death-wish about them. That's why there's always a Terror waiting round the corner.[39]

Espousing neither Carlyle's faith in a past arcadian community nor Kant's belief in a future rational society, Crick offers a static account of human identity that perfectly underpins his undialectical account of history.

Crick's conception of history is ambivalent. Depending on his mood, it is either a kind of defensive fabulation that keeps existential fears at bay by casting life into narrative form or a genuine mode of cognition that provides access to reality. The text does not allow these inconsistencies to be resolved into a pleasing harmony. But the context in which Crick elaborates his views provides important clues to his state of mind and helps to clarify the reasons for his occasional scepticism. Although he is a historian by profession, Crick's impartiality is hampered by his harrowing experiences. He learns as an adolescent about his mother's incest with his grandfather, and he is also largely responsible for the chain of events that culminates in Freddie Parr's murder, Mary's horrendous abortion, and Dick's suicide. As an adult, he faces not only the collapse of his marriage when Mary, unable to cope with the burden of their past, 'cease[s] to belong to reality', but also the sack when his school's headmaster proposes to close the history department. A general fear of impending nuclear war surrounds these events, leading Crick's most gifted student to assert that the 'only important thing about history . . . is that it's got to the point where it's probably about to end'.[40]

Waterland is on this level a contemporary Condition-of-England novel that portrays the country in unremittingly dystopian terms. Crick's narrative is a record of decline. The historical cycle has long since reached its zenith and has steadily been approaching its nadir. The Atkinson family's once great brewing industry has fallen into desuetude, and its personal relations have decayed into incest between father and daughter, producing a brain-damaged suicide as an heir. Tom Crick's life lies in ruins around him, for he has been made redundant and his wife has been committed to a mental asylum. Contemporary society is being decimated by savage government cuts in public spending while the arms race is continued, leaving Crick to wonder what education has to offer 'when deprived of its necessary partner, the future, and faced with – no future at all?'.[41] In addition, fears about the end of history are echoed in anxieties about the end of historiography. Finding the grand explanatory theses no longer tenable, Crick presides over the death of the metaphysical conception of universal history and its rebirth as a form of pragmatism.

There are moments in *Waterland* when Crick, like both his mother and father before him, seeks to evade the reality of history. But the novel's persistent emphasis on his disastrous personal circumstances suggests that his retreat into story-telling can plausibly be seen as the product of his private despair and his oft-acknowledged desire to resist meaninglessness. The novel invites readers to play off its narrator's scepticism against his defence of civilization, his view of history as a form of reclamation, and his avowal that, for all its limitations and imperfections, it is an empirical discipline that has a pedagogic purpose because it 'teaches us . . . to avoid illusion and make-believe . . . to be realistic'. Crick's ambivalence places him somewhere between two extreme views – a positivist conception of history as objective truth or a textualist one that sees it as a form of quasi-literary narrative. *Waterland* thus suggests that although historical knowledge may be incomplete, and its procedures inexact, it nevertheless confronts an object domain that resists being turned into a species of fairy-tale. Reclaimed territory, Crick quite properly reminds his readers, is 'land that was once water, and which, even today, is not quite solid', but it has been reclaimed for all that.[42]

Waterland does not offer this modest conception of history as its last word, however. The trajectory of its narrative discloses just how firmly it belongs to the tradition of the Counter-Enlightenment. *Waterland* rejects Kant's hope that 'after many reformative revolutions, a universal cosmopolitan condition, which Nature has as her ultimate purpose, will come into being as the womb wherein all the original capacities of the human race can develop'.[43] Nor can it conjure up anything remotely like Carlyle's theodicy. The Enlightenment's faith in the beneficent powers of reason is turned on its head. The novel ironizes the Enlightenment's overweening aspirations, signalling its distance from Condorcet's belief that 'the perfectibility of man is truly indefinite', by suggesting that human nature 'cleaves to itself' and 'perpetually travels back to where it came from'.[44] But Crick's Counter-Enlightenment perspective needs to be differentiated from postmodernism's reaction against the

Enlightenment. The latter challenges Enlightenment universalism in the name of heterogeneity and difference; the former does so in the name of a fixed, cyclical theory of history that derives, in turn, from his deeply negative conception of humankind's post-lapsarian nature. Thus *Waterland* turns Kant's faith in Horace's *sapere aude* on its head. The curiosity and critical spirit that Crick enjoins his pupils never to relinquish turns out to have the sort of disastrous consequences that neither Kant nor Condorcet ever predicted. Mary's and Tom's sexual curiosity leads ultimately to death and madness. Dick's desire to have the riddle of his life answered ('D-Dick want know') leads directly to his suicide.[45] Kant's teleology is thus inverted, for 'blind chance takes the place of the guiding thread of reason'.[46] *Waterland* certainly foregrounds the human discontent that Kant saw as the mainspring of human progress, but, in keeping with its Counter-Enlightenment ethos, the novel suggests that the fruit of knowledge thereby produced comes from a cankered tree.

Julian Barnes

Flaubert's Parrot focuses on the problems inherent in the writing of biography and history. The quest for Flaubert's parrot – symbol of the novelist's authentic voice – blurs into the search for a veridical account of the past. The biographer and the historian confront a pile of fragments and traces, out of which they attempt to reconstruct an original wholeness. But for Geoffrey Braithwaite, the novel's middle-aged narrator, any such reconstruction is doomed from the outset:

> It isn't so different, the way we wander through the past. Lost, disordered, fearful, we follow what signs there remain; we read the street names, but cannot be confident where we are. All around is wreckage. . . . We look in at a window. Yes, it's true; despite the carnage some delicate things have survived. A clock still ticks. Prints on the wall remind us that art was once appreciated here. A parrot's perch catches the eye. We look for the parrot. Where is the parrot? We still hear its voice; but all we can see is a bare wooden perch. The bird has flown.

The historian cannot provide a reliable account of the past; she or he hears the parrot's faint squawks but never its full speech. The fragments that are present point inexorably to what is absent; they permit only partial accounts, signalling all the while that vast areas of the past remain irrecoverable. Not surprisingly, then, Braithwaite's search for the authentic Flaubert proves to be inconclusive. Confronted initially by the claims of two stuffed parrots, each of which could have been Flaubert's, he eventually discovers that there are fifty equally plausible candidates in a local museum and wearily concedes defeat: 'Perhaps it was one of them'.[47]

Barnes's preoccupation with the inaccessibility of the past leads him to focus less on the past itself – the object of historical enquiry – than on the modes by which it is apprehended. Metafictional texts such as *Flaubert's Parrot* and *A History of the World in 10½ Chapters* reveal how reliant human beings are on cognitive paradigms and suggest that different paradigms generate dissimilar bodies of knowledge. Both novels concentrate on the role of mediation itself, not only exploring alternative strategies for reading, interpreting, and writing the past but also showing how these very strategies produce competing, often incompatible, accounts of it. The novels' preoccupation with the way that different discourses map reality extends to their respective forms and structures. Although *Flaubert's Parrot* borrows from the genre of detective fiction, being in part an intellectual whodunnit, it is hardly written like one. In fact the novel alerts its readers to its own textuality. It includes different kinds of writing (exam script, critical exegesis, dictionary, biography, autobiography), provides three alternative chronologies of Flaubert's life, which emphasize different key events, and indulges in some peremptory reflections on the state of contemporary fiction. The questing and absurd figure of Braithwaite presides over proceedings, ensuring the novel's forward momentum, but the narrative is constantly retarded (in Shklovsky's phrase) by numerous disruptions. This retardation defamiliarizes the biographical genre and the realist conventions that predominantly underpin it. *Flaubert's Parrot* focuses attention on its multiple narrative models and invites the reader to see that their different ways of mapping a subject – the biography of Flaubert, the historical past – constitute it. *A History of the World*, in turn, adopts a postmodernist version of spatial form. Whereas modernist writers escaped what they saw as the limitations of realism by employing recursive plots and by weaving dense allusive patterns that often drew on myth, Barnes takes this approach in another direction. *A History* is not organized around a single set of characters and a clear plot-line but is divided into what are almost ten-and-a-half separate short stories, which are linked only by shared concerns (the nature of history, the dangers of binary thinking) and recurrent motifs (the ark, the deluge, the apocalypse). Each story is told from a different perspective and in a new register. Like *Flaubert's Parrot*, *A History* offers a refracted view of history. It also provides a whistle-stop tour of the possibilities inherent in the novel genre, making use of first-person, second-person, and third-person narration; male and female narrators; epistolary writing; chronological shifts; meditative chapters on the connectedness of history, love and truth; fables; and apocalyptic fantasies. The text thus becomes a kind of cyclical collage which expunges teleology and totality, the writer acknowledging that he is condemned to traffic in scraps and fragments.

Flaubert's Parrot, for all its frame-breaking devices, is in many respects a more seamless text than *A History*. This is in part because Braithwaite functions as the novel's controlling consciousness and in part because the text is relentlessly recursive, doubling back upon itself in order to enact the hermeneutic circle that it has set itself to explore. *Flaubert's Parrot*, a novel about interpretation, not only discusses the difficulties of its own interpretation but also informs the reader how to interpret it. The novel raises the problem of interpretation early on:

> You can define a net in one of two ways, depending on your point of view. Normally, you would say that it is a meshed instrument designed to catch fish. But you could, with no great injury to logic, reverse the image and define a net as a jocular lexicographer once did: he called it a collection of holes tied together with string.
>
> You can do the same with a biography. The trawling net fills, then the biographer hauls it in, sorts, throws back, stores, fillets and sells. Yet consider what

he doesn't catch: there is always far more of that. The biography stands, fat and worthy-burgherish on the shelf, boastful and sedate: a shilling life will give you all the facts, a ten pound one all the hypotheses as well. But think of everything that got away, that fled with the last deathbed exhalation of the biographee. What chance would the craftiest biographer stand against the subject who saw him coming and decided to amuse himself?

Much of this is typical of Barnes; the emphasis falls on what is lost or inaccessible, on interstices and gaps, on the faint presence of the parrot's voice but the regrettable absence of the bird itself. The twist comes at the end, however, when Braithwaite implies that a subject as self-conscious as Flaubert, who deliberately sets out to frustrate an inquisitive posterity, poses particularly awkward problems for research. The ever-enigmatic, ironic, secretive Flaubert becomes a test-case of historical interpretation for Braithwaite, whose entire narrative is geared towards showing that Flaubert can never really be known. So in the first chapter he provides alternative accounts of Flaubert's work, offering the 'writer as healer'; the 'writer as butcher, the writer as sensitive brute'; the writer as 'a sophisticated parrot' who is, in a parody of French post-structuralism, *'un symbole du Logos'*; the writer either as 'a pertinacious and finished stylist' who commands language or 'as one who considered language tragically insufficient', a passive colluder in the belief that *'on est parlé* – one is spoken'.[48] In the second chapter he offers three different chronologies of Flaubert's life, each of which gives rise to a markedly different picture of the novelist. In the hilarious third chapter he provides a plausible account of Flaubert's relationship with Julie Herbert but admits it is unverifiable because the historical evidence has been destroyed. In the sixth chapter he lampoons literary critics' inaccurate readings of Flaubert's work, ridiculing their pretensions and distortions. In the eleventh chapter he gives a woman's version of Flaubert the man, exposing his insecurities, selfishness, and emotional dishonesty. None of this fazes Braithwaite. Apparently searching for the authentic Flaubert and for an all-encompassing account of his œuvre, he gleefully throws out one hypothesis after another; although he is unable to draw any decisive conclusions from his detective work, he seems to take a positively Barthesian pleasure in the multiplicity of interpretations available to him.

Flaubert's slippery elusiveness is emblematic of the wider problem of apprehending history. The past, Braithwaite claims, is 'a piglet . . . smeared with grease'; those trying to catch it fall over while trying and are 'made to look ridiculous in the process'. So is Braithwaite himself made to look ridiculous in his quest for the past? Well, not exactly, and the reason why this is so takes me back to my earlier claim that the text ironically doubles back upon itself, foregrounding the hermeneutic circle in which it is trapped and thus pre-empting both its own attempts to understand Flaubert and the reader's attempts to interpret Braithwaite and his own narrative. As the text unfolds, it becomes increasingly apparent that Braithwaite is modelling himself on Flaubert. He adopts Flaubert's ironic tone, mimics his disingenuousness, and adjures the reader to make sense of him just as he makes sense of Flaubert: 'you must make your judgment on me as well as on Flaubert'.[49] As Braithwaite embarks on the paper-chase he hopes will lead him to Flaubert, he strews clues about himself in his wake. The reader is urged to construct a biography of Braithwaite while the latter constructs one of Flaubert. But Braithwaite remains as unknowable as his subject. The paradigm he slyly selects for his autobiography constructs him in a way that conceals as much as it reveals. His life-story is a laughably conventional Freudian one: he is sexually impotent and a failed writer; a potentially repressed homosexual; a figure desperate for recognition who dreams of bringing off a literary coup; a buffoon who denies he is a crank while writing to French grocers to enquire if the colour of redcurrant jam is the same now as it was in 1853. These all-too-obvious clues are intended to divert the inattentive reader down a series of blind alleys. Braithwaite describes Flaubert's *Dictionnaire des Idées Réçues* as 'a catalogue of cliches' in which the novelist ridicules the conventional thought of his day for its willingness unthinkingly to follow social norms. His own mischievous account of his life ('How easy it is to set off speculation', he remarks) offers a parallel to the *Dictionary*, for it ironizes not only the desire for a final, decisive account of a life but also the willingness to provide such an account by fitting it to a Procrustean paradigm – in this case a vulgar Freudian one – at the slightest instigation. By this doubling of narratives, Braithwaite's autobiographical story, which leaves the truth largely hidden, mirrors his biographical account of Flaubert, who remains as elusive as his never to be discovered parrot.[50]

There is another sense in which Braithwaite tries to resist the reader's autonomous incursions into his text. He carries out his own interpretation, setting the novel up to be read in a certain way. He structures his narrative in such a way that the reader's approach to it is effectively forestalled because it is directed down certain paths. He impedes interpretation by anticipating the moves by which it might proceed and by setting up his own protocols for how his narrative should be read. His 'clues' about his character are part of this tactic, for he tries to direct the reader's response not only by revealing things about himself in a clearly calculated manner but also by glossing whatever he reveals. He frequently addresses the reader in a quasi-Socratic manner, dispatching potentially awkward questions and objections before they have actually been voiced. Braithwaite thus constructs his own imaginary interlocutor in order to crowd out a reader's alternative responses. He is sanguine about this, even admitting that his desire to control interpretation may be infuriating: 'Do you know the colour of Flaubert's eyes? No, you don't: for the simple reason that I suppressed it a few pages ago. I didn't want you to be tempted by cheap conclusions. See how carefully I look after you. You don't like it? I *know* you don't like it'.[51]

Braithwaite's strategy only appears to invite dialogue and to solicit a response, for his narrative, in keeping with his monomania, is monologic; it seeks to interpellate the reader and thus to produce the terms in which the text is to be read. If interpretation is so problematic, if the seeker of know-ledge (as figured in this novel) is confronted either by fifty parrots among which he cannot choose or by an abandoned perch, can he or she make any claim to knowledge at all? For Braithwaite, Flaubert's parrot – an over-determined symbol – is 'a fluttering, elusive emblem of the writer's voice'. The writer's evasiveness, in turn, functions as an emblem of the slipperiness of the broader historical past, which is variously a greased piglet; a collection of holes tied together by string; a wrecked, labyrinthine city in which most of the signposts have been destroyed; a bare perch. Knowledge of the past seems to be a form of fabulation, 'merely another literary genre'. It is, in any case, always just out of reach:

> The past is a distant, receding coastline and we are all in the same boat. Along the stern rail there is a line of telescopes; each brings the shore into focus at a given distance. If the boat is becalmed, one of the telescopes will be in continual use; it will seem to tell the whole, the unchanging truth. But this is an illusion; and as the boat sets off again, we return to our normal activity: scurrying from one telescope to another, seeing the sharpness fade in one, waiting for the blur to clear in another. And when the blur does clear, we imagine that we have made it do so all by ourselves.[52]

The image of a blurred coastline, dependent on the observer's perspective, suggests that the past can only be known obliquely, and Barnes's multi-perspectival narrative provides the literary form that enacts this view.

In *Flaubert's Parrot* the past is protean and irrecoverable. The novel avoids closure by concluding with 'an answer and not an answer . . . an ending, and not an ending'. *A History* also explores the past but uses indirection in a different manner. Its ten-and-a-half chapters, linked by the recurrent motifs and allusions mentioned earlier, explore the disastrous consequences of binary oppositions that sanction hierarchies of value and principles of exclusion. A key target of the novel is the kind of binary thinking that allows social groups to displace violent instincts onto sacrificial scapegoats. Several oppositions surface and resurface throughout the novel: clean/unclean; sacred/profane; male/female; communication/excommunication; Arab/Jew; nature/civilization; believer/unbeliever. The novel breaks these divisions down, either ironizing the rationales behind them or showing their deadly consequences. In 'The Stowaway', the world according to *anobium domesticum*, the humblest of all the creatures on board the Ark, provides a burlesque of Genesis. But this view of history from below, offered by an 'unclean' stowaway deemed insufficiently worthy to be saved, sounds several of the novel's key concerns: the distinction between the elect and the damned; the role played by religion in sanctioning and promoting such distinctions; the rigorous policing engaged in by representatives of the sacred who forbid the blurring of these boundaries and extirpate transgressors. By disclosing how religious codes often sanction scapegoating, the text foregrounds what René Girard sees as the inescapable connection between violence and the sacred.[53] Miscegenation is expressly forbidden on the Ark. Purity (cleanness) functions as the means by which the group preserves its inviolability, making it easier to identify outsiders as potential sources of pollution and therefore to scapegoat them. As a species, the worm claims, human beings are forever trying to displace responsibility for their own actions onto others: 'The Fall was the serpent's fault, the honest raven was a slacker and a glutton, the goat turned Noah into an alkie'.[54]

A History deconstructs and rejects the various polarities that enable groups to totemize their own practices and belief systems such that those who are excluded can be perceived as unclean, with all the consequences that follow. Barnes's exploration of these issues places him squarely in the territory inhabited by Rushdie. The form and structure of *A History* enacts its author's refusal to recognize hierarchies between social, racial and religious groups; it offers a plethora of narrative modes, which celebrates the novel-genre's heterogeneity, and disrupts the symmetry (purity) of a neat ten-chapter account of the world's history by making its most impassioned claims in a parenthetical aside, a gap in the text. In *Imaginary Homelands* Rushdie observes that *The Satanic Verses* 'rejoices in mongrelization and fears the absolutism of the Pure'.[55] The narrator in 'Parenthesis', who surely speaks for the author here, speaks of love as the 'starting-point for civic virtue', since one 'can't love someone without imaginative sympathy, without beginning to see the world from another point of view'. *A History* is full of alternative viewpoints, ranging from a woodworm's to an astronaut's. It reserves its severest irony for the most zealot-like believers (Spike Tiggler, Amanda Ferguson). Like Rushdie's work, the novel celebrates plurality; its final chapter implicitly rejects all the oppositions that it has dissected in the preceding pages. The narrator's dream of heaven reveals that there will be no judgment, no summing up of a life, no final separation by a godhead of the clean from the unclean. The displacement of guilt onto sacrificial others is ruled out of court, and people are forced to learn the post-metaphysical lesson that they are 'stuck with being themselves'.[56]

A History is a split, fissured text; it not only consists of multiple narrative modes and seemingly unrelated story lines but also celebrates heterogeneity through its treatment of alterity. So does the novel thereby promote a view of history as a vast compendium of different *petits récits* – each told from a different perspective and conceptual system – which can never be encompassed by an overarching metanarrative but can only be played off against one another in the form of a mosaic or collage? It is certainly the case that the novel's spatial form, which establishes links between the text's chapters only on thematic grounds, leaves it open-ended. But the novel confronts head-on the difficulties of writing history; specifically, in a text so full of fables and allegories, it asks whether history is itself a form of fabulation. The issue is initially broached in 'The Survivor', wherein an apparently psychotic woman imagines that nuclear war has finally happened. Her psychiatrist explains that she has displaced her internal conflicts onto an external source: 'the technical term is fabulation. You make up a story to cover the facts you don't know or can't accept. You keep a few true facts and spin a new story round them.' But the protagonist rejects this account: 'We've got to look at things how they are; we can't rely on fabulation any more. It's the only way we'll survive'.[57] Fabulation is later explicitly linked to the writing of history in 'Parenthesis':

> History isn't what happened. History is just what historians tell us. There was a pattern, a plan, a movement, expansion, the march of democracy; it is a tapestry, a flow of events, a complex narrative, connected, explicable. One good story leads to another. First it was kings and archbishops with some offstage divine tinkering, then it was the march of ideas and the movements of masses, then little local events which mean something bigger, but all the time it's connections, progress, meaning, this led to this, this happened because of this. And we, the readers of history, the sufferers from history, we scan the pattern for hopeful conclusions, for the way ahead. And we cling to history as a series of salon pictures, conversation pieces whose participants we can easily reimagine back into life, when all the time it's more like a multi-media collage, with paint applied by decorator's roller rather than camel-hair brush.

The history of the world? Just voices echoing in the dark; images that burn for a few centuries and then fade; stories, old stories that sometimes seem to overlap; strange links, impertinent connections. We lie in our hospital bed of the present. . . . And while we fret and writhe in bandaged uncertainty . . . we fabulate. We make up a story to cover the facts we don't know or can't accept; we keep a few true facts and spin a new story round them. Our panic and our pain are only eased by soothing fabulation; we call it history.

This sceptical, ironic account of the shifting emphases in historians' paradigms and the prevalence of beliefs in human progress seems to uphold the notion of such accounts as mere fables. History, it tells us, is narrative not event, the imposition of order where there is none, and the illusion of teleology where there is absence of meaning.

But this account of history as a form of fabulation is incomplete, which makes sense, given the text's hostility to the falsifications of history that sanction and promote displacement of guilt onto others. What redeems the writing of history from both banal myths of progress and pernicious falsehoods about outsider groups is the possibility that the will to fabulate – born of panic, pain, and the desire to avoid what is threatening to a society's self-perception – can be overcome by a will to truth. In *A History* the civic virtue predicated on the 'imaginative sympathy' that embraces otherness finds its source in a love that is linked to truth: 'I can tell you why to love. Because the history of the world, which only stops at the half-house of love to bulldoze it into rubble, is ridiculous without it. . . . Love won't change the history of the world . . . but it will do something much more important: teach us to stand up to history, to ignore its chin-out strut'.[58]

It is at this point that *A History* approaches Benjamin's 'Theses on the Philosophy of History'. The novel has throughout presented its exploration of multiple perspectives, narrative modes, grids, and paradigms against the background of apocalyptic fears. Benjamin's immensely suggestive but fragmented meditations on history fuse Jewish messianism with Marxist materialism. For Benjamin the 'past carries with it a temporal index by which it is referred to redemption', and 'only a redeemed mankind receives the full-ness of its past'. But this full knowledge is unattainable until the past becomes 'citable in all its moments . . . and that day is Judgment Day'. Because at any given present moment this utopian day is in the future, is deferred, the task of the historian is to resist oppressive accounts of the past: 'In every era the attempt must be made anew to wrest tradition away from a conformism that is about to overpower it. . . . Only that historian will have the gift of fanning the spark of hope in the past who is firmly convinced that *even the dead* will not be safe from the enemy if he wins'. Benjamin is no positivist histori-ographer. But his reading of the traces left by the wreckage of history eschews any compact with fable; utilizing the heuristic model of the constellation, he focuses on fragments from the past that resonate with contradictions in order to make them speak to the present, for 'every image of the past that is not recognized by the present as one of its own concerns threatens to disappear irretrievably'.[59] Barnes's language echoes these Benjaminian sentiments:

Love and truth, yes, that's the prime connection. We all know objective truth is not obtainable, that when some event occurs we shall have a multiplicity of subjective truths which we assess and then fabulate into history, into some God-eyed version of what 'really' happened. This God-eyed version is a fake – a charming, impossible fake. . . . But while we know this, we must still believe that it is 99 per cent obtainable; or if we can't believe this we must believe that 43 per cent objective truth is better than 41 per cent. We must do so, because if we don't we're lost, we fall into beguiling relativity, we value one liar's version as much as another liar's, we throw up our hands at the puzzle of it all, we admit that the victor has the right not just to the spoils but also to the truth.[60]

The last sentence, which is perhaps most noticeably Benjaminian, is also reminiscent of Rushdie's impassioned plea for historical veracity and a polticized conception of the writer's role in 'Outside the Whale', a text that I discuss in the next section. Both novelists see a fundamental part of their task as the obligation to dissent from orthodoxy and to challenge hegemonic discourses. For Barnes, to surrender to fabulation is not only to embrace relativism, thus refusing to differentiate the less accurate from the more accurate, but also to submit to the metanarratives of those who are all too willing to falsify history in the interests of power. To the victor the 'truth' as well as the booty. Those who disbelieve in the possibility of an altruism whose redemptive face is set against domination and the discourses that uphold it 'merely surrender to the history of the world and to someone else's truth'.[61] And as Benjamin warns, the enemy whose 'truths' threaten to overbear even the dead 'has not ceased to be victorious'.[62]

Salman Rushdie

Midnight's Children and *Shame* are both concerned with history – that of India in the first case and that of Pakistan in the second. But what sort of conception of history do their respective narrative strategies urge? The controlling mode of *Midnight's Children* is an exuberant magic realism, whereas that of *Shame* is a self-reflexive form of allegory. Each text emphasizes its fictive qualities, stresses its provenance in the imagination, and distances itself through various literary devices from the historical events it treats. Both novels not only emphasize the difficulties of gaining reliable knowledge of the past but also stress that, since they are fictions rather than historical monographs, they offer refracted interpretations of the occurrences to which they refer. Thus the narrator of *Shame* admits: 'however I choose to write about over-there, I am forced to reflect that world in fragments of broken mirrors'.[63]

Midnight's Children is exemplary in this regard. Its anti-heroic, Shandyan narrator and central protagonist, Saleem Sinai, is an unreliable narrator *par excellence*. He struggles throughout the novel to make sense of the chaotic events in which he is unwittingly caught up. Although he is 'handcuffed to history' and although his life is 'the mirror of [India's] own', he is hard pressed to come up with a coherent account of either. He can neither grasp the detail of his own individual experiences nor get a grip on the totality that surrounds him.[64] Saleem's life, in fact, is the textual homologue of the nation's. A 'swallower of lives', he can only be understood if the reader 'swallow[s] the lot as well'. Even so, the picture can never be complete, for Saleem's perspective is a partial one; like the narrator of *Shame*, he is condemned 'to see [his] own life – its meanings, its structures – in fragments'.

This fragmentation eventually becomes literal when the disintegration of India's hopes for national unity is enacted on his body: 'I have begun to crack all over like an old jug . . . my poor body, singular, unlovely, buffeted by too much history . . . has started coming apart at the seams. In short, I am literally disintegrating . . . I shall eventually crumble into (approximately) six hundred and thirty million particles of anonymous, and necessarily oblivious dust'.[65]

Midnight's Children is at pains to stress the difficulty of reconstructing history, of differentiating fact from fantasy, and of developing a totalizing account of the past. Saleem gets various historical facts wrong and is sometimes aware of this and sometimes not.[66] In the main these are lapses of memory, and *Midnight's Children* is to some extent a novel about the vagaries of memory. Part of Rushdie's original aim was the Proustian 'search for lost time', but in the process of writing the novel his subject became 'the way in which we remake the past to suit our present purposes, using memory as our tool'.[67] The problem of perspective is a related one:

> Reality is a question of perspective; the further you get from the past, the more concrete and plausible it seems – but as you approach the present, it inevitably seems more and more incredible. Suppose yourself in a large cinema, sitting at first in the back row, and gradually moving up, row by row, until your nose is almost pressed against the screen. Gradually the stars' faces dissolve into dancing grain; tiny details assume grotesque proportions; the illusion dissolves – or rather, it becomes clear that the illusion itself *is* reality.

Saleem is unreliable partly because he is a participant in the story he is recounting and partly because he is too close to events and thus lacks the requisite distance: 'we are too close to what is happening, perspective is impossible, later perhaps analysts will say why and wherefore, will adduce underlying economic trends and political developments, but right now we're too close to the cinema-screen, the picture is breaking up into dots, only subjective judgments are possible'.[68]

It proves equally hard to separate fact from fantasy within the textual economy of *Midnight's Children*. Accounts of the War in the Rann of Kutch (1965), for example, are so various and mutually incompatible that it is impossible to ascertain what actually took place. Fiction and reality blur together, rendering the bewildered narrator helpless: 'The war in the Rann lasted until July 1st. That much is fact; but everything else lies concealed beneath the doubly hazy air of unreality and make-believe which affected all goings-on in those days, and especially all events in the phantasmagoric Rann . . . so that the story I am going to tell . . . is as likely to be true as anything; as anything, that is to say, except what we were officially told'. Saleem's attempt to clarify what happened in the Rann is, by his own admission, doomed from the outset. Although he gamely persists, admonishing himself to 'concentrate on good hard facts', his account finally collapses: 'Nothing was real; nothing certain'. Just as he is unable to ascertain what took place during this one particular conflict, so is he more roundly defeated in his efforts to comprehend the overall pattern and meaning of post-Independence Indian history. The text proleptically announces that he will lose his 'struggle against cracks' and ultimately leaves him a broken man: 'No longer connected to history, drained above-and-below, I made my way back to the capital, conscious that an age, which had begun on that long-ago midnight, had come to a sort of end'.[69] *Midnight's Children*, then, is obsessed with the difficulties of reliably recreating the past and offers no glib solutions to the problems it articulates. Its view of history is imbued with uncertainties and hedged about with doubts. But if *Midnight's Children* discloses the frequent interpenetration of reality and fantasy, it also emphasizes the need to differentiate them. The novel is replete with verifiable historical occurrences; it makes detailed reference to events such as the Amritsar massacre, the Rowlatt Act, Brigadier Dyer's Martial Law regulations, the election campaigns of 1957, the India–Pakistan conflicts and the Sino-Indian border disputes, India's nuclear tests, and the state of Emergency in 1975.[70] These historical details not only serve as the novel's scaffolding but also function as the referent against which Saleem's fabulation constantly bumps up. It is not just that this external referent enables Saleem to correct his most obvious factual errors (such as dates) but that it sets limits to his inventiveness. *Midnight's Children* is thus a double-voiced narrative in which a personal discourse of self-discovery and remembrance interacts with, and is constrained by, a public discourse of history and politics. Consider the following passage:

> There followed an illusionist January, a time so still on its surface that 1947 seemed not to have begun at all. (While, of course, in fact . . .) In which the Cabinet Mission – old Pethick-Lawrence, clever Cripps, military A. V. Alexander – saw their scheme for the transfer of power fail. (But of course, in fact it would only be six months until . . .) In which the viceroy, Wavell, understood that he was finished, washed-up, or in our own expressive word, funtoosh. (Which, of course, in fact only speeded things up, because it let in the last of the viceroys, who . . .)[71]

My point here is not to ascertain whether Saleem's account of what really took place is accurate but to show that he believes such an account to be in principle obtainable. He notes that, at the time, it 'was impossible to see the great machineries grinding', but his own retrospective narrative reveals these political machineries to have been busily at work and claims to identify them. He reiterates this view when acknowledging that he is too close to the Emergency to comprehend it but that others will later 'adduce underlying economic trends and political developments'.[72]

Midnight's Children persistently admonishes those who either succumb to private fantasies about the world or distort it for political purposes.[73] Its much-vaunted magic realism thus needs to be carefully assessed, for there is a risk of thinking that the text is making a *general* point about the nature of *all* history. But the novel's chosen narrative mode is inextricable from its particular subject. *Midnight's Children* offers a fictional account of a specific country in a determinate historical period, one that coruscated with competing hopes, dreams, ambitions, intrigues, and myths. To tell this story in flat, realist prose would be to deny the diversity, dynamism, and political confusion of that country at that time. Rushdie's verbal pyrotechnics, I suggest, attempt to do justice to the period's often unreal atmosphere rather than to make some universal claim about the intrinsically fantastic nature of all history. Rushdie's narrative mode does not seek to do away with the distinction between fantasy and reality but shows how strange and unstable was the political reality of the time.

That this is the case can be seen in the way that the very concept of India itself is portrayed as a kind of fantasy:

[A] nation which had never previously existed was about to win its freedom, catapulting us into a world which, although it had five thousand years of history, although it had invented the game of chess and traded with Middle Kingdom Egypt, was nevertheless quite imaginary; into a mythical land, a country which would never exist except by the efforts of a phenomenal collective will – except in a dream we all agreed to dream; it was a mass fantasy shared in varying degrees by Bengali and Punjabi, Madrasi and Jat, and would periodically need the sanctification and renewal which can only be provided by rituals of blood. India, the new myth – a collective fiction in which anything was possible, a fable rivalled only by the two other mighty fantasies: money and God.

The language employed here is ambiguous, double-edged. If India is 'a mythical land' and the product of 'a dream' – a potentially utopian country – then it is also 'quite imaginary' and 'a mass fantasy' – a collective delusion that will regularly result in bloodshed. The text figures these different readings of India through the opposition between the potential of the midnight's children and the exigencies (genuine and manufactured) of Realpolitik, and through the dualistic conflict between Shiva and Saleem. But as the novel approaches its pessimistic climax, it becomes clear that Rushdie's magic realism is actively ranged against delusion and distortion. His most pungent satire is directed at the numerous falsifications of history in the propaganda enveloping the war between India and Pakistan in 1965: 'And on the radio, what destruction, what mayhem! In the first five days of the war Voice of Pakistan announced the destruction of more aircraft than India had ever possessed; in eight days, All-India Radio massacred the Pakistan Army down to, and considerably beyond, the last man'. Because during wartime it is impossible to know precisely what is happening, the text first ramifies into a series of ironic rhetorical questions which allude to key events while acknowledging that the full truth may never be revealed, and then adopts the language of unreality in order to expose the grotesque horrors being concealed:

> Shaheed and I saw many things which were not true, which were not possible, because our boys would not could not have behaved so badly; we saw men in spectacles with heads like eggs being shot in side-streets, we saw the intelligentsia of the city being massacred by the hundred, but it was not true because it could not have been true . . . and Shaheed began his, 'No, buddha – what a thing, Allah, you can't believe your eyes – no, not true, how can it – buddha, tell, what's got into my eyes?' And at last the buddha spoke, knowing Shaheed could not hear: 'O, Shaheeda,' he said, revealing the depths of his fastidiousness, 'a person must sometimes choose what he will see and what he will not; look away, look away from there now.' But Shaheed was staring at a maidan in which lady doctors were being bayoneted before they were raped, and raped again before they were shot. Above them and behind them, the cool white minaret of a mosque stared blindly down upon the scene.[74]

This harrowing passage encapsulates one of the novel's key preoccupations: to look away, or not look away? To confront reality or to evade it? These questions bring us back to the problem of historical knowledge.

The narrator of *Shame* grapples openly with 'the problem of history: what to retain, what to dump, how to hold on to what memory insists on relinquishing, how to deal with change'. Although he seeks to impose his artistic vision onto reality, he is aware that reality may well fight back.

Pakistan, for example, is like a palimpsest; it could only be created by rewriting the past, by 'cover[ing] up Indian history'. But what lies beneath this thin veneer will not be concealed; the past 'refuses to be suppressed . . . is daily doing battle with the present'. *Shame* thus confronts Benjamin's claim in the 'Theses' that the victorious write history to serve their own ends, suppressing all accounts that would question their self-justifications: 'History is natural selection. Mutant versions of the past struggle for dominance. . . . Only the mutations of the strong survive. The weak, the anonymous, the defeated leave few marks: field-patterns, axe-heads, folk-tales, broken pitchers, burial mounds, the fading memory of their youthful beauty. History loves only those who dominate her'.[75] In *Midnight's Children* Saleem's recognition of the way reality resists the overt falsification of such mutant accounts leads him to repudiate a thoroughgoing textualism. Owning up to a conscious 'fib', he quickly reproves himself: 'for the first time, I fell victim to the temptation of every autobiographer, to the illusion that since the past exists only in one's memories and the words which strive vainly to encapsulate them, it is possible to create past events simply by saying they occurred'.[76] He reprimands himself for this falsehood because it is uncomfortably close in tenor to the lies told by the politicians and propagandists against which he has struggled throughout the course of his narrative. (*Shame*'s narrator's 'most damning accusation' is that '[m]en who deny their pasts become incapable of thinking them real'.[77]) When Saleem contemplates a variety of endings to his tale, he is again brought up short: 'but reality is nagging at me. Love does not conquer all, except in the Bombay talkies; rip tear crunch will not be defeated by a mere ceremony; and optimism is a disease'. Saleem has been guilty both of optimism and of hubris. Thus he tells his story as an act of manumission, releasing himself from the bonds of fantasy, and of atonement, leaving the thirty chapters of his memento as thirty jars of pickle 'waiting to be unleashed upon the amnesiac nation'.[78]

Memory and forgetfulness are repeatedly associated with truth and falsehood in *Midnight's Children*, a point underlined by the novel's end. Saleem, who has 'come through amnesia and been shown the extent of its immorality', is horrified at his companions' willingness to forget the recent past. He notes that 'they had mislaid their powers of retention, so that now they had become incapable of judgment, having forgotten everything to which they could compare anything that happened'. His obsessive desire to retain as full a memory of the past as possible thus stands as a *mise-en-abîme* of Rushdie's own purpose in *Midnight's Children*. Saleem readily admits the limitations of his narrative, remarking that 'distortions are inevitable' and that the 'process of revision should be constant and endless'. No simplistic historiographer this, he yet maintains that, despite the distortions and imperfections, his goal 'is to change the flavour in degree, but not in kind'. History, which like the brutal truths of war should be faced, can only meaningfully be evoked if it raises genuine validity claims: 'One day, perhaps, the world may taste the pickles of history. They may be too strong for some palates, their smell may be overpowering, tears may rise to eyes; I hope nevertheless that it will be possible to say of them that they possess the authentic taste of truth'.[79]

Rushdie's conception of history is without question tinged with the uncertainties characteristic of recent postmodernist and New Historicist writing on the subject. This nuanced conception cannot be elided into a hardheaded positivist one, for Rushdie emphasizes the necessary limitations of any given account of past or present. Post-colonial writers cannot 'lay claim to Olympus' because they 'have been forced by cultural displacement to accept the provisional nature of all truths, all certainties'. But this stress on incompleteness and doubt goes hand in hand with a robust defence of values that many postmodernists claim to have discredited. Thus Rushdie consistently invokes universal human rights. He notes of India, for example, that it 'is a paradoxical fact that secularism, which has been much under attack of late, outside India as well as inside it, is the only way of safeguarding the constitutional, civil, human and, yes, religious rights of minority groups'.[80] Rushdie regularly insists on the importance of differentiating truth from falsehood. He writes of official information about the 1965 India–Pakistan war that 'the only certain thing was that it was hopelessly and deliberately misleading';[81] he notes of his lecture 'The New Empire Within Britain' that it was 'distorted, falsified and used against [him]'; and in his devastating critique of Attenborough's *Gandhi* he exposes its falsification of history, describing the portrayal of the Amritsar massacre as 'an unforgivable distortion'.[82] Rushdie's claim that there is a difference between distortion and the recognition that human beings do not have unmediated access to reality does not lead him to abandon emancipatory political and moral aspirations. Literature, he argues, should both 'give the lie to official facts' and confront 'a single, existential question: how are we to live in the world?'.[83] Rushdie's own answer to these issues cannot be extricated from his commitment to a radicalized, always questioned, but still indispensable, Enlightenment legacy. In *Shame*, for example, the opposition between anarchy and dictatorship is countered by a third possibility: 'The third option is the substitution of a new myth for the old one. Here are three such myths, all available from stock at short notice: liberty; equality; fraternity. I recommend them highly'.[84]

Much of the opposition to *The Satanic Verses* runs directly counter to these commitments. But whatever the merits of the case against the novel, it has become obscured by the posturing of both sides, who have all too often succeeded in reducing the complex issues involved to a set of simple dichotomies by providing caricatural versions of their opponents' views. The binary oppositions invoked are as well-worn as they are misleading: censorship/free speech; religion/secularism; fundamentalism/liberalism; East/West. Some liberals have defended a contextless version of free speech, ignoring the many restrictions placed on it in all societies, saying nothing about the inequity of British blasphemy laws, and portraying objections to the novel as the knee-jerk response of unthinking dogmatists.[85] Some Muslims, in turn, have asserted that the book is blasphemous and must simply be banned, ignoring the problem of how a non-believer can be termed a blasphemer, declaring freedom of speech a non-starter, and suggesting that anything less than complete condemnation of the novel is tantamount to a betrayal of the faith.[86] Most disturbing about this opposition between two opposed 'sides' is the monological absolutism that underpins each of them, leading to a conception of one's interlocutors as demonized Others rather than as participants in a properly civic debate. Bikhu Parekh notes how anger over the *fatwa* 'escalated step by even sillier step to a wholly mindless anger first against all *Bradford* Muslims, then against all *British* Muslims, then against all *Muslims*, and ultimately against *Islam* itself'.[87] In this way, liberals transformed an enormously differentiated response to *The Satanic Verses* on the part of Muslim communities – a response characterized by internal debates, conflicts and disagreements – into a uniform desire to ban the book and punish the author, by constructing a monolithic image of Islam. One could hardly find a better example of orientalism at work. But if some liberals have relied on barely concealed racist stereotypes of Islam, some fundamentalist Muslims have constructed a similarly unitary image of a decadent and profane West. Shabbir Akhtar claims that Christianity has been 'totally undermined' by its tolerance of blasphemy, argues that a 'faith which compromises its internal temper of militant wrath is destined for the dustbin of history', and declares that anyone 'who fails to be offended by Rushdie's book *ipso facto* ceases to be a Muslim'.[88] Those who espouse this intransigent position see Rushdie as a threat to the purity of their tradition and seek symbolically to expel him from their communities. On the one hand, both the author and the book are seen in terms of a contagion that threatens the community, and, on the other hand, Rushdie is a threat to himself, a figure described as a 'self-hating Indo-Anglian, totally alienated from his culture'.[89] On these purist views Rushdie is a traitorous and diseased fifth-columnist who seeks to infect the community. The possibility that his is a principled voice of dissent from within a shared, but internally fissured, tradition is summarily dismissed. A remark of Mary Douglas's seems apposite here: 'A polluting person is always in the wrong. He has developed some wrong condition or simply crossed some line which should not have been crossed and this displacement unleashes danger for someone'.[90]

The extremist standpoint that labels Rushdie a pollutant and traitor – a transgressor of fixed boundaries – denies him the status of interlocutor, renders him a non-person, and excludes him from further debate. Rushdie has always seen his work as transgressive, perceiving it as the means by which socially encoded boundaries can be questioned, criticized, and realigned. This view is basic to his conception of the writer's role: 'It seems to me completely legitimate that there should be dissent from orthodoxy, not just about Islam, but about anything'. Because he sees himself as contributing to a dialogue about (among other things) the nature of the intersection of religion and secularism in the late twentieth century, Rushdie refuses to be excluded in the way his opponents desire: 'the idea that what I'm saying is somehow outside Islam is one that I resist. I come from a Muslim tradition. . . . I know about Islam as well, and these people's Islam is not the only Islam'.[91] For Rushdie, to be expelled from the community is to be denied the right to participate in the ongoing process of its historical self-definition. The issue is one of authority – authority over scripts, traditions, and people. As Aziz Al-Azmeh has pointed out, the issue 'is who represents Muslims and who speaks in their name on a range of questions'. He argues that the claims of those who seek to create 'a definitive Islamic monolith' are spurious because they deny the diversity of traditions that comprises Islam in order to create 'a uniformity that has no justification in their histories or traditions'.[92] Rushdie contests this univocality and thus cannot be tolerated. Denied the status of principled dissenter, of spokesperson for views shared by other groups internal to the community, he is treated as an aberrant *individual* to be silenced.

This deracination of the writer finds its counterpart in the liberal defence of *The Satanic Verses*. Those who have supported Rushdie's right to freedom of expression have cut him off from the communities to which he belongs as effectively as his opponents have sought to do. Rushdie's supporters have tended to base their case on his rights and, indispensable though it is, the whole conception of rights is inseparable from the liberal individualist conception of the agent as an autonomous and isolated subject. As communitarian and civic republican critics have long maintained, rights-based views massively undervalue both human beings' fundamentally social character and their obligations to their communities.[93] Supporters of negative liberty focus almost exclusively on the individual's freedom from constraint, on the right to a life as unfettered as possible, but have little to say about concomitant duties and nothing to say about shared conceptions of *eudaimonia*. What is at issue here is not whether or not Rushdie's rights should be protected – they should – but that it is also important to recognize how the liberal defence of them cuts across Rushdie's own sense of himself as a novelist writing within different traditions and communities in order to address their constituent members. To sever him from this context is to render his work close to meaningless. As he himself puts it: 'the point of view from which I have, all my life, attempted [the] process of literary renewal is the result not of the self-hating, deracinated Uncle-Tomism of which some have accused me, but precisely of my determination to create a literary language and literary forms in which the experience of formerly colonized, still-disadvantaged peoples might find full expression'.[94] Rushdie does not so much write back – in a currently fashionable phrase – as write *against* from *within*.

The irony behind the liberalism/fundamentalism and society/individual dichotomies is that Rushdie's entire œuvre resists their simplicities. He explicitly repudiates, for example, the false distinction 'between Western freedoms and Eastern unfreedom'. His eclectic explorations of hybridity, migration, metamorphosis, displacement, ventriloquism, and plurality have challenged such easy oppositions, retaining what is valuable in the different traditions within which he works and discarding what is harmful, while insisting throughout that there is no way for writers like himself to escape the confrontation with diverse cultural perspectives: 'it is completely fallacious to suppose that there is such a thing as a pure, unalloyed tradition from which to draw . . . the very essence of Indian culture is that we possess a mixed tradition'.[95] But this awareness of multiplicity does not lead Rushdie to embrace a contentless pluralism – to valorize alterity and difference as inherently good. It leads him to confront the challenge pluralism poses by acknowledging that the richness of the mix does not sanction political and moral agnosticism. It is here that Rushdie's response to Orwell is of particular interest. Rushdie does not ask whether *Nineteen Eighty-Four*'s O'Brien is right or wrong but argues that he manifests Orwell's *defeatism* in the face of totalitarianism. This defeatism pervades both *Nineteen Eighty-Four*, dooming Winston from the outset, and the essay 'Inside the Whale', which concludes by espousing what amounts to a form of quietism. For Rushdie, the 'quietist option, the exhortation to submit to events, is an intrinsically conservative one'. Passivity, he avers, 'always serves the interests of the status quo' because if 'resistance is useless, those whom one might otherwise resist become omnipotent'.[96]

Rushdie's point is that, even if people cannot have decisive epistemological warrant for their ethical and political beliefs, the beliefs they hold and the actions they predicate upon them have real consequences in the real world. The view that language games are so many different ways of talking about the world but are in no way constrained by its lineaments not only trivializes language but also has far-reaching implications for day-to-day life. It trivializes language because it refuses to recognize that to use a discourse is not to remain locked in a purely linguistic realm but is to adopt a stance *vis-à-vis* the world that has momentous non-linguistic consequences. In Alasdair MacIntyre's words: 'The multiplicity of traditions does not afford a multiplicity of perspectives among which we can move, but a multiplicity of antagonistic commitments, between which only conflict, rational or non-rational, is possible'.[97] To talk of a plurality of language games without recognizing that they sanction and promote particular social practices is to have a disturbingly complacent view of the world. On this view either social reality is remarkably consensual or, where it is not, its conflicts can only be met by one of two responses: political quietism, or the rule of force.

Rushdie's commitment to the distinction between truth and falsehood becomes increasingly clear in this context. So does his impassioned plea for the retention, despite the obvious difficulties involved, of a distinction between accounts of history that are openly distortive and accounts that aim to be as veridical as the limitations of the discipline allow. It is on the basis of precisely this distinction that he articulates a political conception of the writer's function. He responds to the defeatism of Orwell's 'Inside the Whale' as follows: 'The modern world lacks not only hiding places, but certainties. There is no consensus about reality between, for example, the nations of the North and of the South. . . . It becomes necessary to take sides. . . . It seems to me imperative that literature enter such arguments, because what is being disputed is nothing less than *what is the case*, what is truth and what untruth'. Outside the whale, he continues, 'objectivity becomes a great dream, like perfection, an unattainable goal for which one must struggle in spite of the impossibility of success'.[98] Novels such as *Midnight's Children* and *Shame* stress both this unattainability and the obligation to hold on to the ideal it figures forth. It is for this reason that Saleem speaks of the immorality of amnesia, describes his writing as 'the great work of preserving', and claims: 'Morality, judgment, character . . . it all starts with memory'.[99] It thus seems apposite to recall that Winston bases his opposition to O'Brien's falsification of history on memory, and that the Greek word *aletheia* (truth) was closely linked to remembrance.

Rushdie, like Swift and Barnes, offers no easy answers to the problem of historical representation. Novels such as *Midnight's Children*, *Shame*, *Waterland*, *Flaubert's Parrot*, and *A History of the World in 10½ Chapters* testify to the difficulty of knowing the past with any reliability. Their narratives either break down under the strain of reconstructing the past (*Waterland*,

Midnight's Children) or make no attempt at all to offer totalizing accounts (*Flaubert's Parrot, A History*). But although they emphasize uncertainty, discontinuity, and confusion, they insist that these aporias do not invalidate historical knowledge. History, they suggest, must always be incomplete, because it cannot do without the mediation of the interpreter (Crick, Braithwaite, Saleem) and because the sources they use to apprehend the past are not neutral documents but 'interested' interventions. And yet the past, always known indirectly, exerts a pressure on those who would make sense of history. The sources constrain the historian's shaping of events in narrative form because they make explicit reference to events and attempt to explain them. The historian can work with nothing else, and although the sources may be contradictory and difficult to interpret, they not only set strict limits on what can be asserted of the past but also provide the grounds on which any knowledge of the past is in the first place possible. This knowledge is acquired in textual form, but that textuality points back at a recalcitrant historical referent that cannot be wished away. As Arthur Marwick argues, 'to recognize the significance of language is not to agree that there is only language'.[100] This sense of a palpable reality persistently sets limits to the fabulation indulged in by the narrators of these novels. Again and again, they are brought up short by events and actions whose consequences are so direct that, although they may be difficult to comprehend, they cannot be dissolved into language. The distinction between a positivist objectivism and a radical textualism is thus shown to represent a misleading dichotomy. The novels discussed in this chapter refuse to allow the experiences, achievements, errors, conflicts and problems of those who lived in the past, struggling with material forces within specific socio-cultural forms of life, to disappear from view.

Notes

1. Karl Löwith, *Meaning in History: The Theological Implications of the Philosophy of History* (Chicago: University of Chicago Press, 1949), p. vii.
2. Fredric Jameson, *Postmodernism, or The Cultural Logic of Late Capitalism* (London: Verso, 1991), p. 18.
3. Lutz Niethammer in collaboration with Dirk Van Laak, *Posthistoire: Has History Come to an End?*, trans. Patrick Camiller (London: Verso, 1992), p. 3.
4. See Michael S. Roth, 'Introduction', *New Literary History*, 21 (1989–90), pp. 239–51, at pp. 242, 247–50.
5. See, for example, Joan Wallach Scott, *Gender and the Politics of History* (New York: Columbia University Press, 1988), p. 7; and Lionel Gossman, *Between History and Literature* (Cambridge, Mass.: Harvard University Press, 1990), pp. 247–8.
6. See Wallach Scott, *Gender*, p. 8; Gossman, *Between*, p. 248; and John Toews's valuable review article, 'Intellectual History After the Linguistic Turn: The Autonomy of Meaning and the Irreducibility of Experience', *American Historical Review*, 92. 4 (1987), pp. 879–907.
7. See Hayden White, 'The Historical Text as Literary Artefact', *The Writing of History: Literary Form and Historical Understanding* (Madison: Wisconsin University Press, 1978), pp. 41–62; Hayden White, *Metahistory: The Historical Imagination in Nineteenth-Century Europe* (Baltimore: Johns Hopkins University

Press, 1973).

8. This broadly Foucauldian approach has been particularly influential in New Historicist work. See Jean E. Howard and Marion F. O'Connor (eds), *Shakespeare Reproduced: The Text in History and Ideology* (New York and London: Methuen, 1987); Alan Liu, 'The Power of Formalism: The New Historicism', *English Literary History*, 56 (1989), pp. 721–71; Peter Nicholls, 'State of the Art: Old Problems and the New Historicism', *Journal of American Studies*, 23. 3 (1989), pp. 423–34; Lee Patterson, *Negotiating the Past: The Historical Understanding of Medieval Literature* (Madison: University of Wisconsin Press, 1987); H. Aram Veeser (ed.), *The New Historicism* (New York and London: Routledge, 1989); Don E. Wayne, 'New Historicism', *The Encyclopedia of Literture and Criticism*, eds Martin Coyle, Peter Garside, Malcolm Kelsall and John Peck (London: Routledge, 1991).

9. Paul Ricoeur, *The Reality of the Past* (Milwaukee: Marquette University Press, 1984); Dominick LaCapra, *History and Criticism* (Ithaca: Cornell University Press, 1985); John Pocock, *Virtue, Commerce, and History: Essays on Political Thought and History, Chiefly in the Eighteenth Century* (Cambridge: Cambridge University Press, 1985); Quentin Skinner, *Meaning and Context: Quentin Skinner and his Critics*, ed. James Tully (Cambridge, Polity, 1988).

10. Martin Jay, 'Should Intellectual History Take a Linguistic Turn? Reflections on the Habermas–Gadamer Debate', *Modern European Intellectual History: Reappraisals and New Perspectives*, eds Dominick LaCapra and Steve Kaplan (Ithaca: Cornell University Press, 1982), pp. 86–110.

11. LaCapra, *History*, p. 35.

12. Ricoeur, *Reality*, pp. 26, 33.

13. Linda Hutcheon, *A Poetics of Postmodernism: History, Theory, Fiction* (London: Routledge, 1988).

14. Graham Swift, *Waterland* (London: Pan, 1984), p. 53.

15. Julian Barnes, *Flaubert's Parrot* (London: Pan, 1985), pp. 14, 90.

16. Quoted in R. G. Collingwood, *The Idea of History* (Oxford: Oxford University Press, 1946), p. 146.

17. Swift, *Waterland*, p. 122.

18. Thomas Carlye, 'On History', *A Carlyle Reader: Selections from the Writings of Thomas Carlyle*, ed. G. B. Tennyson (Cambridge: Cambridge University Press, 1984), pp. 58–9.

19. For a useful discussion of Carlyle's complex views on history, see John D. Rosenberg, *Carlyle and the Burden of History* (Oxford: Oxford University Press, 1985).

20. Carlyle, 'On History', pp. 60, 61, 59, 59–60, 58, 62–3.

21. Swift, *Waterland*, p. 53.

22. Carlyle, 'On History', p. 58.

23. Swift, *Waterland*, pp. 14, 8.

24. Thomas Carlyle, 'Characteristics', *A Carlyle Reader*, pp. 77–8, 80, 79.

25. Swift, *Waterland*, p. 120. Burke also made this argument in his defence of the English revolutions of the seventeenth century. See Edmund Burke, *Reflections on the Revolution in France*, ed. L. G. Mitchell (Oxford: Oxford University Press, 1993), p. 31. For the French Revolutionaries' desire to restore an old order, see Hannah Arendt's *On Revolution* (London: Faber and Faber, 1963).

26. Swift, *Waterland*, p. 118.

27. Carlyle, 'Characteristics', p. 88.

28. Salman Rushdie, *Midnight's Children* (London: Pan, 1982), pp. 447–8.

29. Swift, *Waterland*, p. 15.

30. Ibid., pp. 194, 17, 52, 179, 227–8, original ellipses.

31. See Ricoeur, *Reality*, p. 2.

32. Swift, *Waterland*, pp. 52, 208, 94.
33. Ibid., p. 291.
34. Ibid., pp. 117–23.
35. Polybius, *The Histories*, trans. W. R. Paton, Vol. 3, Book 6 (London: William Heinemann, 1966), p. 289.
36. Swift, *Waterland*, pp. 207, 291.
37. Immanuel Kant, 'Idea for a Universal History from a Cosmopolitan Point of View', *On History*, ed. Lewis White Beck (Indianapolis, New York: Bobbs-Merrill, 1963), pp. 15, 20, 16.
38. Swift, *Waterland*, pp. 168, 176.
39. Ibid., p. 178.
40. Ibid., pp. 94, 6.
41. Ibid., p. 134.
42. Ibid., pp. 94, 7.
43. Kant, 'Idea', p. 23.
44. Condorcet, *Condorcet: Selected Writings*, ed. Keith Michael Baker (Indianapolis: Bobbs-Merrill, 1976), p. 211; Swift, *Waterland*, p. 177.
45. Swift, *Waterland*, p. 276.
46. Kant, 'Idea', p. 13.
47. Barnes, *Flaubert's*, pp. 60, 190.
48. Ibid., pp. 38, 15, 16, 18, 19.
49. Ibid., pp. 14, 41.
50. Ibid., pp. 13, 38, 180, 86, 97.
51. Ibid., p. 95.
52. Ibid., pp. 14, 38, 60, 90, 101.
53. René Girard, *Violence and the Sacred*, trans. Patrick Gregory (Baltimore: Johns Hopkins University Press, 1977).
54. Julian Barnes, *A History of the World in 10½ Chapters* (New York: Alfred A. Knopf, 1989), p. 29.
55. Salman Rushdie, *Imaginary Homelands: Essays and Criticism, 1981–1991* (London: Granta, 1992), p. 394.
56. Barnes, *History*, pp. 241, 304.
57. Ibid., pp. 109, 111.
58. Ibid., pp. 240, 238.
59. Walter Benjamin, *Illuminations*, ed. Hannah Arendt, trans. Harry Zohn (New York: Schocken, 1978), pp. 254, 255.
60. Barnes, *History*, pp. 243–4.
61. Ibid., p. 244.
62. Benjamin, 'Theses', p. 255.
63. Salman Rushdie, *Shame* (London: Jonathan Cape, 1983), p. 69.
64. Rushdie, *Midnight's*, p. 9.
65. Ibid., pp. 122, 9, 107, 37.
66. Ibid., p.166.
67. Rushdie, *Imaginary*, p. 24.
68. Rushdie, *Midnight's*, pp. 165–6, 435.
69. Ibid., pp. 335, 338, 340, 211, 442.
70. Ibid., pp. 32, 33, 35, 184–5, 292–3, 406, 419.
71. Ibid., p. 64, original ellipses.
72. Ibid., pp. 65, 435.
73. Ibid., pp. 110, 334, 399.
74. Ibid., pp. 112, 339, 375–6.
75. Rushdie, *Shame*, pp. 87–8, 87, 88, 124.
76. Rushdie, *Midnight's*, p. 443.
77. Rushdie, *Shame*, p. 144.

78. Rushdie, *Midnight's*, p. 444, 460.
79. Ibid., pp. 445, 444, 459, 460, 461.
80. Rushdie, *Imaginary*, pp. 12–13, 2–3.
81. Ibid., p. 48.
82. Ibid., pp. 5, 103.
83. Ibid., pp. 14, 18.
84. Rushdie, *Shame*, p. 251.
85. For analyses of the various limitations placed on free speech in all societies, and the claim that free speech should not be seen in purely abstract terms, see Bikhu Parekh, 'The Rushdie Affair and the British Press', *The Salman Rushdie Controversy in Interreligious Perspective*, ed. Dan Cohn-Sherbok (Lewiston, New York: Edwin Mellen, 1990), pp. 71–96.
86. See Munawar A. Anees, *The Kiss of Judas: Affairs of a Brown Sahib* (Kuala Lumpur: Quill, 1989).
87. Parekh, *Controversy*, p. 79.
88. Shabbir Akhtar, in *The Rushdie File*, eds Lisa Appignanesi and Sara Maitland (London: Fourth Estate, 1989), pp. 240, 239.
89. Anees, *Kiss*, p. 29.
90. Mary Douglas, *Purity and Danger: An Analysis of Concepts of Pollution and Taboo* (London: Routledge and Kegan Paul, 1966), p. 113.
91. Rushdie, in *Rushdie File*, pp. 29, 30.
92. Aziz Al-Azmeh, in *Rushdie File*, pp. 71, 230.
93. See Amy Gutman, 'Communitarian Critics of Liberalism', *Philosophy and Public Affairs*, 14. 3 (1985), pp. 308–22; Michael Walzer, 'The Communitarian Critique of Liberalism', *Political Theory*, 18. 1 (1990), pp. 6–23; Adrian Oldfield, *Citizenship and Community: Civic Republicanism and the Modern World* (London: Routledge, 1990); Quentin Skinner, 'The Idea of Negative Liberty: Philosophical and Historical Perspectives', *Philosophy in History: Essays on the Historiography of Philosophy*, eds Richard Rorty, J. B. Schneewind and Quentin Skinner (Cambridge: Cambridge University Press, 1984).
94. Rushdie, *Imaginary*, p. 394.
95. Ibid., pp. 396, 67.
96. Ibid., p. 97.
97. Alasdair MacIntyre, *Whose Justice? Which Rationality?* (London: Duckworth, 1988), p. 368.
98. Rushdie, *Imaginary*, pp. 100, 101.
99. Rushdie, *Midnight's*, pp. 38, 211.
100. Arthur Marwick, '"A Fetishism of Documents"? The Salience of Source-based History', Henry Kozicki (ed.), *Developments in Modern Historiography* (London: Macmillan, 1993), pp. 107–38, at p. 109.

8

Realisms

Beyond Realism and Experimentalism

This book has made no attempt to offer a survey of post-war British fiction. I have focused on a variety of writers who have engaged with post-war issues in different ways, but who have mostly taken realism as their point of departure, even where they have transformed it. This is not true of all of them. Writers such as Compton-Burnett and Green, for example, display little interest in realism; their late-modernist novels belong to a different tradition. Much the same applies to the texts produced by writers such as Carter, Swift, Barnes and Rushdie, whose work is broadly postmodernist in orientation. But where these writers have eschewed realism altogether, they have developed narrative modes that enable them to engage with the implications of moving away from a realist aesthetics and epistemology. Realism has been either utilized and extended in interesting ways by some (Naipaul, Lamming, Berger, Lessing, Wilson, Fowles, Maitland) or confronted by others (Carter, Swift, Barnes, Rushdie). It is in any case revealed to be polyvalent, flexible, and open-ended. Whether it is consciously adopted or rejected, it continues to be a key force-field in post-war writing.

A corollary of my argument that realism changes in different historical periods and that it cannot be reduced to a set of formal features is that British fiction in the post-war period reveals itself to be massively wide-ranging. The notion that this fiction is inward-looking, limited in aspiration, and narrowly traditional is untenable. Realism, even when it is conceived as broadly as in this book, represents only one direction in the post-war novel, albeit a significant one. The post-war period evinces a plethora of writing practices. This suggests that generalizations about its fiction are hard to sustain. It seems clear, however, that whatever novelistic mode a writer chooses he or she cannot but be aware of the challenge to realism posed by modernism, the avant-garde, and postmodernism. It is no accident that 1950s realists such as Amis and Snow waged a vigorous campaign against modernism, portraying it as an art of excess, frivolity, and escapism; they knew that in order to defend an apparently discredited realism they had to mount a robust offensive against the aesthetic doctrines that had superseded it. These writers defined their realism in opposition to modernism; it was the modernism they rejected that gave their novels their bite. Writers who were more sympathetic to modernism, such as Wilson or Berger, also acknowledged that its challenge to realism required the latter to be reconceptualized. A similar concern with the impact of modernism can be discerned in the critical writings and novels of Green, Lessing, Berger, Naipaul, Fowles, Maitland and Rushdie.

But if post-war novelists must somehow confront modernism (and later still, postmodernism) and if many of them do so not by retreating to a naive realism but by incorporating modernist (and postmodernist) insights into their works, then the distinction between 'experimental' and 'realist' fiction must come under scrutiny. I began this book by considering the conflict between these two apparently polarized forms of writing, arguing that certain writers (Snow and Johnson, for example) posited a dichotomy between them in order to argue that the particular aesthetic they favoured represented the only viable option. Other writers dismissed this dualism as misleading and debilitating. Their work not only showed how realism could be extended but also proved influential for writers who came after them. Consider this statement by Ian McEwan:

> The formal experimentation of the late sixties and early seventies came to nothing largely because the stuff was inaccessible and too often unrewarding – no pleasure in the text. And there can surely be no more mileage to be had from demonstrating yet again through self-enclosed 'fictions' that reality is words and words are lies. There is no need to be strangled by that particular loop – the artifice of fiction can be taken for granted. Experimentation in its broadest and most viable sense should have less to do with formal factors like busting up your syntax and scrambling your page order, and more to do with content – the representation of states of mind and the society that forms them.[1]

McEwan, like several of the writers dealt with in this book, takes the artifice of fiction for granted. Part of my undertaking in this book has been to dispute that a clear-cut realism/experimentalism divide has much validity in the post-war period. Although some writers (Brooke-Rose, Brophy, Burns, Johnson) continued to produce overtly *lisible* texts, others preferred to fuse technical innovations with strong social concerns, thereby creating works that make a nonsense of the realism/experimentalism opposition. By focusing primarily on novelists who themselves sought to undermine it, I have tried to show that a significant body of post-war fiction has explored the terrain between these two starkly opposed alternatives.

The novels of Compton-Burnett and Green, which make use of an external narrative mode, have more in common with modernism than realism, but their scrupulous attention to dialogue results in a form of satire that explores fundamentally social questions. Subsequent writers such as Lamming and Naipaul, Berger and Lessing, Wilson and Fowles, take realism as a point of departure for their work but conceive it in markedly different ways. Naipaul and Lamming both focus on the legacy of colonialism. But whereas the former emphasizes the dissonance between his allegiance to a European literary tradition and his experience of the Caribbean as a fractured, sterile region, the latter uses the novel form to confront and overcome the depredations of imperialism. For Berger and Lessing, realism is initially inseparable from the specific conception of it elaborated within Marxist aesthetics, but both writers abandon this conception; Berger develops a Cubist-inspired dialectical form, and Lessing produces texts in which realism splinters into a wide range of alternative narrative modes. Wilson and Fowles remain committed to a liberal humanist view of realism, but their novels extend it in different ways, Wilson making use of multiple perspectives and parody, Fowles employing metafictional tactics and raising existentialist concerns. Carter, Maitland, Swift, Barnes and Rushdie all depart from realism in significant ways. The first two writers engage in a form of cultural critique that explores the social construction of gender identities; the latter three explore the problem of history from a decidedly non-realist set of perspectives. What is clear from any consideration of all these writers is just how wide a variety of strategies, styles, techniques, registers and political viewpoints their enormously differentiated novels employ. There may be some debate as to whether some of the novels I have analyzed should be labelled realist, but there can be little disputing that their disparate fusions of what might be called 'traditional' narrative modes with numerous self-reflexive innovations puts the realism/experimentalism dichotomy in question.

To deny that realism and experimentalism can easily be opposed is only a first step. A corollary of this claim is that neither term can be taken for granted. What it means to be an 'experimental' or 'realist' writer is very much up for grabs in the post-war context, partly because of the historical avant-garde's failure to carry through on the political side of its aesthetic revolt, and partly because postmodernism has virtually turned the modernist impulse to 'make it new' into a contemporary orthodoxy.[2] The proliferation of ever more flamboyant texts, actively promoted by the 'culture industry' and consumed by an eager public, suggests that 'experimental' works have lost any capacity to shock and that it may be 'realist' works which now pack the more powerful punch. It is quite likely that even modernism's shock tactics have been over-rated, as some modernists were themselves aware. Here is Wyndham Lewis, writing in 1937: '"Kill John Bull with Art!" I shouted. And John and Mrs. Bull leapt for joy, in a cynical convulsion. For they felt as safe as houses. So did I'.[3] As Rita Felski has argued, theorists 'who proclaim the subversive power of formal experimentation, fail to consider that the breaking of conventions itself becomes conventional, and the shock effect of any challenge to existing structures of representation is necessarily of limited duration'.[4] It is also important to remember that differences between literary works depend not only on their formal characteristics but also on the contexts in which they are written and read.[5] On the view I am urging, the distinction between experimentalism and realism should be seen as ambiguous and context-dependent, the implications of both terms should be called into question, and realism should be seen as a complex phenomenon, which takes a variety of forms in different historical periods. The claim that experimental writing is inherently radical is as mistaken as the counter-claim that realism is a fundamentally conservative form. Both claims fail to attend to the specificities of content, the situations in which textual interventions operate, and the illocutionary force that such interventions possess.[6]

The work of those writers who do not reject realism outright (Lamming, Naipaul, Berger, Lessing, Fowles, Wilson, Maitland, Rushdie) seeks in distinctive ways to retain realism's strengths, particularly its attention to the social and intersubjective nature of human life, while at the same time confronting the problem of representation. Although the works of this group of novelists are heterogeneous, they all extend realism by disclosing the constitutive function of language and narrative in human beings' production of meaning. This emphasis on the construction of meaning is predominantly the counterpart of a textuality rooted in a particularized and historicized social domain. Thus these novels avow realism's referential impulse but reject any simple reflectionist aesthetic and any straightforward truth-as-correspondence epistemology.

This shift in the forms that realism may take can be understood when it is seen as a tradition. Realism's critics frequently take this as a sign of its ossified character, for they see it as trapped in a moribund aesthetic and a discredited epistemology. Such a view misconstrues the historical nature of tradition. As Alasdair MacIntyre argues, 'what constitutes a tradition is a conflict of interpretations of that tradition, a conflict which itself has a history susceptible of rival interpretations'.[7] On this view, realism is characterized by a general mimetic orientation, but how various novelists, writing for different purposes in different periods, achieve their ends is hugely under-determined. Once we free realism from the genetic fallacy by which texts are compared to its first codification, we can acknowledge its numerous trans-formations and can recognize them as fundamental to an ongoing conflict over the form it should take.

Realism, then, should be differentiated from a narrow association with its nineteenth-century avatars. Post-war fiction has extended the tradition in various ways. The mimetic impulse has been severed from nineteenth-century techniques, allowing novelists to stretch realist forms into new shapes. A glance at the work of twentieth-century writers such as Brecht and Berger shows that the desire to portray the world with the utmost fidelity may go hand in hand with the rejection of particular techniques of rendering it. Brecht attacked Lukács because he discounted the latter's account of realism as formalist and unhistorical. Hence Brecht's dictum: 'Reality changes; in order to represent it, modes of representation must also change'.[8] Berger, in turn, influenced by this non-conventional theory of realism, was to argue that realism embodied an attitude to its subject matter, not a set of con-ventions. For Berger, as for Brecht, realism's 'methods and aims are always changing'.[9] Raymond Tallis makes a valuable point when he argues that antirealists 'confuse the *aims* of realism with certain techniques used to achieve those aims – techniques developed largely by the great nineteenth-century novelists'.[10]

These examples suggest that contemporary realism needs to be seen as an open-ended form, which is oriented to a social domain that it does not reduce to the discursive formations through which it is articulated. Several of the novelists discussed in this book have taken realism in new directions. They have rejected reflectionism and embraced reflexivity. Their texts confront the difficulties entailed by the writer who seeks to represent social reality but grasps that any interpretation of it is in part constituted by the discourses at his or her disposal. It is unsurprising, then, that many of these novels foreground the role played by linguistic codes and narrative forms in the creation of meaning and understanding. They emphasize that the discourses people necessarily use constitute their experience of reality, but they shy away from a textualism that conceives reality to be so fundamentally constructed out of language that it seems to possess no extra-discursive features, which might constrain or shape the way that language configures it. Indeed, the implications for communal life of the tension between language and reality becomes a key preoccupation, and the multi-perspectival texts this tension produces announce that designative accounts of language are insufficient because they hardly begin to explain the complexity of human life. Mark Platts's description of realist semantics exactly captures the kind of language-use these novels exhibit: 'It embodies a picture of our language, and our understanding, grappling with a stubbornly elusive reality. . . . But that reality will always exceed our capacities: we can struggle to achieve *approximately true* beliefs about that reality. . . . But we have to rest with the approximate belief, and ultimately to resign ourselves to (non-complacent) ignorance: for the world, austerely characterised by our language, will always outrun our recognitional capacities'.[11] The novels that emphasize how deeply cognition is embedded in language also insist that it is confronted by a recalcitrant, external world with which it must perforce engage. Out of this tension between word and world emerges a wide range of new realisms.

Realism contra Postmodernism

I argued in my opening chapter that Ricoeur's account of mimesis provides a useful way of thinking about contemporary realisms. Realist fiction, I suggested, does not 'correspond' to reality, does not portray pre-existent events, but offers representations that are plausible by virtue of their rootedness in social reality. Ricoeur, like most of the novelists treated in this book, emphasizes the constitutive role of discourses in the production of knowledge. But while this emphasis enables us to reject discredited 'reflectionist' theories, perhaps it evades the epistemological problems that any account of realist writing should confront? I want now to extend the discussion of literary realism begun in my opening chapter by considering how philosophical realism engages with these problems.

A major problem bedevilling all debates about the nature and validity of realism is that critics tend to conflate epistemology and aesthetics. Terry Lovell has pointed out that realism in epistemology and realism in art are distinct and should be kept separate, since they do not necessarily entail one another.[12] It is also worth bearing in mind that neither kind of realism denotes a widely agreed-upon concept. In a useful review of the philosophical literature, Susan Haack identifies nine different epistemological varieties and concludes that realism is 'multiply ambiguous'.[13] Michael Devitt concurs: 'There is not . . . just one traditional doctrine of realism about the external world: there is a range of related doctrines'.[14] Realism in the arts can be divided into three broad kinds: a general orientation to an external world that it attempts to represent; a nineteenth-century literary and artistic movement; any non-conventional attempt to portray reality in a way believed to be more accurate than that achieved by previous exemplars.

These are only general positions. All who write on realism note its slipperiness as a concept.

Lovell's argument that epistemological realism does not *ipso facto* entail aesthetic realism seems obviously right. There is no necessary reason why an epistemological realist should produce realist art. On the other hand, to be a realist in art is implicitly to be some sort of realist in epistemology, since the belief that art can represent reality rests on a prior conviction that the world can be known. Realism decisively parts company with conventionalism here, but it is important to be clear wherein lies the distinction between them. Despite some of its detractors' claims, it is incorrect to argue that post-structuralist conventionalism entails a Cartesian scepticism about the world's existence; its more subtle position is that knowledge of the world cannot be immediate but must be filtered through some kind of conceptual scheme that in part determines *what* constitutes knowledge. There should by now be little difficulty with the insight that human beings' access to the world is mediated. According to Christopher Norris, however, problems arise when Saussure's heuristic distinction between the signifier and the signified is taken 'for a high point of philosophical principle', for scepticism is likely to follow from this move.[15] The existence of a mind-independent world need not be denied for it to lose its power to constrain accounts of it. If we can only construe the world through some theory or other, and if these theories are incommensurable because they cannot be directly compared with the world itself, then, as Lovell argues, 'the concept of an independent reality ceases to have any force or function'.[16] It is in this sense that conventionalism can be said to deny reality.

Conventionalism is of course closely related to postmodernism. Its epistemological scepticism is one of postmodernism's key signatures. The link between them can be seen by comparing Belsey's *Critical Practice* with some of the positions taken up by writers such as Rorty, Lyotard, and Baudrillard. Towards the end of her book, Belsey explains that she does 'not mean to suggest that the interrogative text is . . . "good" and classic realism ideological, misleading and . . . "bad"'.[17] This is an astonishing statement, because the entire book is based on a polemic against realism and the epistemological and linguistic theories that Belsey thinks underpin it. But it is not difficult to see why she might want to pull back from this position. To favour the interrogative text over the realist text would be implicitly to make a truth-claim of the kind that Belsey's theory of language calls into question. Belsey would be suggesting that the classic realist text somehow falsifies reality (a suggestion which implies that reality exists outside discourse and can be known), whereas the interrogative text, which portrays the world as constructed through discourse, somehow grasps the nature of reality and gets something right about the problems inherent in representing it. Both claims rest on epistemological presuppositions rejected by Belsey's theory, since they tacitly assume that competing accounts of reality can be compared not just with one another but with an external realm that guarantees their truth or falsehood. But any such assumption is ruled out of court, since in Belsey's view language precedes reality. Thus, although *Critical Practice* consistently presents realism negatively and the interrogative text positively, the logic of Belsey's own theoretical position pushes her into denying these respective valuations. The consequences of this view are disastrous, as Adorno long ago pointed out: 'The "all" of the indiscriminately total concept of ideology terminates in nothingness. Once it has ceased to differ from any true consciousness it is no longer fit to criticize a false one'.[18]

This problem confronts all who espouse conventionalist theories. Conventionalism posits the incommensurability of competing language-games and thus *ipso facto* undermines the possibility of making truth-claims even as it urges the plausibility of its own account. The only consistent way out of this dilemma is to reject outright the entire epistemological problematic, to change the conversation. This is the move urged by postmodernists such as Rorty, Baudrillard, and Lyotard. It is not so much a move played within a game as one that breaks the rules in so decisive a way that the old game is transformed. The old game was epistemology, and it had a clear telos: the discovery of a foundation for knowledge. The new game is conversation, and it has no end in sight: one plays for the sake of playing.

Lyotard's celebrated claim that postmodernism is characterized by 'incredulity toward metanarratives' is the *locus classicus* here. Contemporary society is in that text reduced to 'a pragmatics of language particles' that permits of no ordering, no hierarchy. Because the 'grand narrative has lost its credibility' knowledge can no longer be guaranteed by speculative theories. Thus science, which has sought to unify knowledge and has impugned non-scientific discourses, must now accept their mutual incommensurability: 'It is . . . impossible to judge the existence or validity of narrative knowledge on the basis of scientific knowledge and vice versa: the relevant criteria are different. All we can do is gaze in wonderment at the diversity of discursive species, just as we do at the diversity of plant or animal species'. The old metanarratives tried to systematize knowledge, to establish its validity according to rational criteria. But they have gone the way of the dinosaurs; they are displaced by heterogeneous 'petits récits' which eschew any metadiscursive underpinning because they 'are legitimated by the simple fact that they do what they do'.[19] The distinction between theory and ideology is thus swept away, and with it goes the possibility of social critique and future consensus.

Baudrillard's 'Simulacra and Simulations' traverses a similar terrain. Simulation 'is the generation by models of a real without origin or reality: a hyperreal'. We are in the realm of signification, of a textuality comprising all language use, computer networks, and electronic media; the proliferation of images, information, sound-bites, and assorted other simulacra means that any distinction between reality and appearance dissolves. As with Lyotard, the result is an abandonment of the kind of knowledge-claim on which *Ideologiekritik* is predicated. Baudrillard's account of the 'representational imaginary' is explicit: 'With it goes all metaphysics. No more mirror of being and appearances, of the real and its concept'. Simulation contributes to the Derridian undermining of a metaphysics of presence, since 'to simulate is to feign to have what one hasn't' and is thus to imply 'an absence'. For Baudrillard, the consequences are clear: 'namely that truth, reference and objective causes have ceased to exist'.[20] The result, he admits, is a nostalgia for the real, and this nostalgia, manifested as a longing for the *évènements* of 1968 and the days of the *Socialisme où Barbarie* collective, lies just beneath the surface of Baudrillard's apparent celebration of hyperreality. May '68 represents a golden moment during which political activism and intellectual work informed one another. But now 'there is no more *real* dialogue, nor any *real* discussion' since 'the tissue which held together everything underneath is no longer there'.[21] The failure of the Marxist god leads to intellectual polytheism, a substitution of 'signs of the real for the real itself'.[22]

The clearest attack on epistemology has been mounted by Rorty. According to Rorty, modern epistemology began with Descartes and was a mistake. Inaugurating the metaphor of the mirror, it suggested that the world could be reflected onto the mind, that knowledge could be adduced by comparing representations with objects, and that the language in which such representations were formed was straightforwardly designative. For Rorty, this account of language and mind is deeply misleading. Language does not stand in a one-to-one correspondence with the objects of the world; the mind is not a mirror passively recording sense-data; and talk about the comparison of mental states or verbal utterances with their referents is endlessly recursive, since the latter cannot be cognized *an sich*. Reality is apprehended within culturally determined structures of thought and cannot provide us with an Archimedean point from which to survey it dispassionately and describe it objectively. It would therefore be preferable to drop the epistemological tradition altogether and to accept that, because discourses do not grasp 'truth' but disclose 'the potential infinity of vocabularies in which the world can be described', our purpose should be 'to keep the conversation [of mankind] going rather than to find objective truth'.[23] By this move the game is decisively altered.

To make such a move, however, is to become embroiled in a paradox, as Rorty is aware. He seeks to break free from a tradition of thought he believes cannot be sustained, yet because this entails a paradigm-shift he cannot draw on the kinds of argument that would be acceptable (and might prove persuasive) to those who remain committed to the paradigm he is trying to overthrow. In short, if the category of truth is repudiated, what is to guarantee the validity of his own position? If his account is not 'true', does not 'correspond' to a mind-independent reality, what reason could there be for acceding to it? Rorty's response, which may seem disingenuous but is entirely consistent, is to change the subject. His interlocutor is asking him to explain himself in terms of concepts that he rejects and within a language-game he is no longer playing. It is as though he were an ex-cricketer now playing football but being asked to score runs instead of goals. Pragmatism, he explains, 'does not pretend to have a better candidate for doing the same old things which we did when we spoke in the old way' but 'suggests that we might want to stop doing those things and do something else'.[24]

It is not easy to challenge such views without being question-begging in their terms. One continues to play the game but one's opponents have long since left the playing-field. Nevertheless, I want to suggest that the old game is still worth playing for (at least) two reasons: firstly, because postmodernism's assault on epistemology misses its target, is itself question-begging, and results in an unjustified dismissal of realism; secondly, because its account of epistemology has debilitating moral, social, and political consequences.

Postmodernism tends to traduce contemporary epistemology. Defenders of realism apparently believe that philosophy is a mode of enquiry based on *a priori* principles, is foundationalist and transcendental, can provide apodictic certainty, and remains wedded to a correspondence theory of truth by way of which 'nature' is 'mirrored' onto the mind. Hilary Putnam claims that 'the notion of a transcendental match between our representations and the world in itself is nonsense'. Rorty argues that the 'picture which holds traditional philosophy captive is that of the mind as a great mirror, containing various representations – some accurate, some not – and capable of being studied by pure, nonempirical methods'.[25] These views of realism see it as dependent on our having a 'God's Eye View' (Putnam) or our discovering the language that the universe would speak if it could (Rorty).[26] This account of realism is a caricature. To be sure, realism emphasizes the existence of a mind-independent world that precedes and exists outside individuals. It also claims that much of this world can reliably be known. But this in no way commits realism to the discredited views attributed to it by anti-realists. In response to Putnam's assertion that according to meta-physical realism there is only one true way of describing the world, Hartry Field comments that this 'is not a doctrine that any advocate of metaphysical realism ought to hold'. Metaphysical realists, he continues, 'should drop all pretext of being separated from their opponents by some issue about the existence of a uniquely correct theory of the world. A unique and mind-independent world is enough'.[27]

Anti-realists and realists seem to be talking past one another. Why the confusion? One answer might be that the foundationalist project has been so central to philosophy that it is hard for its critics to imagine a realism freed from *a prioristic* and transcendental illusions. Charles Taylor, for example, suggests that Rorty espouses a radical conventionalism because he remains trapped in the categories of the old epistemology. For Rorty, 'to learn that our thoughts don't correspond to things-in-themselves is to conclude that they don't correspond to anything at all. If transcendent entities don't make them true, then nothing makes them true. These were the only game in the epistemic town, and if they go the place has to be closed down'.[28] There are, however, plenty of alternative epistemic games to play. One need not sub-scribe to a belief in the isomorphism of sign and referent to be a realist. In fact, metaphysical realism repudiates most of the views attributed to it by its critics. It acknowledges that there can be no theory-neutral description of the world in either the social or the natural sciences and embraces fallibilism; it rejects the metaphor of the mirror and the 'copy' theories to which it gives rise; and it dissociates itself from *a priori* principles, defending a causal account of truth.[29]

Accounts of realism differ, but most emphasize the gap between human cognition of the world and the world's autonomous existence. Realism is, in this version, non-epistemic; it denies that truth is dependent on human beliefs. Roy Bhaskar, for example, inveighs against the 'epistemic fallacy' by way of which ontology is displaced by epistemology. On Bhaskar's non-epistemic account, realism is not primarily 'a theory of knowledge or truth, but of *being*'. Bhaskar defends the distinction between epistemology and ontology, arguing that although 'there is no way of knowing the world except under particular more or less historically transient descriptions', that which is known 'exists and acts independently of those descriptions'. Because Bhaskar welcomes historicity as an inescapable feature of human life, he willingly admits that knowledge is a social product subject to revision, but he does not on this account concede that there are no rational criteria according to which competing knowledge-claims can be judged. His account of science embraces fallibilism, distinguishes between theory-dependence, which is unavoidable, and theory-determination, which is a false inference, and treats talk of correspondence as a heuristic device.[30]

Alvin Goldman has recently offered a powerful account of realism. Goldman shares Bhaskar's conviction that realism should be construed and defended in non-epistemic terms. He rejects *a priori* foundationalism in favour of an account that combines philosophical enquiry into the nature of knowledge with psychological investigations of cognition that are empirically testable. This approach to epistemology, which is similar to Habermas's concept of 'reconstructive science' and draws on the work of Quine, remains normative. It seeks not to describe what is believed but to evaluate whether beliefs are warranted. It is 'objectivist' (externalist) rather than 'subjectivist' (internalist). Its goal is to account for 'true belief', in contrast to the pragmatist claim that beliefs can only be socially sanctioned and to postmodernist scepticism about the possibility of knowledge. At the same time, however, the theory does not begin from first principles *à la* Descartes, but from established learning. Borrowing Otto Neurath's metaphor, Goldman argues that the epistemological ship cannot be built in a dry dock but must be repaired at sea.

Realism is often characterized, following Michael Dummett, as requiring two features: firstly, bivalence – the view that propositions are either true or false; secondly, verification-transcendence – the view that truth is independent of human beings' capacity to know it. Goldman, like Bhaskar, differentiates these two positions, and whereas he defends the second, arguing that it is essential to the metaphysical realism he upholds, he considers the first to be inessential, since there are many propositions that cannot and need not be thought of in terms of truth or falsehood. His theory is primarily concerned to identify the *nature* of reality; it is only secondarily interested in how or whether human beings reliably cognize reality. Truth is to be distinguished from verification; the way that things are is separable from any account of the way they are.

The standard problem posed for any account of metaphysical realism concerns the adequacy of epistemology to ontology. As I have already indicated, realism is attacked for its reliance on correspondence theory and the designative view of language that is said to underpin it. Among the many objections raised against realism, two are central: firstly, that the world does not consist of ready-made 'facts' or fact-like entities to which propositions could be said to correspond; secondly, that the world is not already organized into categories or kinds, which human beings passively register. Both objections contend that the interaction between world and cognizer crucially depends on the latter's interpretive, organizing, constituting activity. On this account, correspondence can broadly be described as the view that 'the world is structured into truthlike entities (facts), and that truth consists in language or thought mirroring a precategorized world'.[31]

What follows from any such view, clearly, is the whole host of mirror metaphors with all their attendant problems.

This metaphor is surplus to requirements. Correspondence theory may be misleading because it suggests that propositions should 'match' states of affairs, should somehow be isomorphic with them, and this notion allows writers like Rorty gleefully to pillory it. But it is incoherent to construe linguistic propositions as reflections of animate and inanimate entities. Goldman acknowledges the inescapability of human noetic activity and recognizes that any account of knowledge must build human beings' constitutive function into it. He therefore defends a much weaker version of correspondence (although this term could easily be dropped), which replaces the metaphor of the mirror with that of *'fittingness*: the sense in which clothes fit a body'. The emphasis here is not on matching words with objects but on the way that given propositions succeed or fail in making sense of the world by articulating accounts that dovetail with it. The body can be clothed in a wide range of garments, each cut into different shapes and each covering its various parts in any number of different ways. Clothes are not isomorphic with the body, do not reflect or mirror it, do not correspond to it, and do not have to conform to any predetermined style or fashion; but they must fit the body they are to clothe. No analogy can capture the nature of knowledge, but Goldman's metaphor not only does away with discredited 'copy' theories but also accounts for the constitutive role of the intellect:

> Which things a cognizer-speaker chooses to think or say about the world is not determined by the world itself. That is a matter of human noetic activity, lexical resources in the speaker's language, and the like. A sentence or thought sign, in order to have any truth-value, must have an associated set of *conditions of truth*. . . . The satisfaction or nonsatisfaction of these conditions depends upon the world. Truth and falsity, then, consists in the world's 'answering' or 'not answering' to whatever truth-conditions are in question. . . . Notice that *which* truth-conditions must be satisfied is not determined by the world. Conditions of truth are laid down not by the world, but only by thinkers or speakers. This is the sense in which the world is not precategorized, and in which truth does not consist in mirroring of a precategorized world.[32]

Metaphysical realism accepts that knowledge belongs to speakers and is produced through their agency. But it rejects the conventionalist claim that the world is noumenal, remaining forever beyond human grasp, and that therefore all that can be had are different versions (vocabularies, language games), which are non-adjudicable. Thus Michael Devitt writes: 'To say that an object has objective existence is not to say that it is unknowable. It is to say that it is not *constituted by* our knowledge, by our epistemic values, by our capacity to refer to it, by the synthesising power of the mind, by our imposition of concepts, theories, or languages'.[33] The realist, Goldman points out, 'insists on the existence of a wearer: clothes don't make the world'. It is true that unmediated access to an unconceptualized reality is impossible, but this admission only creates difficulties for 'copy' theories that require propositions to mirror *dinge-an-sich*, not for a theory of fittingness: 'The world that I learn *about* is an unconceptualized world. But *what* I learn about this world is that some conceptualization (of mine) fits it. *How* I learn this is by a process that begins with the unconceptualized world but terminates in a conceptualization'.[34]

The idea of fittingness, which is not dissimilar to Robert Nozick's influential concept of 'tracking the truth', relies on a causal theory of knowledge.[35] On Goldman's causal view, knowledge depends less on epistemic justification, as in the Cartesian tradition, and more on non-epistemic causation. This account of knowledge insists that there be a causal link between a state of affairs that makes a proposition about it true and a given person's belief in that proposition.[36] In a sense, the direction is less from mind to world than vice-versa; it is states of affairs that 'cause' propositions to be true or false, in the sense that the former 'answer' the latter.[37] Goldman considers Cartesian standards of justification to be 'too demanding' because they are required to deal scepticism a death-blow. His causal theory, in contrast, settles for the more moderate demand 'that beliefs in the external world be suitably caused, where "suitably" comprehends a process or mechanism that not only produces true belief in the actual situation, but would not produce false belief in relevant counterfactual situations'. This account cannot ultimately rebut scepticism, as Goldman readily concedes. But its modest fallibilist view of knowledge is offered as more accurate, since it describes the kind of discriminations human beings daily have to make and explains how they produce reliable cognition.[38]

Non-epistemic metaphysical realism offers the possibility of reliable knowledge that can distinguish truth from falsehood without falling prey to naive reflectionist accounts of cognition. Language is seen to be constitutive of knowledge, which is always mediated but nevertheless makes contact with a mind-independent reality that constrains what can plausibly be asserted about it. Realism, on this view, offers the possibility of adjudicating between different accounts of the world. It denies that all accounts of reality are radically incommensurable and argues that there are clear rational criteria according to which the truth of conflicting viewpoints can be ascertained.

Realism, Politics, History

The preceding discussion suggests that although epistemological realism and aesthetic realism should not be conflated, neither need depend on reference to simplistic correspondence theories of truth or traditional designative theories of language. Goldman's causal theory of fittingness displaces the reflectionist problematic by building into its procedures an awareness of the constitutive role played by socially embedded individuals and the languages that they have at their disposal. This 'weak' version of correspondence is entirely compatible with Ricoeur's hermeneutic conception of mimesis as 'not simply reduplication but creative reconstruction by means of the mediation of fiction'. Ricoeur breaks out of the reflectionist impasse by arguing that fiction is a form of 'productive reference', which augments our understanding of the reality it redescribes, and not a form of replication or picturing. Drawing on the concept of mimesis as a 'making', Ricoeur argues that 'fiction reveals its ability to transform or transfigure reality only when it is inserted into something as a labour, in short, when it is a work'. Fiction is freed 'from its bondage to picture' when it is conceived in terms of language, not perception, and when the idea of more or less passive reflection is replaced by that of transformative labour.[39]

Goldman works on epistemology, cognition, and psychology; Ricoeur, a wide-ranging philosopher, works primarily on questions relating to the realm of the arts. But both argue that although human beings' access to the world is always mediated this constraint on the kind and extent of knowledge that they can elaborate does not preclude them from making defensible and arbitrable validity claims about the world. The way that literature does this is not by 'mirroring' a pre-existent realm of events but by redescribing the world in a plethora of forms, styles and idioms. The novels I have examined in this book offer the kinds of redescription invoked by Ricoeur. They differ widely from one another in their narrative strategies, their stylistic choices, and their political commitments. Some are firmly rooted in a recognizable social domain, others less so. Some seek to extend realism by focusing on the constitutive and transformative role of language, others reject realism in favour of a cultural critique that explores the construction of social identities and roles. But few of the novels I have discussed rely on a 'reflectionist' aesthetic, and fewer still consider that literary representation is a matter of matching words with objects or of copying reality rather than intervening creatively in it. The form such interventions take differs from text to text, which is why it makes sense to talk of realisms rather than realism, but most novelists refuse to abandon the quest for a knowledge of the past and present that upholds distinctions between truth and falsehood.

Realism in the arts, I have maintained throughout, cannot be aligned with any particular political position or any given set of fictional techniques. It is context-dependent, different from period to period, and upholds a wide range of alternative narrative modes. Realist writers, however, share a general orientation to the world: they believe it has an existence that is independent from the perceptions of the cognizing self, and that the writer's task is to explore that enormously complex world as fully as possible. Reality, as Iris Murdoch remarks, 'is not a given whole'. Nor are individuals asocial beings who can easily command it: 'We are not isolated free choosers, monarchs of all we survey, but benighted creatures sunk in a reality whose nature we are constantly and overwhelmingly tempted to deform by fantasy'.[40]

History and politics lie close to the fore in post-war writers' accounts of reality because they are central to any society's understanding of itself and thus become hotly contested terrains. It has been a central premise of this book that the novels on which I have chosen to focus make powerful interventions in these critical areas. Whereas some post-war writers have chosen to indulge in increasingly sophisticated word-play, making self-referential linguistic puzzles out of their texts, others have struggled with the difficulties of engaging with the past and present. They acknowledge that although fact and fiction frequently blur together in perplexing ways, making it hard to disentangle them, there are times when it is morally and politically imperative to do so. The way that an always recalcitrant reality constrains interpretation of it emerges in most of the novels I have analyzed. Reality demands to be interpreted, but it does not license the free play of just any vocabulary. Indeed, the limits it sets to interpretation are of crucial importance to these texts.

I suggested in my opening chapter that just as realism could not be equated with any particular political stance, so the ways in which it was extended and challenged in the post-war period could not *ipso facto* be related to postmodernism. But the writers discussed in Chapters 6 and 7 belong to a postmodern context in fairly obvious ways. What I have tried to show, however, is that their explorations of identity, gender, history and politics do not uphold postmodernism's more extreme pronouncements. It would be grossly misleading to suggest that such pronouncements (by Baudrillard, for example) characterize postmodernism as a whole, since it is internally fissured. Richard Bernstein thus prefers the Benjaminian 'constellation' to the Adornian 'force-field' in his account of postmodernism, since the former brings out its resistance to a common denominator.[41] For Bernstein, it is not possible to stand outside the postmodern problematic, but it is both possible and necessary to contest it from within. Writers such as Carter, Swift, Barnes and Rushdie participate in precisely this kind of contestation. Their departure from realism results on the one hand in complex examinations of its aporias and limitations, but leads on the other hand to searching analyses of the political consequences of this departure. For if realism's distinctions between truth and falsehood are seen to be discredited, with the result that competing language games are radically incommensurable, then *Ideologiekritik* is fatally undermined.[42] As Perry Anderson puts it: 'The distinction between the true and the false is the ineliminable premise of any rational knowledge. Its central site is evidence'.[43] It is for this reason that the writers whose work I examined in the previous two chapters are not eager to abandon this distinction.

Angela Carter, for example, reminds us that although fiction is free to embroider and embellish, to veer off into the magical, the fantastic, and the surreal, such imaginative daring runs the risk of loosing itself from its moorings in reality; it may dazzle with style but be trivial in content. Lizzie's ironic undercutting of Fevvers's euphoric soliloquies, in *Nights at the Circus*, and Nora's recognition that the world of 'carnival' is an escape from the exigencies of daily life, in *Wise Children*, serve as timely reminders that Carter's playfulness has a serious purpose. The novels of writers such as Swift, Barnes and Rushdie, in turn, try not only to make sense of history and to distinguish between true and false accounts of it but also to confront the moral and political consequences of failing to do so. In *Waterland*, Crick's desire to escape into the realm of fairy-tale is constantly impeded: 'He hasn't begun to ask yet where the stories end and reality begins. But he will, he will'. When reality imposes itself 'in the form of a sodden corpse' it is all of a sudden 'no longer story-time in the land of the Leem'.[44] In *Midnight's Children*, Saleem's redemptive fabulation is similarly foiled: 'but reality is nagging at me. Love does not conquer all, except in the Bombay talkies'.[45] And in *A History of the World in 10½ Chapters*, although the 'God-eyed version' of truth is described as 'a charming, impossible fake', the reader is urged to 'believe that 43 per cent objective truth is better than 41 per cent' because the alternative is a 'beguiling relativity' in which 'we value one liar's version as much as another liar's'.[46] Seyla Benhabib's rejoinder to Lyotard is worth quoting here: 'To deny that the play of language games may not turn into a matter of life and death, and that the intellectual cannot remain the priest of many gods but must take a stance, is cynical'.[47]

These writers all acknowledge that perfect knowledge is unattainable, but they insist on the difference between seeing the past in an undistorted light and casting it in the form of narcissistic projection. Such issues are of course political as well as aesthetic. How the past is understood and how that understanding is passed on are matters of conflict that need to be arbitrated. For Ricoeur, the 'contemporary search for some narrative continuity with the past is not just nostalgic escapism but a contestation of the legislative and planificatory discourse which tends to predominate in bureaucratic societies'.[48] It also currently contests the postmodernist emphasis on the radical contingency of knowledge, the inescapability of multiple language games among which it is impossible to adjudicate, and the consequent inaccessibility of history's referent. To argue against what amounts to a species of cultural relativism, protestations to the contrary notwithstanding, is to engage in a political as well as an epistemological conflict, as both Rushdie and Barnes are aware. Barnes points out that to abandon distinctions between truth and falsehood, however hard they are to establish and maintain, is to 'admit that the victor has the right not just to the spoils but also to the truth'.[49] Rushdie echoes these political sentiments when he asserts that literature must engage in debate over the nature of reality, for 'what is being disputed is nothing less than *what is the case*, what is truth and untruth'. Like Barnes, he admits that objectivity will always elude us, but insists that it represents the 'unattainable goal for which one must struggle in spite of the impossibility of success'.[50] This is so because perspectives that deny the possibility of reliable historical knowledge and see the present as beyond redemption result in a political quietism that plays into the hands of those who are only too willing to employ the metanarratives that best serve their interests. George Iggers is surely right to argue that the 'absence of any over arching direction in history does not mean that there are no forces at work in modern societies which require rational analysis and call for conceptions of historical and social change'.[51] Writers such as Barnes and Rushdie, far from acceding to postmodernist scepticism, contend not only that veridical accounts of the world are possible but also that they are *necessary* if various forms of oppression are to be opposed by rational critique and if the transformation of society is not to recede from view as a political desideratum.

Notes

1. Ian McEwan, 'The State of Fiction: A Symposium', *New Review*, 5. 1 (Summer 1978), pp. 14–76, at p. 51.
2. See Peter Bürger, *Theory of the Avant-Garde*, trans. Michael Shaw (Manchester: Manchester University Press, 1984).

194   *Realisms*

3. Wyndham Lewis, *Blasting and Bombadiering* (London: Calder and Boyars, 1967), p. 36. Lewis was in later years to become a severe critic of experimentation in the arts, arguing that contemporary avant-gardists were doing nothing more than regurgitating work that had long since ceased to have any impact and was simply part of a new orthodoxy. See Wyndham Lewis, *The Demon of Progress in the Arts* (London: Calder and Boyars, 1954).
4. Rita Felski, *Beyond Feminist Aesthetics: Feminist Literature and Social Change* (London: Hutchinson Radius, 1989), p. 159.
5. For more on this point, see Felski, *Beyond*, p. 157.
6. For the concept of illocution, see J. L. Austin, *How to do Things with Words* (Oxford: Oxford University Press, 1975). See also Quentin Skinner, *Meaning and Context: Quentin Skinner and His Critics*, ed. James Tully (Cambridge: Polity, 1988), pp. 231–88.
7. Alasdair MacIntyre, 'Epistemological Crises, Dramatic Narrative and the Philosophy of Science', *The Monist*, 60. 4 (1977), pp. 453–72, at p. 460.
8. Bertolt Brecht, 'Against Georg Lukács', *Aesthetics and Politics: Debates Between Bloch, Lukács, Brecht, Benjamin, Adorno*, ed. Ronald Taylor (London: Verso, 1977), pp. 68–86, at p. 82.
9. John Berger, *Permanent Red: Essays in Seeing* (London: Writers and Readers Publishing Cooperative, 1979), p. 208.
10. Raymond Tallis, *In Defence of Realism* (London: Edward Arnold, 1988), p. 3.
11. Mark de Bretton Platts, *Ways of Meaning: An Introduction to a Philosophy of Language* (London: Routledge and Kegan Paul, 1979), p. 238.
12. Terry Lovell, *Pictures of Reality: Aesthetics, Politics and Pleasure* (London: British Film Institute, 1983), pp. 64, 80.
13. Susan Haack, 'Realism', *Synthese*, 73 (1987), pp. 275–99.
14. Michael Devitt, *Realism and Truth* (Oxford: Blackwell, 1991), p. 13.
15. Christopher Norris, *The Contest of Faculties: Philosophy and Theory after Deconstruction* (London: Methuen, 1985), p. 62.
16. Lovell, *Pictures*, p. 15.
17. Catherine Belsey, *Critical Practice* (London: Methuen, 1980), p. 103.
18. Theodor Adorno, *Negative Dialectics*, trans. E. B. Ashton (London: Routledge and Kegan Paul, 1973), p. 198.
19. Jean-François Lyotard, *The Postmodern Condition: A Report on Knowledge*, trans. Geoff Bennington and Brian Massumi (Manchester: Manchester University Press, 1984), pp. xxiv, xxiv, 26, 23. For recent discussion of Lyotard's work, particularly his considerations of the question of justice, see Jean-François Lyotard, *The Differend: Phrases in Dispute*, trans. Georges Van Den Abbeele (Manchester: Manchester University Press, 1988); Andrew Benjamin (ed.), *Judging Lyotard* (London: Routledge, 1992); Geoffrey Bennington, *Lyotard: Writing the Event* (Manchester: Manchester University Press, 1988).
20. Jean Baudrillard, 'Simulacra and Simulations', *Selected Writings*, ed. Mark Poster (Oxford: Blackwell, 1990), pp. 166, 167, 168.
21. Jean Baudrillard, 'Intellectuals, Commitment and Political Power', *Thesis Eleven*, 10/11 (1984/85), pp. 166–74, at pp. 166, 167, emphases added.
22. Baudrillard, 'Simulacra', p. 167.
23. Richard Rorty, *Philosophy and the Mirror of Nature* (Princeton, New Jersey: Princeton University Press, 1979), pp. 367, 377.
24. Richard Rorty, *Contingency, Irony, and Solidarity* (Cambridge: Cambridge University Press, 1989), p. 9.
25. Hilary Putnam, *Reason, Truth and History* (Cambridge: Cambridge University Press, 1992), p. 134; Rorty, *Philosophy*, p. 12.
26. Putnam, *Reason*, p. 74; Richard Rorty, *Objectivity, Relativism, and Truth* (Cambridge: Cambridge University Press, 1993), p. 80.

27. Hartry Field, 'Realism and Relativism', *Journal of Philosophy*, 79 (1982), pp. 553–67, at pp. 553, 554.
28. Charles Taylor, 'Rorty in the Epistemological Tradition', *Reading Rorty: Critical Responses to Philosophy and the Mirror of Nature (and Beyond)*, ed. Alan Malachowski (Oxford: Blackwell, 1990), pp. 257–75, at p. 271.
29. In addition to Devitt and Field, see Richard Miller, *Fact and Method: Explanation, Confirmation and Reality in the Natural and Social Sciences* (Princeton: Princeton University Press, 1987); Roy Bhaskar, *Scientific Realism and Human Emancipation* (London: Verso, 1987); Roy Bhaskar, *Reclaiming Reality: A Critical Introduction to Contemporary Philosophy* (London: Verso, 1993); Alvin I. Goldman, *Epistemology and Cognition* (Cambridge, Mass.: Harvard University Press, 1986); Alvin I. Goldman, *Liaisons: Philosophy Meets the Cognitive and Social Sciences* (Cambridge, Mass.: MIT, 1992).
30. Bhaskar, *Scientific Realism*, pp. 6, 99, 72, 60, 92.
31. Goldman, *Epistemology*, p. 152.
32. Ibid., pp. 152, 153.
33. Devitt, *Realism*, p. 15.
34. Goldman, *Epistemology*, p. 154. See also Field's argument against an *a priori* conception of epistemology: 'In looking for a theory of truth and a theory of primitive reference we *are* trying to explain the connection between language and (extralinguistic) reality, but we are *not* trying to step outside of our theories of the world in order to do so'. Hartry Field, 'Tarski's Theory of Truth', *Journal of Philosophy*, 89 (1972), p. 373.
35. Robert Nozick, *Philosophical Explanations* (Oxford: Oxford University Press, 1984), pp. 170–1, 175–8, 286–8.
36. Goldman, *Liaisons*, pp. 85–103.
37. Goldman, *Epistemology and Cognition*, p. 36.
38. Ibid., pp. 85, 101, 86.
39. Paul Ricoeur, 'The Function of Fiction in Shaping Reality', *A Ricoeur Reader: Reflection and Imagination*, ed. Mario J. Valdes (Hemel Hempstead: Harvester Wheatsheaf, 1991), pp. 117–36, at pp. 134, 129, 135.
40. Iris Murdoch, 'Against Dryness: A Polemical Sketch', *Encounter* 16. 1 (January 1961), pp. 16–20, at p. 20.
41. See Richard Bernstein, *The New Constellation: The Ethical-Political Horizons of Modernity/Postmodernity* (Oxford: Blackwell, 1991). For a discussion of the differences between these two terms, see Martin Jay, *Adorno* (Cambridge, MA: Harvard University Press, 1984).
42. For a critique of Lyotard's 'chronic confusion between *language-games* and *validity-claims*', see Peter Dews, 'Introduction', *Jürgen Habermas: Autonomy and Solidarity: Interviews* (London: Verso, 1986), pp. 1–34, at p. 22.
43. Perry Anderson, *In the Tracks of Historical Materialism* (London: Verso, 1983), p. 48.
44. Graham Swift, *Waterland* (London: Pan, 1984), pp. 179, 228, 227.
45. Salman Rushdie, *Midnight's Children* (London: Pan, 1982), p. 444.
46. Julian Barnes, *A History of the World in 10½ Chapters* (New York: Alfred A. Knopf, 1989), pp. 243–4.
47. Seyla Benhabib, 'Epistemologies of Postmodernism: A Rejoinder to Jean-François Lyotard', *New German Critique*, 33 (1984), pp. 103–26, at p. 124.
48. Paul Ricoeur, 'The Creativity of Language', Valdes, *A Ricoeur Reader*, pp. 463–81, at p. 473.
49. Barnes, *A History*, p. 244.
50. Salman Rushdie, *Imaginary Homelands: Essays and Criticism, 1981–1991* (London: Granta, 1992), pp. 100, 101.
51. George G. Iggers, 'Rationality and History', *Developments in Modern Historiography*, ed. Henry Kozicki (London: Macmillan, 1993), pp. 19–39, at pp. 35–36.

Index